Lizzie Leigh and other tales /

Elizabeth Cleghorn Gaskell

Lizzie Leigh and other tales /
Gaskell, Elizabeth Cleghorn
British Library, Historical Print Editions
British Library
1865
274 p. : plates. ; 19 cm.
12618.aaa.31

12618 aaa 31

The Old Nurse's Story

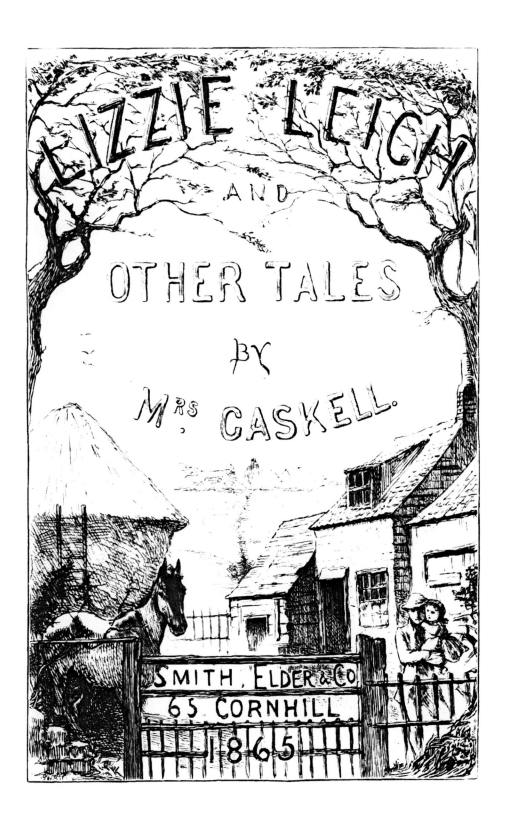

LIZZIE LEIGH

AND

OTHER TALES

BY

MRS GASKELL.

SMITH, ELDER & CO
65 CORNHILL
1865

LIZZIE LEIGH.

AND OTHER TALES.

BY MRS. GASKELL,

AUTHOR OF "MARY BARTON," "NORTH AND SOUTH," "SYLVIA'S
LOVERS," "COUSIN PHILLIS," "CRANFORD," ETC.

ILLUSTRATED EDITION.

LONDON:

SMITH, ELDER AND CO., 65, CORNHILL.

———

M.DCCC.LXV.

CONTENTS.

———◇———

LIZZIE LEIGH;

AND OTHER TALES.

===

LIZZIE LEIGH.

CHAPTER I.

WHEN Death is present in a household on a Christmas Day, the very contrast between the time as it now is, and the day as it has often been, gives a poignancy to sorrow—a more utter blankness to the desolation. James Leigh died just as the far-away bells of Rochdale Church were ringing for morning service on Christmas Day, 1836. A few minutes before his death, he opened his already glazing eyes, and made a sign to his wife, by the faint motion of his lips, that he had yet something to say. She stooped close down, and caught the broken whisper, "I forgive her, Anne! May God forgive me!"

1—3

"Oh, my love, my dear! only get well, and I will never cease showing my thanks for those words. May God in heaven bless thee for saying them. Thou'rt not so restless, my lad! may be—Oh, God!'"

For even while she spoke he died.

They had been two-and-twenty years man and wife; for nineteen of those years their life had been as calm and happy as the most perfect uprightness on the one side, and the most complete confidence and loving submission on the other, could make it. Milton's famous line might have been framed and hung up as the rule of their married life, for he was truly the interpreter, who stood between God and her; she would have considered herself wicked if she had ever dared even to think him austere, though as certainly as he was an upright man, so surely was he hard, stern, and inflexible. But for three years the moan and the murmur had never been out of her heart; she had rebelled against her husband as against a tyrant, with a hidden, sullen rebellion, which tore up the old landmarks of wifely duty and affection, and poisoned the fountains whence gentlest love and reverence had once been for ever springing.

But those last blessed words replaced him on his throne in her heart, and called out penitent anguish for all the bitter estrangement of later years. It was this which made her refuse all the entreaties of her sons, that she would see the kind-hearted neighbours, who called on their way from church, to sympathize and condole. No! she would stay with the dead husband that had spoken tenderly at last, if for three years he had kept silence; who knew but what, if she had only been more gentle and less angrily reserved, he might have relented earlier—and in time?

She sat rocking herself to and fro by the side of the bed, while the footsteps below went in and out; she had been in sorrow too long to have any violent burst of deep grief now; the furrows were well worn in her cheeks, and the tears flowed quietly, if incessantly, all the day long. But when the winter's night drew on, and the neighbours had gone away to their homes, she stole to the window, and gazed out, long and wistfully, over the dark grey moors. She did not hear her son's voice, as he spoke to her from the door, nor his footstep as he drew nearer. She started when he touched her.

"Mother! come down to us. There's no one but Will and me. Dearest mother, we do so want you." The poor lad's voice trembled, and he began to cry. It appeared to require an effort on Mrs. Leigh's part to tear herself away from the window, but with a sigh she complied with his request.

The two boys (for though Will was nearly twenty-one, she still thought of him as a lad) had done everything in their power to make the house-place comfortable for her. She herself, in the old days before her sorrow, had never made a brighter fire or a cleaner hearth, ready for her husband's return home, than now awaited her. The tea things were all put out, and the kettle was boiling; and the boys had calmed their grief down into a kind of sober cheerfulness. They paid her every attention they could think of, but received little notice on her part; she did not resist, she rather submitted to all their arrangements; but they did not seem to touch her heart.

When tea was ended—it was merely the form of tea that had been gone through—Will moved the things away to the dresser. His mother leant back languidly in her chair.

"Mother, shall Tom read you a chapter? He's a better scholar than I."

"Ay, lad!" said she, almost eagerly. "That's it. Read me the Prodigal Son. Ay, ay, lad. Thank thee." ··

Tom found the chapter, and read it in the high-pitched voice which is customary in village schools. His mother bent forward, her lips parted, her eyes dilated; her whole body instinct with eager attention. Will sat with his head depressed and hung down. He knew why that chapter had been chosen; and to him it recalled the family's disgrace. When the reading was ended, he still hung down his head in gloomy silence. But her face was brighter than it had been before for the day. Her eyes looked dreamy, as if she saw a vision; and by-and-by she pulled the Bible towards her, and, putting her finger underneath each word, began to read them aloud in a low voice to herself; she read again the words of bitter sorrow and deep humiliation; but most of all, she paused and brightened over the father's tender reception of the repentant prodigal.

So passed the Christmas evening in the Upclose Farm.

The snow had fallen heavily over the dark waving moorland before the day of the funeral. The black storm-laden dome of heaven lay very still and close upon the white earth, as they carried the body forth out of the house which had known his presence so long as its ruling power. Two and two the mourners followed, making a black procession, in their winding march over the unbeaten snow, to Milne Row Church; now lost in some hollow of the bleak moors, now slowly climbing the heaving ascents. There was no long tarrying after the funeral, for many of the neighbours who accompanied the body to the grave had far to go, and the great white flakes which came slowly down were the boding fore-runners of a heavy storm. One old friend alone accompanied the widow and her sons to their home.

The Upclose Farm had belonged for generations to the Leighs; and yet its possession hardly raised them above the rank of labourers. There was the house and out-buildings, all of an old-fashioned kind, and about seven acres of barren unproductive land, which they had never possessed capital enough to improve; indeed, they could hardly rely upon it for subsistence; and it had been customary to bring up the sons to some trade, such as a wheelwright's or blacksmith's.

James Leigh had left a will in the possession of the old man who accompanied them home. He read it aloud. James had bequeathed the farm to his faithful wife, Anne Leigh, for her life-time, and afterwards to his son William. The hundred and odd pounds in the savings'-bank was to accumulate for Thomas.

After the reading was ended, Anne Leigh sat silent for a time, and then she asked to speak to Samuel Orme alone. The sons went into the back-kitchen, and thence strolled out into the fields regardless of the driving snow. The brothers were dearly fond of each

other, although they were very different in character.
Will, the elder, was like his father, stern, reserved, and
scrupulously upright. Tom (who was ten years younger)
was gentle and delicate as a girl, both in appearance
and character. He had always clung to his mother,
and dreaded his father. They did not speak as they
walked, for they were only in the habit of talking about
facts, and hardly knew the more sophisticated language
applied to the description of feelings.

Meanwhile their mother had taken hold of Samuel
Orme's arm with her trembling hand.

"Samuel, I must let the farm—I must."

"Let the farm! What's come o'er the woman?"

"Oh, Samuel!" said she, her eyes swimming in
tears, "I'm just fain to go and live in Manchester. I
mun let the farm."

Samuel looked, and pondered, but did not speak for
some time. At last he said,—

"If thou hast made up thy mind, there's no speaking again it; and thou must e'en go. Thou'lt be sadly
pottered wi' Manchester ways; but that's not my look
out. Why, thou'lt have to buy potatoes, a thing thou
hast never done afore in all thy born life. Well! it's
not my look out. It's rather for me than again me.
Our Jenny is going to be married to Tom Higginbotham,
and he was speaking of wanting a bit of land to begin
upon. His father will be dying sometime, I reckon,
and then he'll step into the Croft Farm. But meanwhile —"

"Then, thou'lt let the farm," said she, still as eagerly
as ever.

"Ay, ay, he'll take it fast enough, I've a notion.

But I'll not drive a bargain with thee just now; it would not be right; we'll wait a bit."

"No; I cannot wait, settle it out at once."

"Well, well; I'll speak to Will about it. I see him out yonder. I'll step to him and talk it over."

Accordingly he went and joined the two lads, and, without more ado, began the subject to them.

"Will, thy mother is fain to go live in Manchester, and covets to let the farm. Now, I'm willing to take it for Tom Higginbotham; but I like to drive a keen bargain, and there would be no fun chaffering with thy mother just now. Let thee and me buckle to, my lad! and try and cheat each other; it will warm us this cold day."

"Let the farm!" said both the lads at once, with infinite surprise. "Go live in Manchester!"

When Samuel Orme found that the plan had never before been named to either Will or Tom, he would have nothing to do with it, he said, until they had spoken to their mother. Likely she was "dazed" by her husband's death; he would wait a day or two, and not name it to any one; not to Tom Higginbotham himself, or may be he would set his heart upon it. The lads had better go in and talk it over with their mother. He bade them good-day, and left them.

Will looked very gloomy, but he did not speak till they got near the house. Then he said,—

"Tom, go to th' shippon, and supper the cows. I want to speak to mother alone."

When he entered the house-place, she was sitting before the fire, looking into its embers. She did not hear him come in: for some time she had lost her quick perception of outward things.

"Mother! what's this about going to Manchester?" asked he.

"Oh, lad!" said she, turning round, and speaking in a beseeching tone, "I must go and seek our Lizzie. I cannot rest here for thinking on her. Many's the time I've left thy father sleeping in bed, and stole to th' window, and looked and looked my heart out towards Manchester, till I thought I must just set out and tramp over moor and moss straight away till I got there, and then lift up every downcast face till I came to our Lizzie. And often, when the south wind was blowing soft among the hollows, I've fancied (it could but be fancy, thou knowest) I heard her crying upon me; and I've thought the voice came closer and closer, till at last it was sobbing out 'Mother' close to the door; and I've stolen down, and undone the latch before now, and looked out into the still, black night, thinking to see her,—and turned sick and sorrowful when I heard no living sound but the sough of the wind dying away. Oh, speak not to me of stopping here, when she may be perishing for hunger, like the poor lad in the parable." And now she lifted up her voice, and wept aloud.

Will was deeply grieved. He had been old enough to be told the family shame when, more than two years before, his father had had his letter to his daughter returned by her mistress in Manchester, telling him that Lizzie had left her service some time—and why. He had sympathized with his father's stern anger; though he had thought him something hard, it is true, when he had forbidden his weeping, heart-broken wife to go and try to find her poor sinning child, and declared that henceforth they would have no daughter; that she should be as one dead, and her name never more be named at market or at meal time, in blessing or in prayer. He had held his peace, with compressed lips and contracted brow, when the neighbours had noticed to him how poor Lizzie's death had aged both his father and his mother; and how they thought the bereaved couple would never hold up their heads again. He himself had felt as if that one event had made him old before his time; and had envied Tom the tears he had shed over poor, pretty, innocent, dead Lizzie. He thought about her sometimes, till he ground his teeth together, and could have struck her down in her shame. His mother had never named her to him until now.

"Mother!" said he, at last. "She may be dead. Most likely she is."

"No, Will; she is not dead," said Mrs. Leigh. "God will not let her die till I've seen her once again. Thou dost not know how I've prayed and prayed just once again to see her sweet face, and tell her I've forgiven her, though she's broken my heart—she has, Will." She could not go on for a minute or two for the choking sobs. "Thou dost not know that, or thou wouldst not say she could be dead,—for God is very merciful, Will; He is,—He is much more pitiful than man,—I could never ha' spoken to thy father as I did to Him,—and yet thy father forgave her at last. The last words he said were that he forgave her. Thou'lt not be harder than thy father, Will? Do not try and hinder me going to seek her, for it's no use."

Will sat very still for a long time before he spoke. At

last he said, " I'll not hinder you. I think she's dead,
but that's no matter."

" She is not dead," said her mother, with low earnestness. Will took no notice of the interruption.

" We will all go to Manchester for a twelvemonth, and
let the farm to Tom Higginbotham. I'll get blacksmith's
work ; and Tom can have good schooling for awhile,
which he's always craving for. At the end of the year
you'll came back, mother, and give over fretting for
Lizzie, and think with me that she is dead,—and, to
my mind, that would be more comfort than to think of
her living ; " he dropped his voice as he spoke these last
words. She shook her head, but made no answer. He
asked again,—

" Will you, mother, agree to this ? "

" I'll agree to it a-this-ns," said she. " If I hear and
see nought of her for a twelvemonth, me being in Manchester looking out, I'll just ha' broken my heart
fairly before the year's ended, and then I shall know
neither love nor sorrow for her any more, when I'm at
rest in the grave—I'll agree to that, Will."

" Well, I suppose it must be so. I shall not tell
Tom, mother, why we're flitting to Manchester. Best
spare him."

" As thou wilt," said she, sadly, " so that we go,
that's all."

Before the wild daffodils were in flower in the shel-
tered copses round Upclose Farm, the Leighs were
settled in their Manchester home ; if they could ever
grow to consider that place as a home, where there was
no garden or outbuilding, no fresh breezy outlet, no
far-stretching view, over moor and hollow,—no dumb

animals to be tended, and, what more than all they missed, no old haunting memories, even though those remembrances told of sorrow, and the dead and gone.

Mrs. Leigh heeded the loss of all these things less than her sons. She had more spirit in her countenance than she had had for months, because now she had hope; of a sad enough kind, to be sure, but still it was hope. She performed all her household duties, strange and complicated as they were, and bewildered as she was with all the town necessities of her new manner of life; but when her house was " sided," and the boys come home from their work in the evening, she would put on her things and steal out, unnoticed, as she thought, but not without many a heavy sigh from Will, after she had closed the house-door and departed. It was often past midnight before she came back, pale and weary, with almost a guilty look upon her face; but that face so full of disappointment and hope deferred, that Will had never the heart to say what he thought of the folly and hopelessness of the search. Night after night it was renewed, till days grew to weeks, and weeks to months. All this time Will did his duty towards her as well as he could, without having sympathy with her. He stayed at home in the evenings for Tom's sake, and often wished he had Tom's pleasure in reading, for the time hung heavy on his hands as he sat up for his mother.

I need not tell you how the mother spent the weary hours. And yet I will tell you something. She used to wander out, at first as if without a purpose, till she rallied her thoughts, and brought all her energies to bear on the one point; then she went with earnest

patience along the least-known ways to some new part
of the town, looking wistfully with dumb entreaty into
people's faces; sometimes catching a glimpse of a figure
which had a kind of momentary likeness to her child's,
and following that figure with never-wearying perse-
verance, till some light from shop or lamp showed the
cold strange face which was not her daughter's. Once
or twice a kind-hearted passer-by, struck by her look of
yearning woe, turned back and offered help, or asked
her what she wanted. When so spoken to, she answered
only, "You don't know a poor girl they call Lizzie
Leigh, do you?" and when they denied all knowledge,
she shook her head, and went on again. I think they
believed her to be crazy. But she never spoke first to
any one. She sometimes took a few minutes' rest on
the door-steps, and sometimes (very seldom) covered her
face and cried; but she could not afford to lose time and
chances in this way; while her eyes were blinded with
tears, the lost one might pass by unseen.

One evening, in the rich time of shortening autumn-
days, Will saw an old man, who, without being absolutely drunk, could not guide himself rightly along the
foot-path, and was mocked for his unsteadiness of gait
by the idle boys of the neighbourhood. For his father's
sake, Will regarded old age with tenderness, even when
most degraded and removed from the stern virtues which
dignified that father; so he took the old man home, and
seemed to believe his often-repeated assertions, that he
drank nothing but water. The stranger tried to stiffen
himself up into steadiness as he drew nearer home, as if
there were some one there for whose respect he cared
even in his half-intoxicated state, or whose feelings he

feared to grieve. His home was exquisitely clean and neat, even in outside appearance; threshold, window, and window-sill were outward signs of some spirit of purity within. Will was rewarded for his attention by a bright glance of thanks, succeeded by a blush of shame, from a young woman of twenty or thereabouts. She did not speak or second her father's hospitable invitations to him to be seated. She seemed unwilling that a stranger should witness her father's attempts at stately sobriety, and Will could not bear to stay and see her distress. But when the old man, with many a flabby shake of the hand, kept asking him to come again some other evening, and see them, Will sought her downcast eyes, and, though he could not read their veiled meaning, he answered timidly, "If it's agreeable to everybody, I'll come, and thank ye." But there was no answer from the girl, to whom this speech was in reality addressed; and Will left the house, liking her all the better for never speaking.

He thought about her a great deal for the next day or two; he scolded himself for being so foolish as to think of her, and then fell to with fresh vigour, and thought of her more than ever. He tried to depreciate her: he told himself she was not pretty, and then made indignant answer that he liked her looks much better than any beauty of them all. He wished he was not so country-looking, so red-faced, so broad-shouldered; while she was like a lady, with her smooth, colourless complexion, her bright dark hair, and her spotless dress. Pretty or not pretty, she drew his footsteps towards her; he could not resist the impulse that made him wish to see her once more, and find out some fault which should

unloose his heart from her unconscious keeping. But
there she was, pure and maidenly as before. He sat and
looked, answering her father at cross-purposes, while
she drew more and more into the shadow of the chimney-
corner out of sight. Then the spirit that possessed him
(it was not he himself, sure, that did so impudent a
thing!) made him get up and carry the candle to a
different place, under the pretence of giving her more
light at her sewing, but, in reality, to be able to see her
better; she could not stand this much longer, but
jumped up, and said she must put her little niece to
bed; and surely, there never was, before or since, so
troublesome a child of two years old; for though Will
stayed an hour and a half longer, she never came down
again. He won the father's heart, though, by his
capacity as a listener; for some people are not at all
particular, and, so that they themselves may talk on
undisturbed, are not so unreasonable as to expect attention to what they say.

Will did gather this much, however, from the old
man's talk. He had once been quite in a genteel line
of business, but had failed for more money than any
greengrocer he had heard of; at least, any who did not
mix up fish and game with greengrocery proper. This
grand failure seemed to have been the event of his life,
and one on which he dwelt with a strange kind of pride.
It appeared as if at present he rested from his past
exertions (in the bankrupt line), and depended on his
daughter, who kept a small school for very young children. But all these particulars Will only remembered
and understood when he had left the house; at the time
he heard them, he was thinking of Susan. After he had

made good his footing at Mr. Palmer's, he was not long, you may be sure, without finding some reason for returning again and again. He listened to her father, he talked to the little niece, but he looked at Susan, both while he listened and while he talked. Her father kept on insisting upon his former gentility, the details of which would have appeared very questionable to Will's mind, if the sweet, delicate, modest Susan had not thrown an inexplicable air of refinement over all she came near. She never spoke much; she was generally diligently at work; but when she moved, it was so noiselessly, and when she did speak, it was in so low and soft a voice, that silence, speech, motion, and stillness alike seemed to remove her high above Will's reach into some saintly and inaccessible air of glory—high above his reach, even as she knew him! And, if she were made acquainted with the dark secret behind, of his sister's shame, which was kept ever present to his mind by his mother's nightly search among the outcast and forsaken, would not Susan shrink away from him with loathing, as if he were tainted by the involuntary relationship? This was his dread; and thereupon followed a resolution that he would withdraw from her sweet company before it was too late. So he resisted internal temptation, and stayed at home, and suffered and sighed. He became angry with his mother for her untiring patience in seeking for one who, he could not help hoping, was dead rather than alive. He spoke sharply to her, and received only such sad deprecatory answers as made him reproach himself, and still more lose sight of peace of mind. This struggle could not last long without affecting his health; and

Tom, his sole companion through the long evenings,
noticed his increasing languor, his restless irritability,
with perplexed anxiety, and at last resolved to call his
mother's attention to his brother's haggard, careworn
looks. She listened with a startled recollection of Will's
claims upon her love. She noticed his decreasing appe-
tite and half-checked sighs.

"Will, lad! what's come o'er thee?" said she to
him, as he sat listlessly gazing into the fire.

"There's nought the matter with me," said he, as if
annoyed at her remark.

"Nay, lad, but there is." He did not speak again
to contradict her; indeed she did not know if he had
heard her, so unmoved did he look.

"Wouldst like to go back to Upclose Farm?" asked
she, sorrowfully.

"It's just blackberrying time," said Tom.

Will shook his head. She looked at him awhile, as
if trying to read that expression of despondency, and
trace it back to its source.

"Will and Tom could go," said she; "I must stay
here till I've found her, thou know'st," continued she,
dropping her voice.

He turned quickly round, and with the authority he
at all times exercised over Tom, bade him begone to
bed.

When Tom had left the room, he prepared to speak.

CHAPTER II.

"Mother," then said Will, "why will you keep on thinking she's alive? If she were but dead, we need never name her name again. We've never heard nought on her, since father wrote her that letter; we never knew whether she got it or not. She'd left her place before then. Many a one dies in——"

"Oh, my lad! dunnot speak so to me, or my heart will break outright," said his mother, with a sort of cry. Then she calmed herself, for she yearned to persuade him to her own belief. "Thou never asked, and thou'rt too like thy father for me to tell without asking —but it were all to be near Lizzie's old place that I settled down on this side o' Manchester; and the very day at after we came, I went to her old missus, and asked to speak a word wi' her. I had a strong mind to cast it up to her, that she should ha' sent my poor lass away, without telling on it to us first; but she were in black, and looked so sad I could na' find in my heart to threep it up. But I did ask her a bit about our Lizzie. The master would have her turned away at a day's warning (he's gone to t'other place; I hope he'll meet wi' more mercy there than he showed our Lizzie, —I do), and when the missus asked her should she write to us, she says Lizzie shook her head; and when she speered at her again, the poor lass went down on her knees, and begged her not, for she said it would break my heart (as it has done, Will—God knows it has)," said the poor mother, choking with her struggle to keep down her hard, overmastering grief, " and her father would curse her — Oh, God, teach me to be patient." She could not speak for a few minutes,— " and the lass threatened, and said she'd go drown herself in the canal, if the missus wrote home,—and so—

" Well! I'd got a trace of my child,—the missus thought she'd gone to th' workhouse to be nursed; and there I went,—and there, sure enough, she had been, —and they'd turned her out as soon as she were strong, and told her she were young enough to work,—but whatten kind o' work would be open to her, lad, and her baby to keep ? "

Will listened to his mother's tale with deep sympathy, not unmixed with the old bitter shame. But the opening of her heart had unlocked his, and after awhile he spoke.

" Mother! I think I'd e'en better go home. Tom can stay wi' thee. I know I should stay too, but I cannot stay in peace so near—her,—without craving to see her,—Susan Palmer, I mean."

" Has the old Mr. Palmer thou telled me on a daughter ? " asked Mrs. Leigh.

" Ay, he has. And I love her above a bit. And it's because I love her I want to leave Manchester. That's all."

Mrs. Leigh tried to understand this speech for some time, but found it difficult of interpretation.

" Why shouldst thou not tell her thou lov'st her ? Thou'rt a likely lad, and sure o' work. Thou'lt have Upclose at my death; and as for that, I could let thee have it now, and keep mysel' by doing a bit of charring.

It seems to me a very backwards sort o' way of winning her to think of leaving Manchester."

"Oh, mother, she's so gentle and so good,—she's downright holy. She's never known a touch of sin; and can I ask her to marry me, knowing what we do about Lizzie, and fearing worse? I doubt if one like her could ever care for me; but if she knew about my sister, it would put a gulf between us, and she'd shudder up at the thought of crossing it. You don't know how good she is, mother!"

"Will, Will! if she's so good as thou say'st, she'll have pity on such as my Lizzie. If she has no pity for such, she's a cruel Pharisee, and thou'rt best without her."

But he only shook his head, and sighed; and for the time the conversation dropped.

But a new idea sprang up in Mrs. Leigh's head. She thought that she would go and see Susan Palmer, and speak up for Will, and tell her the truth about Lizzie; and according to her pity for the poor sinner, would she be worthy or unworthy of him. She resolved to go the very next afternoon, but without telling any one of her plan. Accordingly she looked out the Sunday clothes she had never before had the heart to unpack since she came to Manchester, but which she now desired to appear in, in order to do credit to Will. She put on her old-fashioned black mode bonnet, trimmed with real lace; her scarlet cloth cloak, which she had had ever since she was married; and always spotlessly clean, she set forth on her unauthorized embassy. She knew the Palmers lived in Crown Street, though where she had heard it she could not tell; and modestly asking her way, she arrived in the street about a quarter to four o'clock. She stopped to inquire the exact number, and the woman whom she addressed told her that Susan Palmer's school would not be loosed till four, and asked her to step in and wait until then at her house.

"For," said she, smiling, "them that wants Susan Palmer wants a kind friend of ours; so we, in a manner, call cousins. Sit down, missus, sit down. I'll wipe the chair, so that it shanna dirty your cloak. My mother used to wear them bright cloaks, and they're right gradely things again a green field."

"Han ye known Susan Palmer long?" asked Mrs. Leigh, pleased with the admiration of her cloak.

"Ever since they comed to live in our street. Our Sally goes to her school."

"Whatten sort of a lass is she, for I ha' never seen her?"

"Well,—as for looks, I cannot say. It's so long since I first knowed her, that I've clean forgotten what I thought of her then. My master says he never saw such a smile for gladdening the heart. But maybe it's not looks you're asking about. The best thing I can say of her looks is, that she's just one a stranger would stop in the street to ask help from if he needed it. All the little childer creeps as close as they can to her; she'll have as many as three or four hanging to her apron all at once."

"Is she cocket at all?"

"Cocket, bless you! you never saw a creature less set up in all your life. Her father's cocket enough. No! she's not cocket any way. You've not heard much of Susan Palmer, I reckon, if you think she's cocket.

She's just one to come quietly in, and do the very thing most wanted; little things, maybe, that any one could do, but that few would think on, for another. She'll bring her thimble wi' her, and mend up after the childer o' nights,—and she writes all Betty Harker's letters to her grandchild out at service,—and she's in nobody's way, and that's a great matter, I take it. Here's the childer running past! School is loosed. You'll find her now, missus, ready to hear and to help. But we none on us frab her by going near her in school-time."

Poor Mrs. Leigh's heart began to beat, and she could almost have turned round and gone home again. Her country breeding had made her shy of strangers, and this Susan Palmer appeared to her like a real born lady by all accounts. So she knocked with a timid feeling at the indicated door, and when it was opened, dropped a simple curtsey without speaking. Susan had her little niece in her arms, curled up with fond endearment against her breast, but she put her gently down to the ground, and instantly placed a chair in the best corner of the room for Mrs. Leigh, when she told her who she was. "It's not Will as has asked me to come," said the mother, apologetically, "I'd a wish just to speak to you myself!"

Susan coloured up to her temples, and stooped to pick up the little toddling girl. In a minute or two Mrs. Leigh began again.

"Will thinks you would na respect us if you knew all; but I think you could na help feeling for us in the sorrow God has put upon us; so I just put on my bonnet, and came off unknownst to the lads. Every

one says you're very good, and that the Lord has
keeped you from falling from His ways; but maybe
you've never yet been tried and tempted as some is.
I'm perhaps speaking too plain, but my heart's welly
broken, and I can't be choice in my words as them
who are happy can. Well now! I'll tell you the truth.
Will dreads you to hear it, but I'll just tell it you.
You mun know,"—but here the poor woman's words
failed her, and she could do nothing but sit rocking
herself backwards and forwards, with sad eyes, straight-
gazing into Susan's face, as if they tried to tell the
tale of agony which the quivering lips refused to utter.
Those wretched, stony eyes forced the tears down Susan's
cheeks, and, as if this sympathy gave the mother strength,
she went on in a low voice,—" I had a daughter once,
my heart's darling. Her father thought I made too much
on her, and that she'd grow marred staying at home;
so he said she mun go among strangers, and learn to
rough it. She were young, and liked the thought of
seeing a bit of the world; and her father heard on a
place in Manchester. Well! I'll not weary you. That
poor girl were led astray; and first thing we heard on
it, was when a letter of her father's was sent back by her
missus, saying she'd left her place, or, to speak right,
the master had turned her into the street soon as he had
heard of her condition—and she not seventeen! "

  She now cried aloud; and Susan wept too. The little
child looked up into their faces, and, catching their
sorrow, began to whimper and wail. Susan took it
softly up, and, hiding her face in its little neck, tried to
restrain her tears, and think of comfort for the mother.
At last she said,—

"Where is she now?"

"Lass! I dunnot know," said Mrs. Leigh, checking her sobs to communicate this addition to her distress. "Mrs. Lomax told me she went——"

"Mrs. Lomax—what Mrs. Lomax?"

"Her as lives in Brabazon Street. She telled me my poor wench went to the workhouse fra there. I'll not speak again the dead; but if her father would but ha' letten me—but he were one who had no notion—no, I'll not say that; best say nought. He forgave her on his death-bed. I daresay I did na go th' right way to work."

"Will you hold the child for me one instant?" said Susan.

"Ay, if it will come to me. Childer used to be fond on me till I got the sad look on my face that scares them, I think."

But the little girl clung to Susan; so she carried it upstairs with her. Mrs. Leigh sat by herself—how long she did not know.

Susan came down with a bundle of far-worn baby-clothes.

"You must listen to me a bit, and not think too much about what I'm going to tell you. Nanny is not my niece, nor any kin to me, that I know of. I used to go out working by the day. One night, as I came home, I thought some woman was following me; I turned to look. The woman, before I could see her face (for she turned it to one side), offered me something. I held out my arms by instinct; she dropped a bundle into them, with a bursting sob that went straight to my heart. It was a baby. I looked round again;

but the woman was gone. She had run away as quick as lightning. There was a little packet of clothes — very few — and as if they were made out of its mother's gowns, for they were large patterns to buy for a baby. I was always fond of babies; and I had not my wits about me, father says; for it was very cold, and when I'd seen as well as I could (for it was past ten) that there was no one in the street, I brought it in and warmed it. Father was very angry when he came, and said he'd take it to the workhouse the next morning, and flyted me sadly about it. But when morning came I could not bear to part with it; it had slept in my arms all night; and I've heard what workhouse bringing-up is. So I told father I'd give up going out working, and stay at home and keep school, if I might only keep the baby; and, after a while, he said if I earned enough for him to have his comforts, he'd let me; but he's never taken to her. Now, don't tremble so—I've but a little more to tell—and maybe I'm wrong in telling it; but I used to work next door to Mrs. Lomax's, in Brabazon Street, and the servants were all thick together; and I heard about Bessy (they called her) being sent away. I don't know that ever I saw her; but the time would be about fitting to this child's age, and I've sometimes fancied it was hers. And now, will you look at the little clothes that came with her—bless her!"

But Mrs. Leigh had fainted. The strange joy and shame, and gushing love for the little child, had over-powered her; it was some time before Susan could bring her round. There she was all trembling, sick with impatience to look at the little frocks. Among them

'Nanny Nanny, my little Nanny

was a slip of paper which Susan had forgotten to name, that had been pinned to the bundle. On it was scrawled in a round, stiff hand,—

"Call her Anne. She does not cry much, and takes a deal of notice. God bless you and forgive me."

The writing was no clue at all; the name "Anne," common though it was, seemed something to build upon. But Mrs. Leigh recognized one of the frocks instantly, as being made out of a part of a gown that she and her daughter had bought together in Rochdale.

She stood up, and stretched out her hands in the attitude of blessing over Susan's bent head.

"God bless you, and show you his mercy in your need, as you have shown it to this little child."

She took the little creature in her arms, and smoothed away her sad looks to a smile, and kissed it fondly, saying over and over again, "Nanny, Nanny, my little Nanny." At last the child was soothed, and looked in her face and smiled back again.

"It has her eyes," said she to Susan.

"I never saw her to the best of my knowledge. I think it must be hers by the frock. But where can she be?"

"God knows," said Mrs. Leigh; "I dare not think she's dead. I'm sure she isn't."

"No; she's not dead. Every now and then a little packet is thrust in under our door, with, may be, two half-crowns in it; once it was half-a-sovereign. Altogether I've got seven-and-thirty shillings wrapped up for Nanny. I never touch it, but I've often thought the poor mother feels near to God when she brings this money. Father wanted to set the policeman to watch, but I said No ; for I was afraid if she was watched she might not come, and it seemed such a holy thing to be checking her in, I could not find in my heart to do it."

"Oh, if we could but find her ! I'd take her in my arms, and we'd just lie down and die together."

"Nay, don't speak so ! " said Susan gently ; "for all that's come and gone, she may turn right at last. Mary Magdalen did, you know."

"Eh ! but I were nearer right about thee than Will. He thought you would never look on him again if you knew about Lizzie. But thou'rt not a Pharisee."

"I'm sorry he thought I could be so hard," said Susan in a low voice, and colouring up. Then Mrs. Leigh was alarmed, and, in her motherly anxiety, she began to fear lest she had injured Will in Susan's estimation.

"You see Will thinks so much of you—gold would not be good enough for you to walk on, in his eye. He said you'd never look at him as he was, let alone his being brother to my poor wench. He loves you so, it makes him think meanly on everything belonging to himself, as not fit to come near ye ; but he's a good lad, and a good son. Thou'lt be a happy woman if thou'lt have him, so don't let my words go against him— don't ! "

But Susan hung her head, and made no answer. She had not known until now, that Will thought so earnestly and seriously about her ; and even now she felt afraid that Mrs. Leigh's words promised her too much happiness, and that they could not be true. At any rate, the instinct of modesty made her shrink from saying anything which might seem like a confession of her own feelings to a third person. Accordingly she turned the conversation on the child.

"I am sure he could not help loving Nanny," said she. "There never was such a good little darling; don't you think she'd win his heart if he knew she was his niece, and perhaps bring him to think kindly on his sister?"

"I dunnot know," said Mrs. Leigh, shaking her head. "He has a turn in his eye like his father, that makes me ——. He's right down good though. But you see, I've never been a good one at managing folk; one severe look turns me sick, and then I say just the wrong thing, I'm so fluttered. Now I should like nothing better than to take Nancy home with me, but Tom knows nothing but that his sister is dead, and I've not the knack of speaking rightly to Will. I dare not do it, and that's the truth. But you mun not think badly of Will. He's so good hissel, that he can't understand how any one can do wrong; and, above all, I'm sure he loves you dearly."

"I don't think I could part with Nancy," said Susan, anxious to stop this revelation of Will's attachment to herself. "He'll come round to her soon; he can't fail; and I'll keep a sharp look-out after the poor mother, and try and catch her the next time she comes with her little parcels of money."

"Ay, lass; we mun get hold of her; my Lizzie. I love thee dearly for thy kindness to her child: but, if thou canst catch her for me, I'll pray for thee when I'm too near my death to speak words; and, while I live, I'll serve thee next to her—she mun come first, thou know'st. God bless thee, lass. My heart is lighter by a deal than it was when I comed in. Them lads will be looking for me home, and I mun go, and leave this little sweet one," kissing it. "If I can take courage, I'll tell Will all that has come and gone between us two. He may come and see thee, mayn't he?"

"Father will be very glad to see him, I'm sure," replied Susan. The way in which this was spoken satisfied Mrs. Leigh's anxious heart that she had done Will no harm by what she had said; and, with many a kiss to the little one, and one more fervent tearful blessing on Susan, she went homewards.

CHAPTER III.

THAT night Mrs. Leigh stopped at home—that only night for many months. Even Tom, the scholar, looked up from his books in amazement; but then he remembered that Will had not been well, and that his mother's attention having been called to the circumstance, it was only natural she should stay to watch him. And no watching could be more tender, or more complete. Her loving eyes seemed never averted from his face—his grave, sad, careworn face. When Tom went to bed the mother left her seat, and, going up to Will, where he sat looking at the fire, but not seeing it, she kissed his forehead, and said,—

"Will! lad, I've been to see Susan Palmer!"

She felt the start under her hand which was placed

on his shoulder, but he was silent for a minute or two. Then he said,—

"What took you there, mother?"

"Why, my lad, it was likely I should wish to see one you cared for; I did not put myself forward. I put on my Sunday clothes, and tried to behave as yo'd ha liked me. At least, I remember trying at first; but after, I forgot all."

She rather wished that he would question her as to what made her forget all. But he only said,—

"How was she looking, mother?"

"Will, thou seest I never set eyes on her before; but she's a good, gentle-looking creature; and I love her dearly, as I've reason to."

Will looked up with momentary surprise; for his mother was too shy to be usually taken with strangers. But, after all, it was natural in this case, for who could look at Susan without loving her? So still he did not ask any questions, and his poor mother had to take courage, and try again to introduce the subject near to her heart. But how?

"Will!" said she (jerking it out, in sudden despair of her own powers to lead to what she wanted to say), "I telled her all."

"Mother! you've ruined me," said he, standing up, and standing opposite to her with a stern white look of affright on his face.

"No! my own dear lad; dunnot look so scared, I have not ruined you!" she exclaimed, placing her two hands on his shoulders, and looking fondly into his face. "She's not one to harden her heart against a mother's sorrow. My own lad, she's too good for that. She's

3

not one to judge and scorn the sinner. She's too deep read in her New Testament for that. Take courage, Will; and thou mayst, for I watched her well, though it is not for one woman to let out another's secret. Sit thee down, lad, for thou look'st very white."

He sat down. His mother drew a stool towards him, and sat at his feet.

"Did you tell her about Lizzie, then?" asked he, hoarse and low.

"I did, I telled her all! and she fell a-crying over my deep sorrow, and the poor wench's sin. And then a light comed into her face, trembling and quivering with some new glad thought; and what dost thou think it was, Will, lad? Nay, I'll not misdoubt but that thy heart will give thanks as mine did, afore God and His angels, for her great goodness. That little Nanny is not her niece, she's our Lizzie's own child, my little grandchild." She could no longer restrain her tears; and they fell hot and fast, but still she looked into his face.

"Did she know it was Lizzie's child? I do not comprehend," said he, flushing red.

"She knows now: she did not at first, but took the little helpless creature in, out of her own pitiful, loving heart, guessing only that it was the child of shame; and she's worked for it, and kept it, and tended it ever sin' it were a mere baby, and loves it fondly. Will! won't you love it?" asked she, beseechingly.

He was silent for an instant; then he said, "Mother, I'll try. Give me time, for all these things startle me. To think of Susan having to do with such a child!"

"Ay, Will! and to think (as may be yet) of Susan having to do with the child's mother! For she is tender and pitiful, and speaks hopefully of my lost one, and will try and find her for me, when she comes, as she does sometimes, to thrust money under the door, for her baby. Think of that, Will. Here's Susan, good and pure as the angels in heaven, yet, like them, full of hope and mercy, and one who, like them, will rejoice over her as repents. Will, my lad, I'm not afeard of you now; and I must speak, and you must listen. I am your mother, and I dare to command you, because I know I am in the right, and that God is on my side. If He should lead the poor wandering lassie to Susan's door, and she comes back crying and sorrowful, led by that good angel to us once more, thou shalt never say a casting-up word to her about her sin, but be tender and helpful towards one 'who was lost and is found;' so may God's blessing rest on thee, and so mayst thou lead Susan home as thy wife."

She stood no longer as the meek, imploring, gentle mother, but firm and dignified, as if the interpreter of God's will. Her manner was so unusual and solemn, that it overcame all Will's pride and stubbornness. He rose softly while she was speaking, and bent his head, as if in reverence at her words, and the solemn injunction which they conveyed. When she had spoken, he said, in so subdued a voice that she was almost surprised at the sound, "Mother, I will."

"I may be dead and gone; but, all the same, thou wilt take home the wandering sinner, and heal up her sorrows, and lead her to her Father's house. My lad! I can speak no more; I'm turned very faint."

He placed her in a chair; he ran for water. She opened her eyes, and smiled.

"God bless you, Will. Oh! I am so happy. It seems as if she were found; my heart is so filled with gladness."

That night Mr. Palmer stayed out late and long. Susan was afraid that he was at his old haunts and habits,—getting tipsy at some public-house: and this thought oppressed her, even though she had so much to make her happy in the consciousness that Will loved her. She sat up long, and then she went to bed, leaving all arranged as well as she could for her father's return. She looked at the little rosy, sleeping girl who was her bed-fellow, with redoubled tenderness, and with many a prayerful thought. The little arms entwined her neck as she lay down, for Nanny was a light sleeper, and was conscious that she, who was loved with all the power of that sweet, childish heart, was near her, and by her, although she was too sleepy to utter any of her half-formed words.

And, by-and-by, she heard her father come home, stumbling uncertain, trying first the windows, and next the door-fastenings, with many a loud, incoherent murmur. The little innocent twined around her seemed all the sweeter and more lovely, when she thought sadly of her erring father. And presently he called aloud for a light. She had left matches and all arranged as usual on the dresser; but, fearful of some accident from fire, in his unusually intoxicated state, she now got up softly, and, putting on a cloak, went down to his assistance.

Alas! the little arms that were unclosed from her soft neck belonged to a light, easily awakened sleeper. Nanny

missed her darling Susy; and terrified at being left
alone in the vast mysterious darkness, which had no
bounds, and seemed infinite, she slipped out of bed, and
tottered, in her little nightgown, towards the door. There
was a light below, and there was Susy and safety! So
she went onwards two steps towards the steep, abrupt
stairs; and then, dazzled with sleepiness, she stood,
she wavered, she fell! Down on her head on the stone
floor she fell! Susan flew to her, and spoke all soft,
entreating, loving words; but her white lids covered up
the blue violets of eyes, and there was no murmur came
out of the pale lips. The warm tears that rained down
did not awaken her; she lay stiff, and weary with her
short life, on Susan's knee. Susan went sick with terror.
She carried her upstairs, and laid her tenderly in bed;
she dressed herself most hastily, with her trembling
fingers. Her father was asleep on the settle downstairs;
and useless, and worse than useless, if awake. But
Susan flew out of the door, and down the quiet, resound-
ing street, towards the nearest doctor's house. Quickly
she went; but as quickly a shadow followed, as if im-
pelled by some sudden terror. Susan rang wildly at
the night-bell,—the shadow crouched near. The doctor
looked out from an upstairs window.

"A little child has fallen down stairs at No. 9, Crown
Street, and is very ill,—dying, I'm afraid. Please, for
God's sake, sir, come directly. No. 9, Crown Street."

"I'll be there directly," said he, and shut the window.

"For that God you have just spoken about—for His
sake—tell me, are you Susan Palmer? Is it my child
that lies a-dying?" said the shadow, springing forwards,
and clutching poor Susan's arm.

" It is a little child of two years old,—I do not know whose it is; I love it as my own. Come with me, whoever you are; come with me."

The two sped along the silent streets,—as silent as the night were they. They entered the house; Susan snatched up the light, and carried it upstairs. The other followed.

She stood with wild, glaring eyes by the bedside, never looking at Susan, but hungrily gazing at the little, white, still child. She stooped down, and put her hand tight on her own heart, as if to still its beating, and bent her ear to the pale lips. Whatever the result was, she did not speak; but threw off the bed-clothes wherewith Susan had tenderly covered up the little creature, and felt its left side.

Then she threw up her arms, with a cry of wild despair.

" She is dead! she is dead!"

She looked so fierce, so mad, so haggard, that, for an instant, Susan was terrified; the next, the holy God had put courage into her heart, and her pure arms were round that guilty, wretched creature, and her tears were falling fast and warm upon her breast. But she was thrown off with violence.

" You killed her—you slighted her—you let her fall down those stairs! you killed her!"

Susan cleared off the thick mist before her, and, gazing at the mother with her clear, sweet, angel eyes, said, mournfully,—

" I would have laid down my own life for her."

" Oh, the murder is on my soul!" exclaimed the wild, bereaved mother, with the fierce impetuosity of one who has none to love her and to be beloved, regard to whom might teach self-restraint.

"Hush!" said Susan, her finger on her lips. "Here is the doctor. God may suffer her to live."

The poor mother turned sharp round. The doctor mounted the stair. Ah! that mother was right; the little child was really dead and gone.

And when he confirmed her judgment, the mother fell down in a fit. Susan, with her deep grief, had to forget herself, and forget her darling (her charge for years), and question the doctor what she must do with the poor wretch, who lay on the floor in such extreme of misery.

"She is the mother!" said she.

"Why did not she take better care of her child?" asked he, almost angrily.

But Susan only said, "The little child slept with me; and it was I that left her."

"I will go back and make up a composing draught; and while I am away you must get her to bed."

Susan took out some of her own clothes, and softly undressed the stiff, powerless form. There was no other bed in the house but the one in which her father slept. So she tenderly lifted the body of her darling; and was going to take it downstairs, but the mother opened her eyes, and, seeing what she was about, she said,—

"I am not worthy to touch her, I am so wicked. I have spoken to you as I never should have spoken; but I think you are very good. May I have my own child to lie in my arms for a little while?"

Her voice was so strange a contrast to what it had been before she had gone into the fit, that Susan hardly recognized it: it was now so unspeakably soft, so irresistibly pleading; the features too had lost their fierce expression, and were almost as placid as death. Susan could not speak, but she carried the little child, and laid it in its mother's arms; then, as she looked at them, something overpowered her, and she knelt down, crying aloud,—

"Oh, my God, my God, have mercy on her, and forgive, and comfort her."

But the mother kept smiling, and stroking the little face, murmuring soft tender words, as if it were alive. She was going mad, Susan thought; but she prayed on, and on, and ever still she prayed with streaming eyes.

The doctor came with the draught. The mother took it, with docile unconsciousness of its nature as medicine. The doctor sat by her; and soon she fell asleep. Then he rose softly, and beckoning Susan to the door, he spoke to her there.

"You must take the corpse out of her arms. She will not awake. That draught will make her sleep for many hours. I will call before noon again. It is now daylight. Good-by."

Susan shut him out; and then, gently extricating the dead child from its mother's arms, she could not resist making her own quiet moan over her darling. She tried to learn off its little placid face, dumb and pale before her.

> Not all the scalding tears of care
> Shall wash away that vision fair;
> Not all the thousand thoughts that rise,
> Not all the sights that dim her eyes,
>   Shall e'er usurp the place
>   Of that little angel-face.

And then she remembered what remained to be done. She saw that all was right in the house; her father was still dead asleep on the settle, in spite of all the noise of the night. She went out through the quiet streets, deserted still, although it was broad daylight, and to where the Leighs lived. Mrs. Leigh, who kept her country hours, was opening her window-shutters. Susan took her by the arm, and, without speaking, went into the house-place. There she knelt down before the astonished Mrs. Leigh, and cried as she had never done before; but the miserable night had overpowered her, and she who had gone through so much calmly, now that the pressure seemed removed could not find the power to speak.

"My poor dear! What has made thy heart so sore as to come and cry a-this-ons? Speak and tell me. Nay, cry on, poor wench, if thou canst not speak yet. It will ease the heart, and then thou canst tell me."

"Nanny is dead!" said Susan. "I left her to go to father, and she fell down stairs, and never breathed again. Oh, that's my sorrow! But I've more to tell. Her mother is come—is in our house! Come and see if it's your Lizzie." Mrs. Leigh could not speak, but, trembling, put on her things and went with Susan in dizzy haste back to Crown Street.

CHAPTER IV.

As they entered the house in Crown Street, they per-
ceived that the door would not open freely on its hinges,
and Susan instinctively looked behind to see the cause
of the obstruction. She immediately recognized the
appearance of a little parcel, wrapped in a scrap of
newspaper, and evidently containing money. She
stooped and picked it up. " Look ! " said she, sorrowfully, " the mother was bringing this for her child last
night."

But Mrs. Leigh did not answer. So near to the
ascertaining if it were her lost child or no, she could
not be arrested, but pressed onwards with trembling
steps and a beating, fluttering heart. She entered the
bedroom, dark and still. She took no heed of the little
corpse over which Susan paused, but she went straight
to the bed, and, withdrawing the curtain, saw Lizzie ;
but not the former Lizzie, bright, gay, buoyant, and
undimmed. This Lizzie was old before her time ; her
beauty was gone ; deep lines of care, and, alas ! of want
(or thus the mother imagined) were printed on the
cheek, so round, and fair, and smooth, when last she
gladdened her mother's eyes. Even in her sleep she
bore the look of woe and despair which was the preva-
lent expression of her face by day ; even in her sleep
she had forgotten how to smile. But all these marks of
the sin and sorrow she had passed through only made
her mother love her the more. She stood looking at

her with greedy eyes, which seemed as though no gazing could satisfy their longing; and at last she stooped down and kissed the pale, worn hand that lay outside the bed-clothes. No touch disturbed the sleeper; the mother need not have laid the hand so gently down upon the counterpane. There was no sign of life, save only now and then a deep sob-like sigh. Mrs. Leigh sat down beside the bed, and, still holding back the curtain, looked on and on, as if she could never be satisfied.

Susan would fain have stayed by her darling one; but she had many calls upon her time and thoughts, and her will had now, as ever, to be given up to that of others. All seemed to devolve the burden of their cares on her. Her father, ill-humoured from his last night's intemperance, did not scruple to reproach her with being the cause of little Nanny's death; and when, after bearing his upbraiding meekly for some time, she could no longer restrain herself, but began to cry, he wounded her even more by his injudicious attempts at comfort; for he said it was as well the child was dead; it was none of theirs, and why should they be troubled with it? Susan wrung her hands at this, and came and stood before her father, and implored him to forbear. Then she had to take all requisite steps for the coroner's inquest: she had to arrange for the dismissal of her school; she had to summon a little neighbour, and send his willing feet on a message to William Leigh, who, she felt, ought to be informed of his mother's whereabouts, and of the whole state of affairs. She asked her messenger to tell him to come and speak to her,—that his mother was at her house. She was thankful that her father sauntered out to have a gossip at the nearest coach-stand, and to relate as many of the night's adventures as he knew; for as yet he was in ignorance of the watcher and the watched, who silently passed away the hours upstairs.

At dinner-time Will came. He looked red, glad, impatient, excited. Susan stood calm and white before him, her soft, loving eyes gazing straight into his.

"Will," said she, in a low, quiet voice, "your sister is upstairs."

"My sister!" said he, as if affrighted at the idea, and losing his glad look in one of gloom. Susan saw it, and her heart sank a little, but she went on as calm to all appearance as ever.

"She was little Nanny's mother, as perhaps you know. Poor little Nanny was killed last night by a fall downstairs." All the calmness was gone; all the suppressed feeling was displayed in spite of every effort. She sat down, and hid her face from him, and cried bitterly. He forgot everything but the wish, the longing to comfort her. He put his arm round her waist, and bent over her. But all he could say, was, "Oh, Susan, how can I comfort you! Don't take on so,—pray don't!" He never changed the words, but the tone varied every time he spoke. At last she seemed to regain her power over herself; and she wiped her eyes, and once more looked upon him with her own quiet, earnest, unfearing gaze.

"Your sister was near the house. She came in on hearing my words to the doctor. She is asleep now, and your mother is watching her. I wanted to tell you all myself. Would you like to see your mother?"

"No!" said he. "I would rather see none but thee. Mother told me thou knew'st all." His eyes were downcast in their shame.

But the holy and pure did not lower or veil her eyes.

She said, "Yes, I know all—all but her sufferings. Think what they must have been!"

He made answer low and stern, "She deserved them all; every jot."

"In the eye of God, perhaps she does. He is the judge; we are not."

"Oh!" she said, with a sudden burst, "Will Leigh! I have thought so well of you; don't go and make me think you cruel and hard. Goodness is not goodness unless there is mercy and tenderness with it. There is your mother, who has been nearly heart-broken, now full of rejoicing over her child—think of your mother."

"I do think of her," said he. "I remember the promise I gave her last night. Thou shouldst give me time. I would do right in time. I never think it o'er in quiet. But I will do what is right and fitting, never fear. Thou hast spoken out very plain to me; and misdoubted me, Susan; I love thee so, that thy words cut me. If I did hang back a bit from making sudden promises, it was because not even for love of thee, would I say what I was not feeling; and at first I could not feel all at once as thou wouldst have me. But I'm not cruel and hard; for if I had been, I should na' have grieved as I have done."

He made as if he were going away; and indeed he did feel he would rather think it over in quiet. But Susan, grieved at her incautious words, which had all the appearance of harshness, went a step or two nearer

—paused—and then, all over blushes, said in a low, soft whisper—

" Oh, Will! I beg your pardon. I am very sorry—won't you forgive me ? "

She who had always drawn back, and been so reserved, said this in the very softest manner; with eyes now uplifted beseechingly, now dropped to the ground. Her sweet confusion told more than words could do; and Will turned back, all joyous in his certainty of being beloved, and took her in his arms, and kissed her.

" My own Susan! " he said.

Meanwhile the mother watched her child in the room above.

It was late in the afternoon before she awoke; for the sleeping draught had been very powerful. The instant she awoke, her eyes were fixed on her mother's face with a gaze as unflinching as if she were fascinated. Mrs. Leigh did not turn away, nor move. For it seemed as if motion would unlock the stony command over herself which, while so perfectly still, she was enabled to preserve. But by-and-by Lizzie cried out in a piercing voice of agony,—

" Mother, don't look at me! I have been so wicked! " and instantly she hid her face, and grovelled among the bedclothes, and lay like one dead—so motionless was she.

Mrs. Leigh knelt down by the bed, and spoke in the most soothing tones.

" Lizzie, dear, don't speak so. I'm thy mother, darling; don't be afeard of me. I never left off loving thee, Lizzie. I was always a-thinking of thee. Thy father forgave thee afore he died." (There was a little

start here, but no sound was heard.) " Lizzie, lass,
I'll do aught for thee; I'll live for thee; only don't be
afeard of me. Whate'er thou art or hast been, we'll
ne'er speak on't. We'll leave th' oud times behind us,
and go back to the Upclose Farm. I but left it to find
thee, my lass; and God has led me to thee. Blessed
be His name. And God is good, too, Lizzie. Thou
hast not forgot thy Bible, I'll be bound, for thou wert
always a scholar. I'm no reader, but I learnt off them
texts to comfort me a bit, and I've said them many a
time a day to myself. Lizzie, lass, don't hide thy head
so, it's thy mother as is speaking to thee. Thy little
child clung to me only yesterday; and if it's gone to be
an angel, it will speak to God for thee. Nay, don't sob
a that 'as; thou shalt have it again in heaven; I know
thou'lt strive to get there, for thy little Nancy's sake—
and listen! I'll tell thee God's promises to them that
are penitent—only doan't be afeard."

Mrs. Leigh folded her hands, and strove to speak
very clearly, while she repeated every tender and merciful text she could remember. She could tell from the
breathing that her daughter was listening; but she was
so dizzy and sick herself when she had ended, that she
could not go on speaking. It was all she could do to
keep from crying aloud.

At last she heard her daughter's voice.

" Where have they taken her to ? " she asked.

" She is downstairs. So quiet, and peaceful, and
happy she looks."

" Could she speak! Oh, if God—if I might but
have heard her little voice! Mother, I used to dream
of it. May I see her once again ?—Oh, mother, if I

strive very hard, and God is very merciful, and I go to heaven, I shall not know her—I shall not know my own again—she will shun me as a stranger, and cling to Susan Palmer and to you. Oh, woe! Oh, woe!" She shook with exceeding sorrow.

In her earnestness of speech she had uncovered her face, and tried to read Mrs. Leigh's thoughts through her looks. And when she saw those aged eyes brimming full of tears, and marked the quivering lips, she threw her arms round the faithful mother's neck, and wept there, as she had done in many a childish sorrow— but with a deeper, a more wretched grief.

Her mother hushed her on her breast; and lulled her as if she were a baby; and she grew still and quiet.

They sat thus for a long, long time. At last Susan Palmer came up with some tea and bread and butter for Mrs. Leigh. She watched the mother feed her sick, unwilling child, with every fond inducement to eat which she could devise; they neither of them took notice of Susan's presence. That night they lay in each other's arms; but Susan slept on the ground beside them.

They took the little corpse (the little, unconscious sacrifice, whose early calling-home had reclaimed her poor wandering mother) to the hills, which in her lifetime she had never seen. They dared not lay her by the stern grandfather in Milne Row churchyard, but they bore her to a lone moorland graveyard, where, long ago, the Quakers used to bury their dead. They laid her there on the sunny slope, where the earliest spring-flowers blow.

Will and Susan live at the Upclose Farm. Mrs. Leigh and Lizzie dwell in a cottage so secluded that, until you drop into the very hollow where it is placed, you do not see it. Tom is a schoolmaster in Rochdale, and he and Will help to support their mother. I only know that, if the cottage be hidden in a green hollow of the hills, every sound of sorrow in the whole upland is heard there—every call of suffering or of sickness for help is listened to by a sad, gentle-looking woman, who rarely smiles (and when she does, her smile is more sad than other people's tears), but who comes out of her seclusion whenever there's a shadow in any household. Many hearts bless Lizzie Leigh, but she—she prays always and ever for forgiveness—such forgiveness as may enable her to see her child once more. Mrs. Leigh is quiet and happy. Lizzie is, to her eyes, something precious— as the lost piece of silver—found once more. Susan is the bright one who brings sunshine to all. Children grow around her and call her blessed. One is called Nanny. Her, Lizzie often takes to the sunny graveyard in the uplands, and while the little creature gathers the daises, and makes chains, Lizzie sits by a little grave and weeps bitterly.

THE WELL OF PEN-MORFA.

CHAPTER I.

OF a hundred travellers who spend a night at Trê-Madoc, in North Wales, there is not one, perhaps, who goes to the neighbouring village of Pen-Morfa. The new town, built by Mr. Maddocks, Shelley's friend, has taken away all the importance of the ancient village—formerly, as its name imports, " the head of the marsh ; " that marsh which Mr. Maddocks drained and dyked, and reclaimed from the Traeth Mawr, till Pen-Morfa, against the walls of whose cottages the winter tides lashed in former days, has come to stand, high and dry, three miles from the sea, on a disused road to Caernarvon. I do not think there has been a new cottage built in Pen-Morfa this hundred years, and many an old one has dates in some obscure corner which tell of the fifteenth century. The joists of timber, where they meet overhead, are blackened with the smoke of centuries. There is one large room, round which the beds are built like cupboards, with wooden doors to open and shut, somewhat in the old Scotch fashion, I imagine ; and below the bed (at least in one instance I can testify that this was the case, and

I was told it was not uncommon) is a great wide wooden drawer, which contained the oat-cake, baked for some months' consumption by the family. They call the promontory of Llŷn (the point at the end of Caernarvon-shire), *Welsh* Wales: I think they might call Pen-Morfa a Welsh Welsh village; it is so national in its ways, and buildings, and inhabitants, and so different from the towns and hamlets into which the English throng in summer. How these said inhabitants of Pen-Morfa ever are distinguished by their names, I, uninitiated, cannot tell. I only know for a fact, that in a family there with which I am acquainted, the eldest son's name is John Jones, because his father's was John Thomas; that the second son is called David Williams, because his grand-father was William Wynn; and that the girls are called indiscriminately by the names of Thomas and Jones. I have heard some of the Welsh chuckle over the way in which they have baffled the barristers at Caernarvon assizes, denying the name under which they had been subpœnaed to give evidence, if they were unwilling wit-nesses. I could tell you of a great deal which is peculiar and wild in these true Welsh people, who are what I suppose we English were a century ago; but I must hasten on to my tale.

I have received great, true, beautiful kindness from one of the members of the family of whom I just now spoke as living at Pen-Morfa; and when I found that they wished me to drink tea with them, I gladly did so, though my friend was the only one in the house who could speak English at all fluently. After tea, I went with them to see some of their friends; and it was then I saw the interiors of the houses of which I have spoken.

It was an autumn evening: we left mellow sunset-light
in the open air when we entered the houses, in which all
seemed dark, save in the ruddy sphere of the firelight,
for the windows were very small, and deep-set in the
thick walls.   Here were an old couple, who welcomed
me in Welsh; and brought forth milk and oat-cake with
patriarchal hospitality. Sons and daughters had married
away from them; they lived alone; he was blind, or
nearly so; and they sat one on each side of the fire, so
old and so still (till we went in and broke the silence)
that they seemed to be listening for death.   At another
house lived a woman stern and severe-looking. She was
busy hiving a swarm of bees, alone and unassisted.   I
do not think my companion would have chosen to speak
to her; but seeing her out in her hill-side garden, she
made some inquiry in Welsh, which was answered in the
most mournful tone I ever heard in my life; a voice of
which the freshness and " timbre " had been choked up
by tears long years ago.   I asked who she was. I dare
say the story is common enough; but the sight of the
woman and her few words had impressed me.   She had
been the beauty of Pen-Morfa; had been in service; had
been taken to London by the family whom she served;
had come down, in a year or so, back to Pen-Morfa, her
beauty gone into that sad, wild, despairing look which I
saw; and she about to become a mother.   Her father
had died during her absence, and left her a very little
money; and after her child was born, she took the little
cottage where I saw her, and made a scanty living by
the produce of her bees.   She associated with no one.
One event had made her savage and distrustful to her
kind.   She kept so much aloof that it was some time

before it became known that her child was deformed, and had lost the use of its lower limbs. Poor thing! When I saw the mother, it had been for fifteen years bedridden. But go past when you would, in the night, you saw a light burning; it was often that of the watching mother, solitary and friendless, soothing the moaning child; or you might hear her crooning some old Welsh air, in hopes to still the pain with the loud monotonous music. Her sorrow was so dignified, and her mute endurance and her patient love won her such respect, that the neighbours would fain have been friends; but she kept alone and solitary. This a most true story. I hope that woman and her child are dead now, and their souls above.

Another story which I heard of these old primitive dwellings I mean to tell at somewhat greater length:—

There are rocks high above Pen-Morfa; they are the same that hang over Trê-Madoc, but near Pen-Morfa they sweep away, and are lost in the plain. Everywhere they are beautiful. The great, sharp ledges, which would otherwise look hard and cold, are adorned with the brightest-coloured moss, and the golden lichen. Close to, you see the scarlet leaves of the crane's-bill, and the tufts of purple heather, which fill up every cleft and cranny; but, in the distance, you see only the general effect of infinite richness of colour, broken, here and there, by great masses of ivy. At the foot of these rocks come a rich, verdant meadow or two; and then you are at Pen-Morfa. The village well is sharp down under the rocks. There are one or two large sloping pieces of stone in that last field, on the road leading to the well, which are always slippery; slippery in the summer's heat, almost as much as in the frost of winter, when some little glassy stream that runs over them is turned into a thin sheet of ice. Many, many years back—a lifetime ago—there lived in Pen-Morfa a widow and her daughter. Very little is required in those out-of-the-way Welsh villages. The wants of the people are very simple. Shelter, fire, a little oat-cake and butter-milk, and garden produce; perhaps some pork and bacon from the pig in winter; clothing, which is prin-cipally of home manufacture, and of the most enduring kind : these take very little money to purchase, especially in a district into which the large capitalists have not yet come, to buy up two or three acres of the peasants ; and nearly every man about Pen-Morfa owned, at the time of which I speak, his dwelling and some land beside.

Eleanor Gwynn inherited the cottage (by the roadside, on the left hand as you go from Trê-Madoc to Pen-Morfa) in which she and her husband had lived all their married life, and a small garden sloping southwards, in which her bees lingered before winging their way to the more distant heather. She took rank among her neigh-bours as the possessor of a moderate independence—not rich, and not poor. But the young men of Pen-Morfa thought her very rich in the possession of a most lovely daughter. Most of us know how very pretty Welsh women are ; but, from all accounts, Nest Gwynn (Nest, or Nesta, is the Welsh for Agnes) was more regularly beautiful than any one for miles round. The Welsh are still fond of triads, and " as beautiful as a summer's morning at sunrise, as a white seagull on the green sea wave, and as Nest Gwynn," is yet a saying in that district. Nest knew she was beautiful, and delighted in

it. Her mother sometimes checked her in her happy
pride, and sometimes reminded her that beauty was a
great gift of God (for the Welsh are a very pious
people); but when she began her little homily, Nest
came dancing to her, and knelt down before her, and
put her face up to be kissed, and so, with a sweet interruption, she stopped her mother's lips. Her high spirits
made some few shake their heads, and some called her a
flirt and a coquette; for she could not help trying to
please all, both old and young, both men and women.
A very little from Nest sufficed for this; a sweet, glit-
tering smile, a word of kindness, a merry glance, or a
little sympathy; all these pleased and attracted: she
was like the fairy-gifted child, and dropped inestimable
gifts. But some, who had interpreted her smiles and
kind words rather as their wishes led them, than as they
were really warranted, found that the beautiful, beaming
Nest could be decided and saucy enough; and so they
revenged themselves by calling her a flirt. Her mother
heard it, and sighed; but Nest only laughed.

It was her work to fetch water for the day's use from
the well I told you about. Old people say it was the
prettiest sight in the world to see her come stepping
lightly and gingerly over the stones with the pale of water
balanced on her head; she was too adroit to need to
steady it with her hand. They say, now that they can
afford to be charitable and speak the truth, that in all
her changes to other people, there never was a better
daughter to a widowed mother than Nest. There is a
picturesque old farmhouse under Moel Gwynn, on the
road from Trê-Madoc to Criccaeth, called by some Welsh
name which I now forget; but its meaning in English

is "The End of Time;" a strange, boding, ominous name. Perhaps, the builder meant his work to endure till the end of time. I do not know; but there the old house stands, and will stand for many a year. When Nest was young, it belonged to one Edward Williams; his mother was dead, and people said he was on the look-out for a wife. They told Nest so, but she tossed her head and reddened, and said she thought he might look long before he got one; so it was not strange that one morning when she went to the well, one autumn morning when the dew lay heavy on the grass, and the thrushes were busy among the mountain-ash berries, Edward Williams happened to be there, on his way to the coursing match near, and somehow his greyhounds threw her pail of water over in their romping play, and she was very long in filling it again; and when she came home she threw her arms round her mother's neck, and, in a passion of joyous tears, told her that Edward Williams, of "The End of Time," had asked her to marry him, and that she had said "Yes."

Eleanor Gwynn shed her tears too; but they fell quietly when she was alone. She was thankful Nest had found a protector—one suitable in age and apparent character, and above her in fortune; but she knew she should miss her sweet daughter in a thousand household ways; miss her in the evenings by the fireside; miss her when at night she wakened up with a start from a dream of her youth, and saw her fair face lying calm in the moonlight, pillowed by her side. Then she forgot her dream, and blessed her child, and slept again. But who could be so selfish as to be sad when Nest was so supremely happy; she danced and sang more than ever; and then sat silent, and smiled to herself: if spoken to, she started and came back to the present with a scarlet blush, which told what she had been thinking of.

That was a sunny, happy, enchanted autumn. But the winter was nigh at hand; and with it came sorrow. One fine frosty morning, Nest went out with her lover— she to the well, he to some farming business, which was to be transacted at the little inn of Pen-Morfa. He was late for his appointment; so he left her at the entrance of the village, and hastened to the inn; and she, in her best cloak and new hat (put on against her mother's advice; but they were a recent purchase, and very becoming), went through the Dol Mawr, radiant with love and happiness. One who lived until lately, met her going down towards the well that morning, and said he turned round to look after her—she seemed unusually lovely. He wondered at the time at her wearing her Sunday clothes; for the pretty, hooded blue-cloth cloak is kept among the Welsh women as a church and market garment, and not commonly used, even on the coldest days of winter, for such household errands as fetching water from the well. However, as he said, " It was not possible to look in her face, and 'fault' anything she wore." Down the sloping stones the girl went blithely with her pail. She filled it at the well; and then she took off her hat, tied the strings together, and slung it over her arm. She lifted the heavy pail and balanced it on her head. But, alas! in going up the smooth, slippery, treacherous rock, the encumbrance of her cloak— it might be such a trifle as her slung hat—something, at any rate, took away her evenness of poise; the freshet had frozen on the slanting stone, and was one

coat of ice ; poor Nest fell, and put out her hip. No
more flushing rosy colour on that sweet face ; no more
look of beaming innocent happiness ; instead, there was
deadly pallor, and filmy eyes, over which dark shades
seemed to chase each other as the shoots of agony grew
more and more intense. She screamed once or twice ;
but the exertion (involuntary, and forced out of her by
excessive pain) overcame her, and she fainted. A child,
coming an hour or two afterwards, on the same errand,
saw her lying there, ice-glued to the stone, and thought
she was dead. It flew crying back.

"Nest Gwynn is dead! Nest Gwynn is dead!" and,
crazy with fear, it did not stop until it had hid its head
in its mother's lap. The village was alarmed, and all
who were able went in haste towards the well. Poor
Nest had often thought she was dying in that dreary
hour; had taken fainting for death, and struggled
against it ; and prayed that God would keep her alive
till she could see her lover's face once more ; and when
she did see it, white with terror, bending over her, she
gave a feeble smile, and let herself faint away into unconsciousness.

Many a month she lay on her bed unable to move.
Sometimes she was delirious, sometimes worn-out into
the deepest depression. Through all, her mother
watched her with tenderest care. The neighbours
would come and offer help. They would bring presents
of country dainties; and I do not suppose that there
was a better dinner than ordinary cooked in any household in Pen-Morfa parish, but a portion of it was sent
to Eleanor Gwynn, if not for her sick daughter, to try
and tempt her herself to eat and be strengthened; for

to no one would she delegate the duty of watching over
her child. Edward Williams was for a long time most
assiduous in his inquiries and attentions ; but by-and-
by (ah! you see the dark fate of poor Nest now), he
slackened, so little at first that Eleanor blamed herself
for her jealousy on her daughter's behalf, and chid her
suspicious heart. But as spring ripened into summer,
and Nest was still bedridden, Edward's coolness was
visible to more than the poor mother. The neighbours
would have spoken to her about it, but she shrunk from
the subject as if they were probing a wound. "At any
rate," thought she, "Nest shall be strong before she is
told about it. I will tell lies—I shall be forgiven—but
I must save my child; and when she is stronger, perhaps I may be able to comfort her. Oh! I wish she
would not speak to him so tenderly and trustfully, when
she is delirious. I could curse him when she does." And
then Nest would call for her mother, and Eleanor would
go and invent some strange story about the summonses
Edward had had to Caernarvon assizes, or to Harlech
cattle market. But at last she was driven to her wit's
end ; it was three weeks since he had even stopped at the
door to inquire, and Eleanor, mad with anxiety about
her child, who was silently pining off to death for want
of tidings of her lover, put on her cloak, when she had
lulled her daughter to sleep one fine June evening, and
set off to "The End of Time." The great plain which
stretches out like an amphitheatre, in the half-circle of
hills formed by the ranges of Moel Gwynn and the Trê-
Madoc Rocks, was all golden-green in the mellow light
of sunset. To Eleanor it might have been black with
winter frost—she never noticed outward things till she

reached "The End of Time;" and there, in the little
farm-yard, she was brought to a sense of her present
hour and errand by seeing Edward. He was examining
some hay, newly stacked; the air was scented by its
fragrance, and by the lingering sweetness of the breath
of the cows. When Edward turned round at the footstep and saw Eleanor, he coloured and looked confused;
however, he came forward to meet her in a cordial
manner enough.

"It's a fine evening," said he. "How is Nest? But,
indeed, you're being here is a sign she is better. Won't
you come in and sit down?" He spoke hurriedly, as if
affecting a welcome which he did not feel.

"Thank you. I'll just take this milking-stool and
sit down here. The open air is like balm, after being
shut up so long."

"It is a long time," he replied, "more than five
months."

Mrs. Gwynn was trembling at heart. She felt an
anger which she did not wish to show; for, if by any
manifestations of temper or resentment she lessened or
broke the waning thread of attachment which bound
him to her daughter, she felt she should never forgive
herself. She kept inwardly saying, "Patience, patience!
he may be true, and love her yet;" but her indignant
convictions gave her words the lie.

"It's a long time, Edward Williams, since you've
been near us to ask after Nest," said she. "She may
be better, or she may be worse, for aught you know."
She looked up at him reproachfully, but spoke in a
gentle, quiet tone.

"I—you see the hay has been a long piece of work.

The weather has been fractious—and a master's eye is needed. Besides," said he, as if he had found the reason for which he sought to account for his absence, " I have heard of her from Rowland Jones. I was at the surgery for some horse-medicine—he told me about her :" and a shade came over his face, as he remembered what the doctor had said. Did he think that shade would escape the mother's eye ?

" You saw Rowland Jones ! Oh, man-alive, tell me what he said of my girl ! He'll say nothing to me, but just hems and haws the more I pray him. But you will tell me. You *must* tell me." She stood up and spoke in a tone of command, which his feeling of independence, weakened just then by an accusing conscience, did not enable him to resist. He strove to evade the question, however.

" It was an unlucky day that ever she went to the well !"

" Tell me what the doctor said of my child," repeated Mrs. Gwynn. " Will she live, or will she die ? " He did not dare to disobey the imperious tone in which this question was put.

" Oh, she will live, don't be afraid. The doctor said she would live." He did not mean to lay any peculiar emphasis on the word " live," but somehow he did, and she, whose every nerve vibrated with anxiety, caught the word.

" She will live !" repeated she. " But there is something behind. Tell me, for I will know. If you won't say, I'll go to Rowland Jones to-night, and make him tell me what he has said to you."

There had passed something in this conversation-between himself and the doctor, which Edward did not wish to have known; and Mrs. Gwynn's threat had the desired effect. But he looked vexed and irritated.

"You have such impatient ways with you, Mrs. Gwynn," he remonstrated.

"I am a mother asking news of my sick child," said she. "Go on. What did he say? She'll live—" as if giving the clue.

"She'll live, he has no doubt of that. But he thinks —now don't clench your hands so—I can't tell you if you look in that way; you are enough to frighten a man."

"I'm not speaking," said she, in a low, husky tone. "Never mind my looks: she'll live——"

"But she'll be a cripple for life. There! you would have it out," said he, sulkily.

"A cripple for life," repeated she, slowly. "And I'm one-and-twenty years older than she is!" She sighed heavily.

"And, as we're about it, I'll just tell you what is in my mind," said he, hurried and confused. "I've a deal of cattle; and the farm makes heavy work, as much as an able healthy woman can do. So you see——" He stopped, wishing her to understand his meaning without words. But she would not. She fixed her dark eyes on him, as if reading his soul, till he flinched under her gaze.

"Well," said she, at length, "say on. Remember, I've a deal of work in me yet, and what strength is mine is my daughter's."

"You're very good. But, altogether, you must be aware, Nest will never be the same as she was."

"And you've not yet sworn in the face of God to take her for better, for worse; and, as she is worse"— she looked in his face, caught her breath, and went on —"as she is worse, why, you cast her off, not being church-tied to her. Though her body may be crippled, her poor heart is the same—alas!—and full of love for you. Edward, you don't mean to break it off because of our sorrows. You're only trying me, I know," said she, as if begging him to assure her that her fears were false. "But, you see, I'm a foolish woman—a poor, foolish woman—and ready to take fright at a few words." She smiled up in his face; but it was a forced, doubting smile, and his face still retained its sullen, dogged aspect.

"Nay, Mrs. Gwynn," said he, "you spoke truth at first. Your own good sense told you Nest would never be fit to be any man's wife—unless, indeed, she could catch Mr. Griffiths of Tynwntyrybwlch; he might keep her a carriage, maybe." Edward really did not mean to be unfeeling; but he was obtuse, and wished to carry off his embarrassment by a kind of friendly joke, which he had no idea would sting the poor mother as it did. He was startled at her manner.

"Put it in words like a man. Whatever you mean by my child, say it for yourself, and don't speak as if my good sense had told me anything. I stand here, doubting my own thoughts, cursing my own fears. Don't be a coward. I ask you whether you and Nest are troth-plight?"

"I am not a coward. Since you ask me, I answer, Nest and I *were* troth-plight; but we *are* not. I cannot—no one would expect me to wed a cripple. It's

your own doing I've told you now; I had made up my
mind, but I should have waited a bit before telling
you."

"Very well," said she, and she turned to go away;
but her wrath burst the flood-gates, and swept away
discretion and forethought. She moved, and stood in
the gateway. Her lips parted, but no sound came; with
an hysterical motion, she threw her arms suddenly up to
heaven, as if bringing down lightning towards the grey
old house to which she pointed as they fell, and then she
spoke :—

"The widow's child is unfriended. As surely as the
Saviour brought the son of a widow from death to life,
for her tears and cries, so surely will God and His angels
watch over my Nest, and avenge her cruel wrongs." She
turned away weeping, and wringing her hands.

Edward went in-doors; he had no more desire to
reckon his stores; he sat by the fire, looking gloomily
at the red ashes. He might have been there half an
hour or more, when some one knocked at the door. He
would not speak. He wanted no one's company. Another
knock, sharp and loud. He did not speak. Then the
visitor opened the door, and, to his surprise—almost to
his affright—Eleanor Gwynn came in.

"I knew you were here. I knew you could not go
out into the clear, holy night as if nothing had happened.
Oh! did I curse you? If I did, I beg you to forgive
me; and I will try and ask the Almighty to bless you,
if you will but have a little mercy—a very little. It
will kill my Nest if she knows the truth now—she is so
very weak. Why, she cannot feed herself, she is so low
and feeble. You would not wish to kill her, I think,

Edward!" She looked at him, as if expecting an answer; but he did not speak. She went down on her knees on the flags by him.

"You will give me a little time, Edward, to get her strong, won't you, now? I ask it on my bended knees! Perhaps, if I promise never to curse you again, you will come sometimes to see her, till she is well enough to know how all is over, and her heart's hopes crushed. Only say you'll come for a month or so, as if you still loved her—the poor cripple, forlorn of the world. I'll get her strong, and not tax you long." Her tears fell too fast for her to go on.

"Get up, Mrs. Gwynn," Edward said. "Don't kneel to me. I have no objection to come and see Nest, now and then, so that all is clear between you and me. Poor thing! I'm sorry, as it happens, she's so taken up with the thought of me."

"It was likely, was not it? and you to have been her husband before this time, if—oh, miserable me! to let my child go and dim her bright life! But you'll forgive me, and come sometimes, just for a little quarter of an hour, once or twice a week. Perhaps she'll be asleep sometimes when you call, and then, you know, you need not come in. If she were not so ill, I'd never ask you."

So low and humble was the poor widow brought, through her exceeding love for her daughter.

—◦—

CHAPTER II.

Nest revived during the warm summer weather. Edward
came to see her, and stayed the allotted quarter of an
hour; but he dared not look her in the face. She was,
indeed, a cripple : one leg was much shorter than the
other, and she halted on a crutch. Her face, formerly
so brilliant in colour, was wan and pale with suffering;
the bright roses were gone, never to return. Her large
eyes were sunk deep down in their hollow, cavernous
sockets; but the light was in them still, when Edward
came. Her mother dreaded her returning strength—
dreaded, yet desired it; for the heavy burden of her
secret was most oppressive at times, and she thought
Edward was beginning to weary of his enforced attentions. One October evening she told her the truth.
She even compelled her rebellious heart to take the cold,
reasoning side of the question; and she told her child
that her disabled frame was a disqualification for ever
becoming a farmer's wife. She spoke hardly, because
her inner agony and sympathy was such, she dared not
trust herself to express the feelings that were rending
her. But Nest turned away from cold reason; she
revolted from her mother; she revolted from the world.
She bound her sorrow tight up in her breast, to corrode
and fester there.

Night after night, her mother heard her cries and
moans—more pitiful, by far, than those wrung from her
by bodily pain a year before; and night after night, if

her mother spoke to soothe, she proudly denied the existence of any pain but what was physical, and consequent upon her accident.

"If she would but open her sore heart to me—to me, her mother," Eleanor wailed forth in prayer to God, "I would be content. Once it was enough to have my Nest all my own. Then came love, and I knew it would never be as before; and then I thought the grief I felt, when Edward spoke to me, was as sharp a sorrow as could be; but this present grief, O Lord, my God, is worst of all; and Thou only, Thou, canst help!"

When Nest grew as strong as she was ever likely to be on earth, she was anxious to have as much labour as she could bear. She would not allow her mother to spare her anything. Hard work—bodily fatigue—she seemed to crave. She was glad when she was stunned by exhaustion into a dull insensibility of feeling. She was almost fierce when her mother, in those first months of convalescence, performed the household tasks which had formerly been hers; but she shrank from going out of doors. Her mother thought that she was unwilling to expose her changed appearance to the neighbours' remarks, but Nest was not afraid of that; she was afraid of their pity, as being one deserted and cast off. If Eleanor gave way before her daughter's imperiousness, and sat by while Nest "tore" about her work with the vehemence of a bitter heart, Eleanor could have cried, but she durst not; tears, or any mark of commiseration, irritated the crippled girl so much, she even drew away from caresses. Everything was to go on as it had been before she had known Edward; and so it did, outwardly; but they trod carefully, as if the ground on which they moved was hollow—deceptive. There was no more careless ease; every word was guarded, and every action planned. It was a dreary life to both. Once, Eleanor brought in a little baby, a neighbour's child, to try and tempt Nest out of herself, by her old love of children. Nest's pale face flushed as she saw the innocent child in her mother's arms; and, for a moment, she made as if she would have taken it; but then she turned away, and hid her face behind her apron, and murmured, "I shall never have a child to lie in my breast, and call me mother!" In a minute she arose, with compressed and tightened lips, and went about her household work, without her noticing the cooing baby again, till Mrs. Gwynn, heart-sick at the failure of her little plan, took it back to its parents.

One day the news ran through Pen-Morfa that Edward Williams was about to be married. Eleanor had long expected this intelligence. It came upon her like no new thing, but it was the filling-up of her cup of woe. She could not tell Nest. She sat listlessly in the house, and dreaded that each neighbour who came in would speak about the village news. At last some one did. Nest looked round from her employment, and talked of the event with a kind of cheerful curiosity as to the particulars, which made her informant go away, and tell others that Nest had quite left off caring for Edward Williams. But when the door was shut, and Eleanor and she were left alone, Nest came and stood before her weeping mother like a stern accuser.

"Mother, why did not you let me die? Why did you keep me alive for this?" Eleanor could not speak, but she put her arms out towards her girl. Nest turned away, and Eleanor cried aloud in her soreness of spirit. Nest came again.

"Mother, I was wrong. You did your best. I don't know how it is I am so hard and cold. I wish I had died when I was a girl, and had a feeling heart."

"Don't speak so, my child. God has afflicted you sore, and your hardness of heart is but for a time. Wait a little. Don't reproach yourself, my poor Nest. I understand your ways. I don't mind them, love. The feeling heart will come back to you in time. Anyways, don't think you're grieving me; because, love, that may sting you when I'm gone; and I'm not grieved, my darling. Most times, we're very cheerful, I think."

After this, mother and child were drawn more together. But Eleanor had received her death from these sorrowful, hurrying events. She did not conceal the truth from herself; nor did she pray to live, as some months ago she had done, for her child's sake; she had found out that she had no power to console the poor wounded heart. It seemed to her as if her prayers had been of no avail; and then she blamed herself for this thought.

There are many Methodist preachers in this part of Wales. There was a certain old man, named David Hughes, who was held in peculiar reverence because he had known the great John Wesley. He had been captain of a Caernarvon slate-vessel; he had traded in the Mediterranean, and had seen strange sights. In those early days (to use his own expression) he had lived without God in the world; but he went to mock John Wesley, and was converted by the white-haired patriarch, and remained to pray. Afterwards he became one of

tho earnest, self-denying, much-abused band of itinerant
preachers who went forth under Wesley's direction, to
spread abroad a more earnest and practical spirit of
religion. His rambles and travels were of use to him.
They extended his knowledge of the circumstances in
which men are sometimes placed, and enlarged his
sympathy with the tried and tempted. His sympathy,
combined with the thoughtful experience of fourscore
years, made him cognisant of many of the strange secrets
of humanity; and when younger preachers upbraided the
hard hearts they met with, and despaired of the sinners,
he " suffered long, and was kind."

When Eleanor Gwynn lay low on her death-bed, David
Hughes came to Pen-Morfa. He knew her history, and
sought her out. To him she imparted the feelings I
have described.

"I have lost my faith, David. The tempter has
come, and I have yielded. I doubt if my prayers have
been heard. Day and night have I prayed that I might
comfort my child in her great sorrow; but God has not
heard me. She has turned away from me, and refused
my poor love. I wish to die now; but I have lost my
faith, and have no more pleasure in the thought of going
to God. What must I do, David?"

She hung upon his answer; and it was long in
coming.

" I am weary of earth," said she, mournfully, " and
can I find rest in death even, leaving my child desolate
and broken-hearted ? "

" Eleanor," said David, " where you go, all things
will be made clear; and you will learn to thank God
for the end of what now seems grievous and heavy to

be borne. Do you think your agony has been greater than the awful agony in the Garden—or your prayers more earnest than that which He prayed in that hour when the great drops of blood ran down his face like sweat? We know that God heard Him, although no answer came to Him through the dread silence of that night. God's times are not our times. I have lived eighty and one years, and never yet have I known an earnest prayer fall to the ground unheeded. In an unknown way, and when no one looked for it, maybe, the answer came; a fuller, more satisfying answer than heart could conceive of, although it might be different to what was expected. Sister, you are going where in His light you will see light; you will learn there that in very faithfulness he has afflicted you!"

"Go on—you strengthen me," said she.

After David Hughes left that day, Eleanor was calm as one already dead, and past mortal strife. Nest was awed by the change. No more passionate weeping—no more sorrow in the voice; though it was low and weak, it sounded with a sweet composure. Her last look was a smile; her last word a blessing.

Nest, tearless, streeked the poor worn body. She laid a plate with salt upon it on the breast, and lighted candles for the head and feet. It was an old Welsh custom; but when David Hughes came in, the sight carried him back to the time when he had seen the chapels in some old Catholic cathedral. Nest sat gazing on the dead with dry, hot eyes.

"She is dead," said David, solemnly; "she died in Christ. Let us bless God, my child. He giveth and He taketh away."

"She is dead," said Nest, "my mother is dead. No one loves me now."

She spoke as if she were thinking aloud, for she did not look at David, or ask him to be seated.

"No one loves you now? No human creature, you mean. You are not yet fit to be spoken to concerning God's infinite love. I, like you, will speak of love for human creatures. I tell you if no one loves you, it is time for you to begin to love." He spoke almost severely (if David Hughes ever did); for, to tell the truth, he was repelled by her hard rejection of her mother's tenderness, about which the neighbours had told him.

"Begin to love!" said she, her eyes flashing. "Have I not loved? Old man, you are dim, and worn-out. You do not remember what love is." She spoke with a scornful kind of pitying endurance. "I will tell you how I have loved by telling you the change it has wrought in me. I was once the beautiful Nest Gwynn; I am now a cripple, a poor, wan-faced cripple, old before my time. That is a change, at least people think so." She paused and then spoke lower. "I tell you, David Hughes, that outward change is as nothing compared to the change in my nature caused by the love I have felt—and have had rejected. I was gentle once, and if you spoke a tender word, my heart came towards you as natural as a little child goes to its mammy. I never spoke roughly, even to the dumb creatures, for I had a kind feeling for all. Of late (since I loved, old man), I have been cruel in my thoughts to every one. I have turned away from tenderness with bitter indifference. Listen!" she spoke in a hoarse whisper. "I will own

THE WELL OF PEN-MORFA.

it. I have spoken hardly to her," pointing towards the corpse,—" her who was ever patient, and full of love for me. She did not know," she muttered, " she is gone to the grave without knowing how I loved her— I had such strange, mad, stubborn pride in me."

" Come back, mother! Come back," said she, crying wildly to the still, solemn corpse; " come back as a spirit or a ghost—only come back, that I may tell you how I have loved you. '

But the dead never come back.

The passionate adjuration ended in tears—the first she had shed. When they ceased, or were absorbed into long quivering sobs, David knelt down. Nest did not kneel, but bowed her head. He prayed, while his own tears fell fast. He rose up. They were both calm.

" Nest," said he, " your love has been the love of youth—passionate, wild, natural to youth. Hencefor- ward, you must love like Christ, without thought of self, or wish for return. You must take the sick and the weary to your heart, and love them. That love will lift you up above the storms of the world into God's own peace. The very vehemence of your nature proves that you are capable of this. I do not pity you. You do not require pity. You are powerful enough to trample down your own sorrows into a blessing for others ; and to others you will be a blessing. I see it before you, I see in it the answer to your mother's prayer."

The old man's dim eyes glittered as if they saw a vision; the fire-light sprang up, and glinted on his long white hair. Nest was awed as if she saw a prophet, and a prophet he was to her.

When next David Hughes came to Pen-Morfa, he
asked about Nest Gwynn, with a hovering doubt as to
the answer.   The inn-folk told him she was living still
in the cottage, which was now her own.

"But would you believe it, David," said Mrs. Thomas,
"she has gone and taken Mary Williams to live with
her?   You remember Mary Williams, I'm sure."

No! David Hughes remembered no Mary Williams at
Pen-Morfa.

"You must have seen her, for I know you've called
at Thomas Griffiths', where the parish boarded her?"

"You don't mean the half-witted woman—the poor
crazy creature?"

"But I do!" said Mrs. Thomas.

"I have seen her sure enough, but I never thought
of learning her name.   And Nest Gwynn has taken her
to live with her."

"Yes!   I thought I should surprise you.   She might
have had many a decent girl for companion.   My own
niece, her that is an orphan, would have gone, and
been thankful.   Besides, Mary Williams is a regular
savage at times: John Griffiths says there were days
when he used to beat her till she howled again, and yet
she would not do as he told her.   Nay, once, he says, if
he had not seen her eyes glare like a wild beast, from
under the shadow of the table where she had taken
shelter, and got pretty quickly out of her way, she would
have flown upon him, and throttled him.   He gave Nest
fair warning of what she must expect, and he thinks
some day she will be found murdered."

David Hughes thought a while.   "How came Nest to
take her to live with her?" asked he.

"Well! Folk say John Griffiths did not give her enough to eat. Half-wits, they tell me, take more to feed them than others, and Eleanor Gwynn had given her oat-cake, and porridge a time or two, and most likely spoken kindly to her (you know Eleanor spoke kind to all), so some months ago, when John Griffiths had been beating her, and keeping her without food to try and tame her, she ran away, and came to Nest's cottage in the dead of night, all shivering and starved, for she did not know Eleanor was dead, and thought to meet with kindness from her, I've no doubt; and Nest remembered how her mother used to feed and comfort the poor idiot, and made her some gruel, and wrapped her up by the fire. And, in the morning, when John Griffiths came in search of Mary, he found her with Nest, and Mary wailed so piteously at the sight of him, that Nest went to the parish officers, and offered to take her to board with her for the same money they gave to him. John says he was right glad to be off his bargain."

David Hughes knew there was a kind of remorse which sought relief in the performance of the most difficult and repugnant tasks. He thought he could understand how, in her bitter repentance for her conduct towards her mother, Nest had taken in the first helpless creature that came seeking shelter in her name. It was not what he would have chosen, but he knew it was God that had sent the poor wandering idiot there.

He went to see Nest the next morning. As he drew near the cottage—it was summer time, and the doors and windows were all open—he heard an angry passionate kind of sound that was scarcely human. That sound prevented his approach from being heard; and, standing at the threshold, he saw poor Mary Williams pacing backwards and forwards in some wild mood. Nest, cripple as she was, was walking with her, speaking low soothing words, till the pace was slackened, and time and breathing was given to put her arm around the crazy woman's neck, and soothe her by this tender caress into the quiet luxury of tears—tears which give the hot brain relief. Then David Hughes came in. His first words, as he took off his hat, standing on the lintel, were—"The peace of God be upon this house." Neither he nor Nest recurred to the past, though solemn recollections filled their minds. Before he went, all three knelt and prayed; for, as Nest told him, some mysterious influence of peace came over the poor half-wit's mind, when she heard the holy words of prayer; and often when she felt a paroxysm coming on, she would kneel and repeat a homily rapidly over, as if it were a charm to scare away the Demon in possession; sometimes, indeed, the control over herself requisite for this effort was enough to dispel the fluttering burst. When David rose up to go, he drew Nest to the door.

" You are not afraid, my child ? " asked he.

" No," she replied. " She is often very good and quiet. When she is not, I can bear it."

" I shall see your face on earth no more," said he. " God bless you! " He went on his way. Not many weeks after, David Hughes was borne to his grave.

The doors of Nest's heart were opened—opened wide by the love she grew to feel for crazy Mary, so helpless, so friendless, so dependent upon her. Mary loved her back again, as a dumb animal loves its blind master. It was happiness enough to be near her. In general, she was only too glad to do what she was bidden by Nest. But there were times when Mary was overpowered by the glooms and fancies of her poor disordered brain. Fearful times! No one knew how fearful. On those days, Nest warned the little children who loved to come and play around her, that they must not visit the house. The signal was a piece of white linen hung out of a side window. On those days, the sorrowful and sick waited in vain for the sound of Nest's lame approach. But what she had to endure was only known to God, for she never complained. If she had given up the charge of Mary, or if the neighbours had risen, out of love and care for her life, to compel such a step, she knew what hard curses and blows, what starvation and misery, would await the poor creature.

She told of Mary's docility, and her affection, and her innocent, little sayings; but she never told the details of the occasional days of wild disorder, and driving insanity.

Nest grew old before her time, in consequence of her accident. She knew that she was as old at fifty as many are at seventy. She knew it partly by the vividness with which the remembrance of the days of her youth came back to her mind, while the events of yesterday were dim and forgotten. She dreamt of her girlhood and youth. In sleep, she was once more the beautiful Nest Gwynn, the admired of all beholders, the light-hearted girl, beloved by her mother. Little circumstances connected with those early days, forgotten since the very time when they occurred, came back to her mind, in her waking hours. She had a scar on the palm of her left hand, occasioned by the fall of a branch of a tree, when

she was a child. It had not pained her since the first
two days after the accident; but now it began to hurt
her slightly; and clear in her ears was the crackling
sound of the treacherous, rending wood; distinct before
her rose the presence of her mother, tenderly binding up
the wound. With these remembrances came a longing
desire to see the beautiful, fatal well once more before
her death. She had never gone so far since the day
when, by her fall there, she lost love and hope, and her
bright glad youth. She yearned to look upon its waters
once again. This desire waxed as her life waxed. She
told it to poor crazy Mary.

"Mary!" said she, "I want to go to the Rock Well.
If you will help me, I can manage it. There used to be
many a stone in the Dol Mawr on which I could sit and
rest. We will go to-morrow morning before folks are
astir."

Mary answered briskly, "Up, up! To the Rock
Well. Mary will go. Mary will go." All day long
she kept muttering to herself, "Mary will go."

Nest had the happiest dream that night. Her mother
stood beside her—not in the flesh, but in the bright
glory of a blessed spirit. And Nest was no longer
young—neither was she old—"they reckon not by days,
nor years, where she was gone to dwell;" and her
mother stretched out her arms to her with a calm, glad
look of welcome. She awoke; the woodlark was singing
in the near copse—the little birds were astir, and rust-
ling in their leafy nests. Nest arose, and called Mary.
The two set out through the quiet lane. They went
along slowly and silently. With many a pause they
crossed the broad Dol Mawr, and carefully descended

the sloping stones, on which no trace remained of the hundreds of feet that had passed over them since Nest was last there. The clear water sparkled and quivered in the early sunlight, the shadows of the birch-leaves were stirred on the ground; the ferns—Nest could have believed that they were the very same ferns which she had seen thirty years before—hung wet and dripping where the water overflowed—a thrush chanted matins from a hollybush near—and the running stream made a low, soft, sweet accompaniment. All was the same. Nature was as fresh and young as ever. It might have been yesterday that Edward Williams had overtaken her, and told her his love—the thought of his words—his handsome looks—(he was a gray, hard-featured man by this time), and then she recalled the fatal wintry morning when joy and youth had fled; and as she remembered that faintness of pain, a new, a real faintness—no echo of the memory—came over her. She leant her back against a rock, without a moan or sigh, and died! She found immortality by the well-side, instead of her fragile, perishing youth. She was so calm and placid that Mary (who had been dipping her fingers in the well, to see the waters drop off in the gleaming sunlight), thought she was asleep, and for some time continued her amusement in silence. At last, she turned, and said,—

"Mary is tired. Mary wants to go home." Nest did not speak, though the idiot repeated her plaintive words. She stood and looked till a strange terror came over her—a terror too mysterious to be borne.

"Mistress, wake! Mistress, wake!" she said, wildly, shaking the form.

But Nest did not awake. And the first person who

came to the well that morning found crazy Mary sitting, awestruck, by the poor dead Nest. They had to get the poor creature away by force, before they could remove the body.

Mary is in Trê-Madoc workhouse. They treat her pretty kindly, and, in general, she is good and tractable. Occasionally, the old paroxysms come on; and, for a time, she is unmanageable. But some one thought of speaking to her about Nest. She stood arrested at the name; and, since then, it is astonishing to see what efforts she makes to curb her insanity; and when the dread time is past, she creeps up to the matron, and says, "Mary has tried to be good. Will God let her go to Nest now?"

THE HEART OF JOHN MIDDLETON.

———◆◇◆———

I was born at Sawley, where the shadow of Pendle Hill falls at sunrise. I suppose Sawley sprang up into a village in the time of the monks, who had an abbey there. Many of the cottages are strange old places; others, again, are built of the abbey stones, mixed up with the shale from the neighbouring quarries; and you may see many a quaint bit of carving worked into the walls, or forming the lintels of the doors. There is a row of houses, built still more recently, where one Mr. Peel came to live there for the sake of the water-power, and gave the place a fillip into something like life; though a different kind of life, as I take it, from the grand, slow ways folks had when the monks were about.

Now it was—six o'clock, ring the bell, throng to the factory; sharp home at twelve; and even at night, when work was done, we hardly knew how to walk slowly; we had been so bustled all day long. I can't recollect the time when I did not go to the factory. My father used to drag me there when I was quite a little fellow, in order

6

to wind reels for him. I never remember my mother.
I should have been a better man than I have been, if I
had only had a notion of the sound of her voice, or the
look on her face.

My father and I lodged in the house of a man who
also worked in the factory. We were sadly thronged in
Sawley, so many people came from different parts of the
country to earn a livelihood at the new work; and it was
some time before the row of cottages I have spoken
of could be built. While they were building, my
father was turned out of his lodgings for drinking and
being disorderly, and he and I slept in the brick-kiln;
that is to say, when we did sleep o' nights; but, often
and often, we went poaching; and many a hare and
pheasant have I rolled up in clay, and roasted in the
embers of the kiln. Then, as followed to reason, I was
drowsy next day over my work; but father had no mercy
on me for sleeping, for all he knew the cause of it, but
kicked me where I lay, a heavy lump on the factory floor,
and cursed and swore at me till I got up for very fear,
and to my winding again. But, when his back was
turned, I paid him off with heavier curses than he had
given me, and longed to be a man, that I might be
revenged on him. The words I then spoke I would not
now dare to repeat; and worse than hating words, a
hating heart went with them. I forget the time when I
did not know how to hate. When I first came to read,
and learnt about Ishmael, I thought I must be of his
doomed race, for my hand was against every man, and
every man's against me. But I was seventeen or more
before I cared for my book enough to learn to read.

After the row of works was finished, father took one,

and set up for himself, in letting lodgings. I can't say much for the furnishing; but there was plenty of straw, and we kept up good fires; and there is a set of people who value warmth above everything. The worst lot about the place lodged with us. We used to have a supper in the middle of the night; there was game enough, or if there was not game, there was poultry to be had for the stealing. By day, we all made a show of working in the factory. By night, we feasted and drank.

Now this web of my life was black enough, and coarse enough; but, by-and-by, a little golden, filmy thread began to be woven in; the dawn of God's mercy was at hand.

One blowy October morning, as I sauntered lazily along to the mill, I came to the little wooden bridge over a brook that falls into the Bribble. On the plank there stood a child, balancing the pitcher on her head, with which she had been to fetch water. She was so light on her feet that, had it not been for the weight of the pitcher, I almost believe the wind would have taken her up, and wafted her away as it carries off a blow-ball in seed-time; her blue cotton dress was blown before her, as if she were spreading her wings for a flight; she turned her face round, as if to ask me for something, but when she saw who it was, she hesitated, for I had a bad name in the village, and I doubt not she had been warned against me. But her heart was too innocent to be distrustful; so she said to me, timidly,—

"Please, John Middleton, will you carry me this heavy jug just over the bridge?"

It was the very first time I had ever been spoken to

6—2

gently.   I was ordered here and there by my father and
his rough companions; I was abused, and cursed by
them if I failed in doing what they wished; if I succeeded, there came no expression of thanks or gratitude.
I was informed of facts necessary for me to know.   But
the gentle words of request or entreaty were aforetime
unknown to me, and now their tones fell on my ear soft
and sweet as a distant peal of bells.   I wished that I
knew how to speak properly in reply; but though we
were of the same standing as regarded worldly circumstances, there was some mighty difference between us,
which made me unable to speak in her language of soft
words and modest entreaty.   There was nothing for me
but to take up the pitcher in a kind of gruff, shy silence,
and carry it over the bridge, as she had asked me.   When
I gave it her back again, she thanked me and tripped
away, leaving me, wordless, gazing after her like an
awkward lout as I was.   I knew well enough who she
was.   She was grandchild to Eleanor Hadfield, an aged
woman, who was reputed as a witch by my father and
his set, for no other reason, that I can make out, than
her scorn, dignity, and fearlessness of rancour.   It was
true we often met her in the grey dawn of the morning,
when we returned from poaching, and my father used to
curse her, under his breath, for a witch, such as were
burnt long ago on Pendle Hill top; but I had heard
that Eleanor was a skilful sick nurse, and ever ready to
give her services to those who were ill; and I believe
that she had been sitting up through the night (the
night that we had been spending under the wild heavens,
in deeds as wild), with those who were appointed to die.
Nelly was her orphan granddaughter; her little hand-

maiden; her treasure; her one ewe lamb. Many and
many a day have I watched by the brook-side, hoping
that some happy gust of wind, coming with opportune
bluster down the hollow of the dale, might make me
necessary once more to her. I longed to hear her speak
to me again. I said the words she had used to myself,
trying to catch her tone; but the chance never came
again. I do not know that she ever knew how I watched
for her there. I found out that she went to school, and
nothing would serve me but that I must go too. My
father scoffed at me; I did not care. I knew nought of
what reading was, nor that it was likely that I should
be laughed at; I, a great hulking lad of seventeen or
upwards, for going to learn my A, B, C, in the midst
of a crowd of little ones. I stood just this way in my
mind. Nelly was at school; it was the best place for
seeing her, and hearing her voice again. Therefore I
would go too. My father talked, and swore, and threatened, but I stood to it. He said I should leave school,
weary of it in a month. I swore a deeper oath than
I like to remember, that I would stay a year, and come
out a reader and a writer. My father hated the notion
of folks learning to read, and said it took all the spirit
out of them; besides, he thought he had a right to
every penny of my wages, and though, when he was in
good humour, he might have given me many a jug of
ale, he grudged my twopence a week for schooling.
However, to school I went. It was a different place to
what I had thought it before I went inside. The girls
sat on one side, and the boys on the other; so I was
not near Nelly. She, too, was in the first class; I
was put with the little toddling things that could hardly

run alone. The master sat in the middle, and kept pretty strict watch over us. But I could see Nelly, and hear her read her chapter; and even when it was one with a long list of hard names, such as the master was very fond of giving her, to show how well she could hit them off without spelling, I thought I had never heard a prettier music. Now and then she read other things. I did not know what they were, true or false; but I listened because she read; and, by-and-by, I began to wonder. I remember the first word I ever spoke to her was to ask her (as we were coming out of school) who was the Father of whom she had been reading, for when she said the words "Our Father," her voice dropped into a soft, holy kind of low sound, which struck me more than any loud reading, it seemed so loving and tender.. When I asked her this, she looked at me with her great blue wondering eyes, at first shocked; and then, as it were, melted down into pity and sorrow, she said in the same way, below her breath, in which she read the words, "Our Father,"—

"Don't you know? It is God."

"God?"

"Yes; the God that grandmother tells me about."

"Tell me what she says, will you?" So we sat down on the hedge-bank, she a little above me, while I looked up into her face, and she told me all the holy texts her grandmother had taught her, as explaining all that could be explained of the Almighty. I listened in silence, for indeed I was overwhelmed with astonishment. Her knowledge was principally rote-knowledge; she was too young for much more; but we, in Lancashire, speak a rough kind of Bible language, and the texts seemed very clear to me. I rose up, dazed and overpowered. I was going away in silence, when I bethought me of my manners, and turned back, and said, "Thank you," for the first time I ever remember saying it in my life. That was a great day for me, in more ways than one.

I was always one who could keep very steady to an object when once I had set it before me. My object was to know Nelly. I was conscious of nothing more. But it made me regardless of all other things. The master might scold, the little ones might laugh; I bore it all without giving it a second thought. I kept to my year, and came out a reader and writer; more, however, to stand well in Nelly's good opinion, than because of my oath. About this time, my father committed some bad, cruel deed, and had to fly the country. I was glad he went; for I had never loved or cared for him, and wanted to shake myself clear of his set. But it was no easy matter. Honest folk stood aloof; only bad men held out their arms to me with a welcome. Even Nelly seemed to have a mixture of fear now with her kind ways towards me. I was the son of John Middleton, who, if he were caught, would be hung at Lancaster Castle. I thought she looked at me sometimes with a sort of sorrowful horror. Others were not forbearing enough to keep their expression of feeling confined to looks. The son of the overlooker at the mill never ceased twitting me with my father's crime; he now brought up his poaching against him, though I knew very well how many a good supper he himself had made on game which had been given him to make him and his father wink at late hours in the morning.

And how were such as my father to come honestly by game?

This lad, Dick Jackson, was the bane of my life. He was a year or two older than I was, and had much power over the men who worked at the mill, as he could report to his father what he chose. I could not always hold my peace when he "threaped" me with my father's sins, but gave it him back sometimes in a storm of passion. It did me no good; only threw me farther from the company of better men, who looked aghast and shocked at the oaths I poured out—blasphemous words learnt in my childhood, which I could not forget now that I would fain have purified myself of them; while all the time Dick Jackson stood by, with a mocking smile of intelligence; and when I had ended, breathless and weary with spent passion, he would turn to those whose respect I longed to earn, and ask if I were not a worthy son of my father, and likely to tread in his steps. But this smiling indifference of his to my miserable vehemence was not all, though it was the worst part of his conduct, for it made the rankling hatred grow up in my heart, and overshadow it like the great gourd-tree of the prophet Jonah. But his was a merciful shade, keeping out the burning sun; mine blighted what it fell upon.

What Dick Jackson did besides, was this. His father was a skilful overlooker, and a good man. Mr. Peel valued him so much, that he was kept on, although his health was failing; and when he was unable, through illness, to come to the mill, he deputed his son to watch over, and report the men. It was too much power for one so young—I speak it calmly now. Whatever Dick

Jackson became, he had strong temptations when he was young, which will be allowed for hereafter. But at the time of which I am telling, my hate raged like a fire. I believed that he was the one sole obstacle to my being received as fit to mix with good and honest men. I was sick of crime and disorder, and would fain have come over to a different kind of life, and have been industrious, sober, honest, and right-spoken (I had no idea of higher virtue then), and at every turn Dick Jackson met me with his sneers. I have walked the night through, in the old abbey field, planning how I could outwit him, and win men's respect in spite of him. The first time I ever prayed, was underneath the silent stars, kneeling by the old abbey walls, throwing up my arms, and asking God for the power of revenge upon him.

I had heard that if I prayed earnestly, God would give me what I asked for, and I looked upon it as a kind of chance for the fulfilment of my wishes. If earnestness would have won the boon for me, never were wicked words so earnestly spoken. And oh, later on, my prayer was heard, and my wish granted! All this time I saw little of Nelly. Her grandmother was failing, and she had much to do in-doors. Besides, I believed I had read her looks aright, when I took them to speak of aversion; and I planned to hide myself from her sight, as it were, until I could stand upright before men, with fearless eyes, dreading no face of accusation. It was possible to acquire a good character; I would do it— I did it: but no one brought up among respectable untempted people can tell the unspeakable hardness of the task. In the evenings I would not go forth among

the village throng; for the acquaintances that claimed
me were my father's old associates, who would have
been glad enough to enlist a strong young man like me
in their projects; and the men who would have shunned
me and kept aloof, were the steady and orderly.   So I
stayed in-doors, and practised myself in reading.   You
will say, I should have found it easier to earn a good
character away from Sawley, at some place where neither
I nor my father was known.   So I should; but it would
not have been the same thing to my mind.   Besides,
representing all good men, all goodness to me, in Sawley
Nelly lived.   In her sight I would work out my life, and
fight my way upwards to men's respect.   Two years
passed on.   Every day I strove fiercely; every day my
struggles were made fruitless by the son of the overlooker; and I seemed but where I was—but where I
must ever be esteemed by all who knew me—but as the
son of the criminal—wild, reckless, ripe for crime myself.
Where was the use of my reading and writing?   These
acquirements were disregarded and scouted by those
among whom I was thrust back to take my portion.   I
could have read any chapter in the Bible now; and
Nelly seemed as though she would never know it.   I
was driven in upon my books; and few enough of them
I had.   The pedlars brought them round in their packs,
and I bought what I could.   I had the *Seven Champions*,
and the *Pilgrim's Progress;* and both seemed to me
equally wonderful, and equally founded on fact.   I got
Byron's *Narrative*, and Milton's *Paradise Lost;* but I
lacked the knowledge which would give a clue to all.
Still they afforded me pleasure, because they took me
out of myself, and made me forget my miserable

position, and made me unconscious (for the time at least) of my one great passion of hatred against Dick Jackson.

When Nelly was about seventeen her grandmother died. I stood aloof in the churchyard, behind the great yew-tree, and watched the funeral. It was the first religious service that ever I heard; and, to my shame, as I thought, it affected me to tears. The words seemed so peaceful and holy that I longed to go to church, but I durst not, because I had never been. The parish church was at Bolton, far enough away to serve as an excuse for all who did not care to go. I heard Nelly's sobs filling up every pause in the clergyman's voice; and every sob of hers went to my heart. She passed me on her way out of the churchyard; she was so near I might have touched her; but her head was hanging down, and I durst not speak to her. Then the question arose, what was to become of her? She must earn her living! was it to be as a farm-servant, or by working at the mill? I knew enough of both kinds of life to make me tremble for her. My wages were such as to enable me to marry, if I chose; and I never thought of woman, for my wife, but Nelly. Still, I would not have married her now, if I could; for, as yet, I had not risen up to the character which I determined it was fit that Nelly's husband should have. When I was rich in good report, I would come forwards, and take my chance, but until then I would hold my peace. I had faith in the power of my long-continued dogged breasting of opinion. Sooner or later it must, it should, yield, and I be received among the ranks of good men. But, meanwhile, what was to become of Nelly? I

reckoned up my wages; I went to inquire what the
board of a girl would be who should help her in her
household work, and live with her as a daughter, at the
house of one of the most decent women of the place;
she looked at me suspiciously.   I kept down my temper,
and told her I would never come near the place; that I
would keep away from that end of the village, and that
the girl for whom I made the inquiry should never know
but what the parish paid for her keep.   It would not do;
she suspected me; but I know I had power over myself
to have kept my word; and besides, I would not for
worlds have had Nelly put under any obligation to me,
which should speck the purity of her love, or dim it by
a mixture of gratitude,—the love that I craved to earn,
not for my money, not for my kindness, but for myself.
I heard that Nelly had met with a place in Bolland; and
I could see no reason why I might not speak to her once
before she left our neighbourhood.   I meant it to be a
quiet friendly telling her of my sympathy in her sorrow.
I felt I could command myself.   So, on the Sunday
before she was to leave Sawley, I waited near the wood-
path, by which I knew that she would return from afternoon church.   The birds made such a melodious warble,
such a busy sound among the leaves, that I did not hear
approaching footsteps till they were close at hand; and
then there were sounds of two persons' voices.   The
wood was near that part of Sawley where Nelly was
staying with friends; the path through it led to their
house, and theirs only, so I knew it must be she, for I
had watched her setting out to church alone.

But who was the other?

The blood went to my heart and head, as if I were

shot, when.I saw that it was Dick Jackson. Was this the end of it all? In the steps of sin which my father had trod, I would rush to my death and my doom. Even where I stood I longed for a weapon to slay him. How dared he come near my Nelly? She too,—I thought her faithless, and forgot how little I had ever been to her in outward action; how few words, and those how uncouth, I had ever spoken to her; and I hated her for a traitress. These feelings passed through me before I could see, my eyes and head were so dizzy and blind. When I looked I saw Dick Jackson holding her hand, and speaking quick and low and thick, as a man speaks in great vehemence. She seemed white and dismayed; but all at once, at some word of his (and what it was she never would tell me), she looked as though she defied a fiend, and wrenched herself out of his grasp. He caught hold of her again, and began once more the thick whisper that I loathed. I could bear it no longer, nor did I see why I should. I stepped out from behind the tree where I had been lying. When she saw me, she lost her look of one strung up to desperation, and came and clung to me; and I felt like a giant in strength and might. I held her with one arm, but I did not take my eyes off him; I felt as if they blazed down into his soul, and scorched him up. He never spoke, but tried to look as though he defied me. At last, his eyes fell before mine, I dared not speak; for the old horrid oaths thronged up to my mouth; and I dreaded giving them way, and terrifying my poor, trembling Nelly.

At last, he made to go past me: I drew her out of the pathway. By instinct she wrapped her garments round her, as if to avoid his accidental touch; and he was stung by this, I suppose—I believe—to the mad, miserable revenge he took. As my back was turned to him, in an endeavour to speak some words to Nelly that might soothe her into calmness, she, who was looking after him, like one fascinated with terror, saw him take a sharp, shaley stone, and aim it at me. Poor darling! she clung round me as a shield, making her sweet body into a defence for mine. It hit her, and she spoke no word, kept back her cry of pain, but fell at my feet in a swoon. He—the coward!—ran off as soon as he saw what he had done. I was with Nelly alone in the green gloom of the wood. The quivering and leaf-tinted light made her look as if she were dead. I carried her, not knowing if I bore a corpse or not, to her friend's house. I did not stay to explain, but ran madly for the doctor.

Well! I cannot bear to recur to that time again. Five weeks I lived in the agony of suspense; from which my only relief was in laying savage plans for revenge. If I hated him before, what think ye I did now? It seemed as if earth could not hold us twain, but that one of us must go down to Gehenna. I could have killed him; and would have done it without a scruple, but that seemed too poor and bold a revenge. At length—oh! the weary waiting—oh! the sickening of my heart—Nelly grew better; as well as she was ever to grow. The bright colour had left her cheek; the mouth quivered with repressed pain, the eyes were dim with tears that agony had forced into them; and I loved her a thousand times better and more than when she was bright and blooming! What was best of all, I began to perceive that she cared for me. I know her grandmother's friends warned her against me, and told

her I came of a bad stock; but she had passed the point
where remonstrance from bystanders can take effect—
she loved me as I was, a strange mixture of bad and
good, all unworthy of her. We spoke together now, as
those do whose lives are bound up in each other. I
told her I would marry her as soon as she had recovered
her health. Her friends shook their heads; but they
saw she would be unfit for farm-service or heavy work,
and they perhaps thought, as many a one does, that a
bad husband was better than none at all. Anyhow, we
were married; and I learnt to bless God for my happiness, so far beyond my deserts. I kept her like a lady.
I was a skilful workman, and earned good wages; and
every want she had I tried to gratify. Her wishes were
few and simple enough, poor Nelly! If they had been
ever so fanciful, I should have had my reward in the
new feeling of the holiness of home. She could lead me
as a little child, with the charm of her gentle voice, and
her ever-kind words. She would plead for all when I
was full of anger and passion; only Dick Jackson's
name passed never between our lips during all that
time. In the evening she lay back in her beehive chair,
and read to me. I think I see her now, pale and weak,
with her sweet, young face, lighted by her holy, earnest
eyes, telling me of the Saviour's life and death, till they
were filled with tears. I longed to have been there, to
have avenged him on the wicked Jews. I liked Peter
the best of all the disciples. But I got the Bible myself,
and read the mighty act of God's vengeance, in the Old
Testament, with a kind of triumphant faith that, sooner
or later, He would take my cause in hand, and revenge
me on mine enemy.

In a year or so, Nelly had a baby—a little girl, with eyes just like hers, that looked, with a grave openness, right into yours. Nelly recovered but slowly. It was just before winter, the cotton-crop had failed, and master had to turn off many hands. I thought I was sure of being kept on, for I had earned a steady character, and did my work well; but once again it was permitted that Dick Jackson should do me wrong. He induced his father to dismiss me among the first in my branch of the business; and there was I, just before winter set in, with a wife and new-born child, and a small enough store of money to keep body and soul together, till I could get to work again. All my savings had gone by Christmas Eve, and we sat in the house, foodless for the morrow's festival. Nelly looked pinched and worn; the baby cried for a larger supply of milk than its poor, starving mother could give it. My right hand had not forgot its cunning, and I went out once more to my poaching. I knew where the gang met; and I knew what a welcome back I should have,—a far warmer and more hearty welcome than good men had given me when I tried to enter their ranks. On the road to the meeting-place I fell in with an old man,—one who had been a companion to my father in his early days.

"What, lad!" said he, "art thou turning back to the old trade? It's the better business, now that cotton has failed."

"Ay," said I, "cotton is starving us outright. A man may bear a deal himself, but he'll do aught bad and sinful to save his wife and child."

"Nay, lad," said he, "poaching is not sinful; it goes against man's laws, but not against God's."

I was too weak to argue or talk much. I had not tasted food for two days. But I murmured, " At any rate, I trusted to have been clear of it for the rest of my days. It led my father wrong at first. I have tried and I have striven. Now I give all up. Right or wrong shall be the same to me. Some are fore-doomed ; and so am I." And as I spoke, some notion of the futurity that would separate Nelly, the pure and holy, from me, the reckless and desperate one, came over me with an irrepressible burst of anguish. Just then the bells of Bolton-in-Bolland struck up a glad peal, which came over the woods, in the solemn midnight air, like the sons of the morning shouting for joy—they seemed so clear and jubilant. It was Christmas Day : and I felt like an outcast from the gladness and the salvation. Old Jonah spoke out :—

" Yon's the Christmas bells. I say, Johnny, my lad, I've no notion of taking such a spiritless chap as thou into the thick of it, with thy rights and thy wrongs. We don't trouble ourselves with such fine lawyer's stuff, and we bring down the ' varmint' all the better. Now, I'll not have thee in our gang, for thou art not up to the fun, and thou'd hang fire when the time came to be doing. But I've a shrewd guess that plaguy wife and child of thine are at the bottom of thy half-and-half joining. Now, I was thy father's friend afore he took to them helter-skelter ways, and I've five shillings and a neck of mutton at thy service. I'll not list a fasting man ; but if thou'lt come to us with a full stomach, and say, ' I like your life, my lads, and I'll make one of you with pleasure, the first shiny night,' why, we'll give you a welcome and a half ; but, to-night, make no more

7

ado, but turn back with me for the mutton and the money."

I was not proud: nay, I was most thankful. I took the meat, and boiled some broth for my poor Nelly. She was in a sleep, or a faint, I know not which; but I roused her, and held her up in bed, and fed her with a teaspoon, and the light came back to her eyes, and the faint, moonlight smile to her lips; and when she had ended, she said her innocent grace, and fell asleep, with her baby on her breast. I sat over the fire, and listened to the bells, as they swept past my cottage on the gusts of the wind. I longed and yearned for the second coming of Christ, of which Nelly had told me. The world seemed cruel, and hard, and strong—too strong for me; and I prayed to cling to the hem of His garment, and be borne over the rough places when I fainted, and bled, and found no man to pity or help me, but poor old Jonah, the publican and sinner. All this time my own woes and my own self were uppermost in my mind, as they are in the minds of most who have been hardly used. As I thought of my wrongs, and my sufferings, my heart burned against Dick Jackson; and as the bells rose and fell, so my hopes waxed and waned, that in those mysterious days, of which they were both the remembrance and the prophecy, he would be purged from off the earth. I took Nelly's Bible, and turned, not to the gracious story of the Saviour's birth, but to the records of the former days, when the Jews took such wild revenge upon all their opponents. I was a Jew,—a leader among the people. Dick Jackson was as Pharaoh, as the King Agag, who walked delicately, thinking the bitterness of death was past,—in short, he was the conquered enemy, over whom I gloated, with my Bible in my hand—that Bible which contained our Saviour's words on the Cross. As yet, those words seemed faint and meaningless to me, like a tract of country seen in the starlight haze; while the histories of the Old Testament were grand and distinct in the blood-red colour of sunset. By-and-by that night passed into day, and little piping voices came round, carol-singing. They wakened Nelly. I went to her as soon as I heard her stirring.

"Nelly," said I, "there's money and food in the house; I will be off to Padiham seeking work, while thou hast something to go upon."

"Not to-day," said she; "stay to-day with me. If thou wouldst only go to church with me this once"—for you see I had never been inside a church but when we were married, and she was often praying me to go; and now she looked at me, with a sigh just creeping forth from her lips, as she expected a refusal. But I did not refuse. I had been kept away from church before because I dared not go; and now I was desperate, and dared do anything. If I did look like a heathen in the face of all men, why, I was a heathen in my heart; for I was falling back into all my evil ways. I had resolved if my search of work at Padiham should fail, I would follow my father's footsteps, and take with my own right hand and by my strength of arm what it was denied me to obtain honestly. I had resolved to leave Sawley, where a curse seemed to hang over me; so, what did it matter if I went to church, all unbe-knowing what strange ceremonies were there performed? I walked thither as a sinful man—sinful in my heart.

Nelly hung on my arm, but even she could not get me to speak. I went in; she found my places, and pointed to the words, and looked up into my eyes with hers, so full of faith and joy. But I saw nothing but Richard Jackson—I heard nothing but his loud nasal voice, making response, and desecrating all the holy words. He was in broadcloth of the best—I in my fustian jacket. He was prosperous and glad—I was starving and desperate. Nelly grew pale, as she saw the expression in my eyes; and she prayed ever, and ever more fervently as the thought of me tempted by the Devil even at that very moment came more fully before her.

By-and-by she forgot even me, and laid her soul bare before God, in a long, silent, weeping prayer, before we left the church. Nearly all had gone; and I stood by her, unwilling to disturb her, unable to join her. At last she rose up, heavenly calm. She took my arm, and we went home through the woods, where all the birds seemed tame and familiar. Nelly said she thought all living creatures knew it was Christmas Day, and rejoiced, and were loving together. I believed it was the frost that had tamed them; and I felt the hatred that was in me, and knew that whatever else was loving, I was full of malice and uncharitableness, nor did I wish to be otherwise. That afternoon I bade Nelly and our child farewell, and tramped to Padiham. I got work— how I hardly know; for stronger and stronger came the force of the temptation to lead a wild, free life of sin; legions seemed whispering evil thoughts to me, and only my gentle, pleading Nelly to pull me back from the great gulf. However, as I said before, I got work, and set off homewards to move my wife and child to that neighbourhood. I hated Sawley, and yet I was fiercely indignant to leave it, with my purposes unaccomplished. I was still an outcast from the more respectable, who stood afar off from such as I; and mine enemy lived and flourished in their regard. Padiham, however, was not so far away for me to despair—to relinquish my fixed determination. It was on the eastern side of the great Pendle Hill, ten miles away—maybe. Hate will overleap a greater obstacle. I took a cottage on the Fell, high up on the side of the hill. We saw a long black moorland slope before us, and then the grey stone houses of Padiham, over which a black cloud hung, different from the blue wood or turf smoke about Sawley. The wild winds came down and whistled round our house many a day when all was still below. But I was happy then. I rose in men's esteem. I had work in plenty. Our child lived and throve. But I forgot not our country proverb—"Keep a stone in thy pocket for seven years: turn it, and keep it seven years more; but have it ever ready to cast at thine enemy when the time comes."

One day a fellow-workman asked me to go to a hill-side preaching. Now, I never cared to go to church; but there was something newer and freer in the notion of praying to God right under His great dome; and the open air had had a charm to me ever since my wild boy-hood. Besides, they said, these ranters had strange ways with them, and I thought it would be fun to see their way of setting about it; and this ranter of all others had made himself a name in our parts. Accordingly we went; it was a fine summer's evening, after work was done. When we got to the place we saw such a crowd as I

never saw before—men, women, and children; all ages
were gathered together, and sat on the hill-side. They
were care-worn, diseased, sorrowful, criminal; all that
was told on their faces, which were hard and strongly
marked. In the midst, standing in a cart, was the
ranter. When I first saw him, I said to my companion,
"Lord! what a little man to make all this pother! I
could trip him up with one of my fingers," and then
I sat down, and looked about me a bit. All eyes were
fixed on the preacher; and I turned mine upon him too.
He began to speak; it was in no fine-drawn language,
but in words such as we heard every day of our lives,
and about things we did every day of our lives. He did
not call our shortcomings pride or worldliness, or plea-
sure-seeking, which would have given us no clear notion
of what he meant, but he just told us outright what we
did, and then he gave it a name, and said that it was
accursed, and that we were lost if we went on so doing.

By this time the tears and sweat were running down
his face; he was wrestling for our souls. We wondered
how he knew our innermost lives as he did, for each
one of us saw his sin set before him in plain-spoken
words. Then he cried out to us to repent; and spoke
first to us, and then to God, in a way that would have
shocked many—but it did not shock me. I liked strong
things; and I liked the bare, full truth: and I felt
brought nearer to God in that hour—the summer darkness creeping over us, and one after one the stars coming
out above us, like the eyes of the angels watching us
—than I had ever done in my life before. When he
had brought us to our tears and sighs, he stopped his
loud voice of upbraiding, and there was a hush, only

broken by sobs and quivering moans, in which I heard
through the gloom the voices of strong men in anguish
and supplication, as well as the shriller tones of women.
Suddenly he was heard again; by this time we could
not see him; but his voice was now tender as the voice
of an angel, and he told us of Christ, and implored
us to come to Him. I never heard such passionate
entreaty. He spoke as if he saw Satan hovering near
us in the dark, dense night, and as if our only safety
lay in a very present coming to the Cross; I believe he
did see Satan; we know he haunts the desolate old hills,
awaiting his time, and now or never it was with many
a soul. At length there was a sudden silence; and by
the cries of those nearest to the preacher, we heard
that he had fainted. We had all crowded round him,
as if he were our safety and our guide; and he was
overcome by the heat and the fatigue, for we were the
fifth set of people whom he had addressed that day.
I left the crowd who were leading him down, and took a
lonely path myself.

Here was the earnestness I needed. To this weak
and weary fainting man, religion was a life and a passion.
I look back now, and wonder at my blindness as to what
was the root of all my Nelly's patience and long-suffer-
ing; for I thought, now I had found out what religion
was, and that hitherto it had been all an unknown thing
to me.

Henceforward, my life was changed. I was zealous
and fanatical. Beyond the set to whom I had affiliated
myself, I had no sympathy. I would have persecuted
all who differed from me, if I had only had the power.
I became an ascetic in all bodily enjoyments. And,

strange and inexplicable mystery, I had some thoughts
that by every act of self-denial I was attaining to my
unholy end, and that, when I had fasted and prayed
long enough, God would place my vengeance in my
hands.   I have knelt by Nelly's bedside, and vowed to
live a self-denying life, as regarded all outward things,
if so that God would grant my prayer. . I left it in His
hands.   I felt sure he would trace out the token and
the word; and Nelly would listen to my passionate
words, and lie awake sorrowful and heart-sore through
the night; and I would get up and make her tea, and
rearrange her pillows, with a strange and wilful blindness that my bitter words and blasphemous prayers had
cost her miserable, sleepless nights.   My Nelly was
suffering yet from that blow.   How or where the stone
had hurt her, I never understood; but in consequence
of that one moment's action, her limbs became numb
and dead, and, by slow degrees, she took to her bed,
from whence she was never carried alive.   There she lay,
propped up by pillows, her meek face ever bright, and
smiling forth a greeting; her white, pale hands ever
busy with some kind of work; and our little Grace was
as the power of motion to her.   Fierce as I was away
from her, I never could speak to her but in my gentlest
tones.   She seemed to me as if she had never wrestled
for salvation as I had; and when away from her, I
resolved many a time and oft, that I would rouse her
up to her state of danger when I returned home that
evening—even if strong reproach were required I would
rouse her up to her soul's need.   But I came in and
heard her voice singing softly some holy word of patience,
some psalm which, maybe, had comforted the martyrs,

and when I saw her face like the face of an angel, full
of patience and happy faith, I put off my awakening
speeches till another time.

One night, long ago, when I was yet young and
strong, although my years were past forty, I sat alone
in my houseplace. Nelly was always in bed, as I have
told you, and Grace lay in a cot by her side. I believed
them to be both asleep; though how they could sleep I
could not conceive, so wild and terrible was the night.
The wind came sweeping down from the hill-top in great
beats, like the pulses of heaven; and, during the pauses,
while I listened for the coming roar, I felt the earth
shiver beneath me. The rain beat against windows and
doors, and sobbed for entrance. I thought the Prince
of the Air was abroad; and I heard, or fancied I heard,
shrieks come on the blast, like the cries of sinful souls
given over to his power.

The sounds came nearer and nearer. I got up and
saw to the fastenings of the door, for though I cared
not for mortal man, I did care for what I believed
was surrounding the house, in evil might and power.
But the door shook as though it, too, were in deadly
terror, and I thought the fastenings would give way. I
stood facing the entrance, lashing my heart up to defy
the spiritual enemy that I looked to see, every instant,
in bodily presence; and the door did burst open; and
before me stood—what was it? man or demon? a grey-
haired man, with poor, worn clothes all wringing wet,
and he himself battered and piteous to look upon, from
the storm he had passed through.

"Let me in!" he said. "Give me shelter. I am
poor, or I would reward you. And I am friendless,

too," he said, looking up in my face, like one seeking what he cannot find. In that look, strangely changed, I knew that God had heard me; for it was the old cowardly look of my life's enemy. Had he been a stranger, I might not have welcomed him; but as he was mine enemy, I gave him welcome in a lordly dish. I sat opposite to him. "Whence do you come?" said I. "It is a strange night to be out on the fells."

He looked up at me sharp; but in general he held his head down like a beast or hound.

"You won't betray me. I'll not trouble you long. As soon as the storm abates, I'll go."

"Friend!" said I, "what have I to betray?" and I trembled lest he should keep himself out of my power and not tell me. "You come for shelter, and I give you of my best. Why do you suspect me?"

"Because," said he, in his abject bitterness, "all the world is against me. I never met with goodness or kindness; and now I am hunted like a wild beast. I'll tell you—I'm a convict returned before my time. I was a Sawley man" (as if I, of all men, did not know it!), "and I went back, like a fool, to the old place. They've hunted me out where I would fain have lived rightly and quietly, and they'll send me back to that hell upon earth, if they catch me. I did not know it would be such a night. Only let me rest and get warm once more, and I'll go away. Good, kind man, have pity upon me!" I smiled all his doubts away; I promised him a bed on the floor, and I thought of Jael and Sisera. My heart leaped up like a war-horse at the sound of the trumpet, and said, "Ha, ha, the Lord hath heard my prayer and supplication; I shall have vengeance at last!"

He did not dream who I was. He was changed; so that I, who had learned his features with all the diligence of hatred, did not, at first, recognize him; and he thought not of me, only of his own woe and affright. He looked into the fire with the dreamy gaze of one whose strength of character, if he had any, is beaten out of him, and cannot return at any emergency whatsoever. He sighed and pitied himself, yet could not decide on what to do. I went softly about my business, which was to make him up a bed on the floor, and, when he was lulled to sleep and security, to make the best of my way to Padiham, and summon the constable, into whose hands I would give him up, to be taken back to his " hell upon earth." I went into Nelly's room. She was awake and anxious. I saw she had been listening to the voices.

" Who is there ? " said she. " John, tell me; it sounded like a voice I knew. For God's sake, speak ! "

I smiled a quiet smile. " It is a poor man, who has lost his way. Go to sleep, my dear—I shall make him up on the floor. I may not come for some time. Go to sleep;" and I kissed her. I thought she was soothed, but not fully satisfied. However, I hastened away before there was any further time for questioning. I made up the bed, and Richard Jackson, tired out, lay down and fell asleep. My contempt for him almost equalled my hate. If I were avoiding return to a place which I thought to be a hell upon earth, think you I would have taken a quiet sleep under any man's roof till, somehow or another, I was secure. Now comes this man, and, with incontinence of tongue, blabs out the very thing he most should conceal, and then lies down to a good, quiet, snoring sleep. I looked again. His face was old,

and worn, and miserable.   So should mine enemy look.
And yet it was sad to gaze upon him, poor, hunted
creature!

I would gaze no more, lest I grew weak and pitiful.
Thus I took my hat, and softly opened the door.   The
wind blew in, but did not disturb him, he was so utterly
weary.   I was out in the open air of night.   The storm
was ceasing, and, instead of the black sky of doom that
I had seen when I last looked forth, the moon was come
out, wan and pale, as if wearied with the fight in the
heavens, and her white light fell ghostly and calm on
many a well-known object.   Now and then, a dark, torn
cloud was blown across her home in the sky; but they
grew fewer and fewer, and at last she shone out steady
and clear.   I could see Padiham down before me.   I
heard the noise of the watercourses down the hill-side.
My mind was full of one thought, and strained upon
that one thought, and yet my senses were most acute and
observant.   When I came to the brook, it was swollen
to a rapid, tossing river; and the little bridge, with its
hand-rail, was utterly swept away.   It was like the
bridge at Sawley, where I had first seen Nelly; and I
remembered that day even then in the midst of my
vexation at having to go round.   I turned away from
the brook, and there stood a little figure facing me.   No
spirit from the dead could have affrighted me as it did;
for I saw it was Grace, whom I had left in bed by her
mother's side.

She came to me, and took my hand.   Her bare feet
glittered white in the moonshine, and sprinkled the
light upwards, as they plashed through the pool.

"Father," said she, "mother bade me say this."

Then pausing to gather breath and memory, she repeated these words, like a lesson of which she feared to forget a syllable :—

"Mother says, 'There is a God in heaven; and in His house are many mansions. If you hope to meet her there, you will come back and speak to her; if you are to be separate for ever and ever, you will go on, and may God have mercy on her and on you!' Father, I have said it right—every word."

I was silent. At last, I said,—

"What made mother say this? How came she to send you out?"

"I was asleep, father, and I heard her cry. I wakened up, and I think you had but just left the house, and that she was calling for you. Then she prayed, with the tears rolling down her cheeks, and kept saying—'Oh, that I could walk!—oh, that for one hour I could run and walk!' So I said, 'Mother, I can run and walk. Where must I go?' And she clutched at my arm, and bade God bless me, and told me not to fear, for that He would compass me about, and taught me my message: and now, father, dear father, you will meet mother in heaven, won't you, and not be separate for ever and ever?" She clung to my knees, and pleaded once more in her mother's words. I took her up in my arms, and turned homewards.

"Is yon man there, on the kitchen floor?" asked I.

"Yes!" she answered. At any rate, my vengeance was not out of my power yet.

When we got home I passed him, dead asleep.

In our room, to which my child guided me, was Nelly. She sat up in bed, a most unusual attitude for her, and one of which I thought she had been incapable of attaining to without help. She had her hands clasped, and her face rapt, as if in prayer; and when she saw me, she lay back with a sweet ineffable smile. She could not speak at first; but when I came near, she took my hand and kissed it, and then she called Grace to her, and made her take off her cloak and her wet things, and dressed in her short scanty nightgown, she slipped in to her mother's warm side; and all this time my Nelly never told me why she summoned me : it seemed enough that she should hold my hand, and feel that I was there. I believed she had read my heart; and yet I durst not speak to ask her. At last, she looked up. "My husband," said she, "God has saved you and me from a great sorrow this night." I would not understand, and I felt her look die away into disappointment.

"That poor wanderer in the house-place is Richard Jackson, is it not?"

I made no answer. Her face grew white and wan.

"Oh," said she, "this is hard to bear. Speak what is in your mind, I beg of you. I will not thwart you harshly; dearest John, only speak to me."

"Why need I speak? You seem to know all."

"I do know that his is a voice I can never forget; and I do know the awful prayers you have prayed; and I know how I have lain awake, to pray that your words might never be heard; and I am a powerless cripple. I put my cause in God's hands. You shall not do the man any harm. What you have it in your thoughts to do, I cannot tell. But I know that you cannot do it. My eyes are dim with a strange mist; but some voice tells me that you will forgive even Richard Jackson.

Dear husband—dearest John, it is so dark, I cannot see you : but speak once to me."

I moved the candle ; but when I saw her face, I saw what was drawing the mist over those loving eyes—how strange and woeful that she could die ! Her little girl lying by her side looked in my face, and then at her ; and the wild knowledge of death shot through her young heart, and she screamed aloud.

Nelly opened her eyes once more. They fell upon the gaunt, sorrow-worn man who was the cause of all. He roused him from his sleep, at that child's piercing cry, and stood at the doorway, looking in. He knew Nelly, and understood where the storm had driven him to shelter. He came towards her :—

" Oh, woman—dying woman—you have haunted me in the loneliness of the Bush far away—you have been in my dreams for ever—the hunting of men has not been so terrible as the hunting of your spirit,—that stone—that stone ! " He fell down by her bedside in an agony ; above which her saint-like face looked on us all, for the last time, glorious with the coming light of heaven. She spoke once again :—

" It was a moment of passion ; I never bore you malice for it. I forgive you; and so does John, I trust."

Could I keep my purpose there ? It faded into nothing. But, above my choking tears, I strove to speak clear and distinct, for her dying ear to hear, and her sinking heart to be gladdened.

" I forgive you, Richard ; I will befriend you in your trouble."

She could not see ; but, instead of the dim shadow of

death stealing over her face, a quiet light came over it, which we knew was the look of a soul at rest.

That night I listened to his tale for her sake ; and I learned that it is better to be sinned against than to sin. In the storm of the night mine enemy came to me ; in the calm of the grey morning I led him forth, and bade him " God speed." And a woe had come upon me, but the burning burden of a sinful, angry heart was taken off. I am old now, and my daughter is married. I try to go about preaching and teaching in my rough, rude way; and what I teach is, how Christ lived and died, and what was Nelly's faith of love.

THE OLD NURSE'S STORY.

You know, my dears, that your mother was an orphan, and an only child; and I daresay you have heard that your grandfather was a clergyman up in Westmoreland, where I come from. I was just a girl in the village school, when, one day, your grandmother came in to ask the mistress if there was any scholar there who would do for a nurse-maid; and mighty proud I was, I can tell ye, when the mistress called me up, and spoke to my being a good girl at my needle, and a steady, honest girl, and one whose parents were very respectable, though they might be poor. I thought I should like nothing better than to serve the pretty young lady, who was blushing as deep as I was, as she spoke of the coming baby, and what I should have to do with 'it. However, I see you don't care so much for this part of my story, as for what you think is to come, so I'll tell you at once. I was engaged and settled at the parsonage before Miss Rosamond (that was the baby, who is now your mother) was born. To be sure, I had little enough to do with her when she came, for she was never

8

out of her mother's arms, and slept by her all night
long; and proud enough was I sometimes when missis
trusted her to me.   There never was such a baby before
or since, though you've all of you been fine enough in
your turns; but for sweet, winning ways, you've none
of you come up to your mother.   She took after her
mother, who was a real lady born; a Miss Furnivall, a
grand-daughter of Lord Furnivall's, in Northumberland.
I believe she had neither brother nor sister, and had
been brought up in my lord's family till she had married
your grandfather, who was just a curate, son to a shopkeeper in Carlisle—but a clever, fine gentleman as ever
was—and one who was a right-down hard worker in his
parish, which was very wide, and scattered all abroad
over the Westmoreland Fells.   When your mother, little
Miss Rosamond, was about four or five years old, both
her parents died in a fortnight—one after the other.
Ah! that was a sad time.   My pretty young mistress
and me was looking for another baby, when my master
came home from one of his long rides, wet and tired,
and took the fever he died of; and then she never held
up her head again, but just lived to see her dead baby,
and have it laid on her breast, before she sighed away
her life.   My mistress had asked me, on her death-bed,
never to leave Miss Rosamond; but if she had never
spoken a word, I would have gone with the little child
to the end of the world.

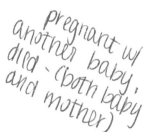

The next thing, and before we had well stilled our
sobs, the executors and guardians came to settle the
affairs.   They were my poor young mistress's own
cousin, Lord Furnivall, and Mr. Esthwaite, my master's
brother, a shopkeeper in Manchester; not so well to do

then as he was afterwards, and with a large family rising
about him. Well! I don't know if it were their settling, or because of a letter my mistress wrote on her
death-bed to her cousin, my lord; but somehow it was
settled that Miss Rosamond and me were to go to
Furnivall Manor House, in Northumberland, and my
lord spoke as if it had been her mother's wish that she
should live with his family, and as if he had no objec-
tions, for that one or two more or less could make no
difference in so grand a household. So, though that
was not the way in which I should have wished the
coming of my bright and pretty pet to have been looked
at—who was like a sunbeam in any family, be it never
so grand—I was well pleased that all the folks in the
Dale should stare and admire, when they heard I was
going to be young lady's-maid at my Lord Furnivall's at
Furnivall Manor.

But I made a mistake in thinking we were to go and
live where my lord did. It turned out that the family
had left Furnivall Manor House fifty years or more. I
could not hear that my poor young mistress had ever been
there, though she had been brought up in the family;
and I was sorry for that, for I should have liked Miss
Rosamond's youth to have passed where her mother's
had been.

My lord's gentleman, from whom I asked as many
questions as I durst, said that the Manor House was at
the foot of the Cumberland Fells, and a very grand
place; that an old Miss Furnivall, a great-aunt of my
lord's, lived there, with only a few servants; but that it
was a very healthy place, and my lord had thought
that it would suit Miss Rosamond very well for a few

8—2

years, and that her being there might perhaps amuse his old aunt.

I was bidden by my lord to have Miss Rosamond's things ready by a certain day. He was a stern, proud man, as they say all the Lords Furnivall were; and he never spoke a word more than was necessary. Folk did say he had loved my young mistress; but that, because she knew that his father would object, she would never listen to him, and married Mr. Esthwaite; but I don't know. He never married, at any rate. But he never took much notice of Miss Rosamond; which I thought he might have done if he had cared for her dead mother. He sent his gentleman with us to the Manor House, telling him to join him at Newcastle that same evening; so there was no great length of time for him to make us known to all the strangers before he, too, shook us off; and we were left, two lonely young things (I was not eighteen) in the great old Manor House. It seems like yesterday that we drove there. We had left our own dear parsonage very early, and we had both cried as if our hearts would break, though we were travelling in my lord's carriage, which I thought so much of once. And now it was long past noon on a September day, and we stopped to change horses for the last time at a little smoky town, all full of colliers and miners. Miss Rosamond had fallen asleep, but Mr. Henry told me to waken her, that she might see the park and the Manor House as we drove up. I thought it rather a pity; but I did what he bade me, for fear he should complain of me to my lord. We had left all signs of a town, or even a village, and were then inside the gates of a large wild park—not like the parks here in the south, but with rocks, and the noise of running water, and gnarled thorn-trees, and old oaks, all white and peeled with age.

The road went up about two miles, and then we saw a great and stately house, with many trees close around it, so close that in some places their branches dragged against the walls when the wind blew; and some hung broken down; for no one seemed to take much charge of the place;—to lop the wood, or to keep the moss-covered carriage-way in order. Only in front of the house all was clear. The great oval drive was without a weed; and neither tree nor creeper was allowed to grow over the long, many-windowed front; at both sides of which a wing projected, which were each the ends of other side fronts; for the house, although it was so desolate, was even grander than I expected. Behind it rose the Fells, which seemed unenclosed and bare enough; and on the left hand of the house, as you stood facing it, was a little, old-fashioned flower-garden, as I found out afterwards. A door opened out upon it from the west front; it had been scooped out of the thick, dark wood for some old Lady Furnivall; but the branches of the great forest-trees had grown and over-shadowed it again, and there were very few flowers that would live there at that time.

When we drove up to the great front entrance, and went into the hall, I thought we should be lost—it was so large, and vast, and grand. There was a chandelier all of bronze, hung down from the middle of the ceiling; and I had never seen one before, and looked at it all in amaze. Then, at one end of the hall, was a great fire-place, as large as the sides of the houses in my country, with massy andirons and dogs to hold the wood; and by it were heavy, old-fashioned sofas. At the opposite end of the hall, to the left as you went in —on the western side—was an organ built into the wall, and so large that it filled up the best part of that end. Beyond it, on the same side, was a door; and opposite, on each side of the fire-place, were also doors leading to the east front; but those I never went through as long as I stayed in the house, so I can't tell you what lay beyond.

The afternoon was closing in, and the hall, which had no fire lighted in it, looked dark and gloomy, but we did not stay there a moment. The old servant, who had opened the door for us, bowed to Mr. Henry, and took us in through the door at the further side of the great organ, and led us through several smaller halls and passages into the west drawing-room, where he said that Miss Furnivall was sitting. Poor little Miss Rosamond held very tight to me, as if she were scared and lost in that great place; and as for myself, I was not much better. The west drawing-room was very cheerful-looking, with a warm fire in it, and plenty of good, comfortable furniture about. Miss Furnivall was an old lady not far from eighty, I should think, but I do not know. She was thin and tall, and had a face as full of fine wrinkles as if they had been drawn all over it with a needle's point. Her eyes were very watchful to make up, I suppose, for her being so deaf as to be obliged to use a trumpet. Sitting with her, working at the same great piece of tapestry, was Mrs. Stark, her maid and companion, and almost as old as she was. She had lived with Miss Furnivall ever since they both were

young, and now she seemed more like a friend than a
servant; she looked so cold, and grey, and stony, as if
she had never loved or cared for any one; and I don't
suppose she did care for any one, except her mistress;
and, owing to the great deafness of the latter, Mrs. Stark
treated her very much as if she were a child. Mr. Henry
gave some message from my lord, and then he bowed
good-by to us all,—taking no notice of my sweet little
Miss Rosamond's out-stretched hand—and left us standing there, being looked at by the two old ladies through
their spectacles.

I was right glad when they rung for the old footman
who had shown us in at first, and told him to take us to
our rooms. So we went out of that great drawing-room,
and into another sitting-room, and out of that, and then
up a great flight of stairs, and along a broad gallery—
which was something like a library, having books all
down one side, and windows and writing-tables all down
the other—till we came to our rooms, which I was not
sorry to hear were just over the kitchens; for I began
to think I should be lost in that wilderness of a house.
There was an old nursery, that had been used for all
the little lords and ladies long ago, with a pleasant fire
burning in the grate, and the kettle boiling on the hob,
and tea-things spread out on the table; and out of that
room was the night-nursery, with a little crib for Miss
Rosamond close to my bed. And old James called up
Dorothy, his wife, to bid us welcome; and both he and
she were so hospitable and kind, that by-and-by Miss
Rosamond and me felt quite at home; and by the time
tea was over, she was sitting on Dorothy's knee, and
chattering away as fast as her little tongue could go.

I soon found out that Dorothy was from Westmoreland, and that bound her and me together, as it were; and I would never wish to meet with kinder people than were old James and his wife. James had lived pretty nearly all his life in my lord's family, and thought there was no one so grand as they. He even looked down a little on his wife; because, till he had married her, she had never lived in any but a farmer's household. But he was very fond of her, as well he might be. They had one servant under them, to do all the rough work. Agnes they called her; and she and me, and James and Dorothy, with Miss Furnivall and Mrs. Stark, made up the family; always remembering my sweet little Miss Rosamond! I used to wonder what they had done before she came, they thought so much of her now. Kitchen and drawing-room, it was all the same. The hard, sad Miss Furnivall, and the cold Mrs. Stark, looked pleased when she came fluttering in like a bird, playing and pranking hither and thither, with a continual murmur, and pretty prattle of gladness. I am sure, they were sorry many a time when she flitted away into the kitchen, though they were too proud to ask her to stay with them, and were a little surprised at her taste; though to be sure, as Mrs. Stark said, it was not to be wondered at, remembering what stock her father had come of. The great, old rambling house was a famous place for little Miss Rosamond. She made expeditions all over it, with me at her heels; all, except the east wing, which was never opened, and whither we never thought of going. But in the western and northern part was many a pleasant room; full of things that were curiosities to us, though they might not have been to people who had seen more. The windows were darkened by the sweeping boughs of the trees, and the ivy which had overgrown them: but, in the green gloom, we could manage to see old China jars and carved ivory boxes, and great heavy books, and, above all, the old pictures!

Once, I remember, my darling would have Dorothy go with us to tell us who they all were; for they were all portraits of some of my lord's family, though Dorothy could not tell us the names of every one. We had gone through most of the rooms, when we came to the old state drawing-room over the hall, and there was a picture of Miss Furnivall; or, as she was called in those days, Miss Grace, for she was the younger sister. Such a beauty she must have been! but with such a set, proud look, and such scorn looking out of her handsome eyes, with her eyebrows just a little raised, as if she wondered how any one could have the impertinence to look at her, and her lip curled at us, as we stood there gazing. She had a dress on, the like of which I had never seen before, but it was all the fashion when she was young: a hat of some soft white stuff like beaver, pulled a little over her brows, and a beautiful plume of feathers sweeping round it on one side; and her gown of blue satin was open in front to a quilted white stomacher.

"Well, to be sure!" said I, when I had gazed my fill. "Flesh is grass, they do say; but who would have thought that Miss Furnivall had been such an out-and-out beauty, to see her now?"

"Yes," said Dorothy. "Folks change sadly. But if what my master's father used to say was true, Miss

Furnivall, the elder sister, was handsomer than Miss Grace. Her picture is here somewhere ; but, if I show it you, you must never let on, even to James, that you have seen it. Can the little lady hold her tongue, think you ? " asked she.

I was not so sure, for she was such a little sweet, bold, open-spoken child, so I set her to hide herself; and then I helped Dorothy to turn a great picture, that leaned with its face towards the wall, and was not hung up as the others were. To be sure, it beat Miss Grace for beauty ; and, I think, for scornful pride, too, though in that matter it might be hard to choose. I could have looked at it an hour, but Dorothy seemed half frightened at having shown it to me, and hurried it back again, and bade me run and find Miss Rosamond, for that there were some ugly places about the house, where she should like ill for the child to go. I was a brave, high-spirited girl, and thought little of what the old woman said, for I liked hide-and-seek as well as any child in the parish ; so off I ran to find my little one.

As winter drew on, and the days grew shorter, I was sometimes almost certain that I heard a noise as if some one was playing on the great organ in the hall. I did not hear it every evening ; but, certainly, I did very often, usually when I was sitting with Miss Rosamond, after I had put her to bed, and keeping quite still and silent in the bedroom. Then I used to hear it booming and swelling away in the distance. The first night, when I went down to my supper, I asked Dorothy who had been playing music, and James said very shortly that I was a gowk to take the wind soughing among the trees for music: but I saw Dorothy look at him very fearfully,

and Bessy, the kitchen-maid, said something beneath
her breath, and went quite white. I saw they did not
like my question, so I held my peace till I was with
Dorothy alone, when I knew I could get a good deal out
of her. So, the next day, I watched my time, and I
coaxed and asked her who it was that played the organ;
for I knew that it was the organ and not the wind well
enough, for all I had kept silence before James. But
Dorothy had had her lesson, I'll warrant, and never a
word could I get from her. So then I tried Bessy,
though I had always held my head rather above her, as I
was evened to James and Dorothy, and she was little
better than their servant. So she said I must never,
never tell; and if I ever told, I was never to say *she*
had told me; but it was a very strange noise, and she
had heard it many a time, but most of all on winter
nights, and before storms; and folks did say it was the
old lord playing on the great organ in the hall, just as
he used to do when he was alive; but who the old lord
was, or why he played, and why he played on stormy
winter evenings in particular, she either could not or
would not tell me. Well! I told you I had a brave
heart; and I thought it was rather pleasant to have
that grand music rolling about the house, let who would
be the player; for now it rose above the great gusts of
wind, and wailed and triumphed just like a living creature, and then it fell to a softness most complete, only
it was always music, and tunes, so it was nonsense to
call it the wind. I thought at first, that it might be
Miss Furnivall who played, unknown to Bessy; but, one
day when I was in the hall by myself, I opened the
organ and peeped all about it and around it, as I had

done to the organ in Crosthwaite Church once before,
and I saw it was all broken and destroyed inside, though
it looked so brave and fine ; and then, though it was noon-
day, my flesh began to creep a little, and I shut it up,
and run away pretty quickly to my own bright nursery ;
and I did not like hearing the music for some time after
that, any more than James and Dorothy did. All this
time Miss Rosamond was making herself more and more
beloved. The old ladies liked her to dine with them at
their early dinner. James stood behind Miss Furnivall's
chair, and I behind Miss Rosamond's all in state ; and
after dinner, she would play about in a corner of the
great drawing-room as still as any mouse, while Miss
Furnivall slept, and I had my dinner in the kitchen.
But she was glad enough to come to me in the nursery
afterwards ; for, as she said, Miss Furnivall was so sad,
and Mrs. Stark so dull ; but she and I were merry
enough ; and, by-and-by, I got not to care for that weird
rolling music, which did one no harm, if we did not
know where it came from.

That winter was very cold. In the middle of October
the frosts began, and lasted many, many weeks. I
remember one day, at dinner, Miss Furnivall lifted up
her sad, heavy eyes, and said to Mrs. Stark, "I am
afraid we shall have a terrible winter," in a strange kind
of meaning way. But Mrs. Stark pretended not to hear,
and talked very loud of something else. My little lady
and I did not care for the frost ; not we ! As long as it
was dry, we climbed up the steep brows behind the house,
and went up on the Fells, which were bleak and bare
enough, and there we ran races in the fresh, sharp air ;
and once we came down by a new path, that took us past

the two old gnarled holly-trees, which grew about half-way down by the east side of the house. But the days grew shorter and shorter, and the old lord, if it was he, played away, more and more stormily and sadly, on the great organ. One Sunday afternoon—it must have been towards the end of November—I asked Dorothy to take charge of little missey when she came out of the draw-ing-room, after Miss Furnivall had had her nap; for it was too cold to take her with me to church, and yet I wanted to go. And Dorothy was glad enough to promise, and was so fond of the child, that all seemed well; and Bessy and I set off very briskly, though the sky hung heavy and black over the white earth, as if the night had never fully gone away, and the air, though still, was very biting and keen.

"We shall have a fall of snow," said Bessy to me. And sure enough, even while we were in church, it came down thick, in great large flakes—so thick, it almost darkened the windows. It had stopped snowing before we came out, but it lay soft, thick, and deep beneath our feet, as we tramped home. Before we got to the hall, the moon rose, and I think it was lighter then—what with the moon, and what with the white dazzling snow—than it had been when we went to church, between two and three o'clock. I have not told you that Miss Furni-vall and Mrs. Stark never went to church; they used to read the prayers together, in their quiet, gloomy way; they seemed to feel the Sunday very long without their tapestry-work to be busy at. So when I went to Dorothy in the kitchen, to fetch Miss Rosamond and take her up-stairs with me, I did not much wonder when the old woman told me that the ladies had kept the child with

them, and that she had never come to the kitchen, as I
had bidden her, when she was tired of behaving pretty
in the drawing-room.   So I took off my things and
went to find her, and bring her to her supper in the
nursery.   But when I went into the best drawing-room,
there sat the two old ladies, very still and quiet, dropping
out a word now and then, but looking as if nothing so
bright and merry as Miss Rosamond had ever been near
them.   Still I thought she might be hiding from me;
it was one of her pretty ways,—and that she had persuaded them to look as if they knew nothing about her;
so I went softly peeping under this sofa, and behind that
chair, making believe I was sadly frightened at not
finding her.

"What's the matter, Hester?" said Mrs. Stark,
sharply.   I don't know if Miss Furnivall had seen me,
for, as I told you, she was very deaf, and she sat quite
still, idly staring into the fire, with her hopeless face.
"I'm only looking for my little Rosy Posy," replied I,
still thinking that the child was there, and near me,
though I could not see her.

"Miss Rosamond is not here," said Mrs. Stark.
"She went away, more than an hour ago, to find
Dorothy."   And she, too, turned and went on looking
into the fire.

My heart sank at this, and I began to wish I had
never left my darling.   I went back to Dorothy and
told her.   James was gone out for the day, but she,
and me, and Bessy took lights, and went up into the
nursery first; and then we roamed over the great,
large house, calling and entreating Miss Rosamond to
come out of her hiding-place, and not frighten us to

death in that way.   But there was no answer ; no
sound.

"Oh!" said I, at last, "can she have got into the
east wing and hidden there ? "

But Dorothy said it was not possible, for that she
herself had never been in there ; that the doors were
always locked, and my lord's steward had the keys, she
believed ; at any rate, neither she nor James had ever
seen them : so I said I would go back, and see if, after
all, she was not hidden in the drawing-room, unknown
to the old ladies ; and if I found her there, I said, I
would whip her well for the fright she had given me ; but
I never meant to do it.   Well, I went back to the west
drawing-room, and I told Mrs. Stark we could not find
her anywhere, and asked for leave to look all about the
furniture there, for I thought now that she might have
fallen asleep in some warm, hidden corner ; but no !
we looked—Miss Furnivall got up and looked, trembling
all over—and she was nowhere there ; then we set off
again, every one in the house, and looked in all the
places we had searched before, but we could not find
her.   Miss Furnivall shivered and shook so much, that
Mrs. Stark took her back into the warm drawing-room ;
but not before they had made me promise to bring her
to them when she was found.   Well-a-day! I began to
think she never would be found, when I bethought me
to look out into the great front court, all covered with
snow.   I was upstairs when I looked out ; but, it was
such clear moonlight, I could see, quite plain, two little
footprints, which might be traced from the hall-door and
round the corner of the east wing.   I don't know how I
got down, but I tugged open the great stiff hall-door,

and, throwing the skirt of my gown over my head for a cloak, I ran out. I turned the east corner, and there a black shadow fell on the snow; but when s came again into the moonlight, there were the little footmarks going up—up to the Fells. It was bitter cold; so cold, that the air almost took the skin off my face as I ran; but I ran on, crying to think how my poor little darling must be perished and frightened. I was within sight of the holly-trees, when I saw a shepherd coming down the hill, bearing something in his arms wrapped in his maud. He shouted to me, and asked me if I had lost a bairn; and, when I could not speak for crying, he bore towards me, and I saw my wee bairnie lying still, and white, and stiff in his arms, as if she had been dead. He told me he had been up the Fells to gather in his sheep, before the deep cold of night came on, and that under the holly-trees (black marks on the hill-side, where no other bush was for miles around) he had found my little lady—my lamb—my queen—my darling—stiff and cold, in the terrible sleep which is frost-begotten. Oh! the joy and the tears of having her in my arms once again! for I would not let him carry her; but took her, maud and all, into my own arms, and held her near my own warm neck and heart, and felt the life stealing slowly back again into her little gentle limbs. But she was still insensible when we reached the hall, and I had no breath for speech. We went in by the kitchen-door.

"Bring the warming-pan," said I; and I carried her upstairs, and began undressing her by the nursery fire, which Bessy had kept up. I called my little lammie all the sweet and playful names I could think of,—even while my eyes were blinded by my tears; and at last, oh! at length she opened her large blue eyes. Then I put her into her warm bed, and sent Dorothy down to tell Miss Furnivall that all was well; and I made up my mind to sit by my darling's bedside the live-long night. She fell away into a soft sleep as soon as her pretty head had touched the pillow, and I watched by her till morning light; when she wakened up bright and clear—or so I thought at first—and, my dears, so I think now.

She said, that she had fancied that she should like to go to Dorothy, for that both the old ladies were asleep, and it was very dull in the drawing-room; and that, as she was going through the west lobby, she saw the snow through the high window falling—falling—soft and steady; but she wanted to see it lying pretty and white on the ground; so she made her way into the great hall; and then, going to the window, she saw it bright and soft upon the drive; but while she stood there, she saw a little girl, not so old as she was, "but so pretty," said my darling, "and this little girl beckoned to me to come out; and oh, she was so pretty and so sweet, I could not choose but go." And then this other little girl had taken her by the hand, and side by side the two had gone round the east corner.

"Now you are a naughty little girl, and telling stories," said I. "What would your good mamma, that is in heaven, and never told a story in her life, say to her little Rosamond, if she heard her—and I daresay she does—telling stories!"

"Indeed, Hester," sobbed out my child, "I'm telling you true. Indeed I am."

"Don't tell me!" said I, very stern. "I tracked

9

you by your foot-marks through the snow; there were
only yours to be seen : and if you had had a little
girl to go hand-in-hand with you up the hill, don't
you think the footprints would have gone along with
yours ?"

"I can't help it, dear, dear Hester," said she, crying,
"if they did not; I never looked at her feet, but she
held my hand fast and tight in her little one, and it was
very, very cold.   She took me up the Fell-path, up to
the holly-trees; and there I saw a lady weeping and
crying; but when she saw me, she hushed her weeping,
and smiled very proud and grand, and took me on her
knee, and began to lull me to sleep; and that's all,
Hester—but that is true; and my dear mamma knows
it is," said she, crying.   So I thought the child was in
a fever, and pretended to believe her, as she went over
her story—over and over again, and always the same.
At last Dorothy knocked at the door with Miss Rosamond's breakfast; and she told me the old ladies were
down in the eating parlour, and that they wanted to
speak to me.   They had both been into the night-nursery
the evening before, but it was after Miss Rosamond was
asleep; so they had only looked at her—not asked me
any questions.

"I shall catch it," thought I to myself, as I went
along the north gallery.   "And yet," I thought, taking
courage, "it was in their charge I left her; and it's
they that's to blame for letting her steal away unknown
and unwatched.   So I went in boldly, and told my story.
I told it all to Miss Furnivall, shouting it close to her
ear; but when I came to the mention of the other little
girl out in the snow, coaxing and tempting her out, and

wiling her up to the grand and beautiful lady by the holly-tree, she threw her arms up—her old and withered arms—and cried aloud, " Oh! Heaven forgive! Have mercy!"

Mrs. Stark took hold of her; roughly enough, I thought; but she was past Mrs. Stark's management, and spoke to me, in a kind of wild warning and authority.

" Hester! keep her from that child! It will lure her to her death! That evil child! Tell her it is a wicked, naughty child." Then, Mrs. Stark hurried me out of the room; where, indeed, I was glad enough to go; but Miss Furnivall kept shrieking out, " Oh, have mercy! Wilt Thou never forgive! It is many a long year ago——"

I was very uneasy in my mind after that. I durst never leave Miss Rosamond, night or day, for fear lest she might slip off again, after some fancy or other; and all the more, because I thought I could make out that Miss Furnivall was crazy, from their odd ways about her; and I was afraid lest something of the same kind (which might be in the family, you know) hung over my darling. And the great frost never ceased all this time; and, whenever it was a more stormy night than usual, between the gusts, and through the wind, we heard the old lord playing on the great organ. But, old lord, or not, wherever Miss Rosamond went, there I followed; for my love for her, pretty, helpless orphan, was stronger than my fear for the grand and terrible sound. Besides, it rested with me to keep her cheerful and merry, as beseemed her age. So we played together, and wandered together, here and there, and everywhere; for I never dared to lose sight of her again in that large and

rambling house. And so it happened, that one afternoon, not long before Christmas-day, we were playing
together on the billiard-table in the great hall (not that
we knew the right way of playing, but she liked to roll
the smooth ivory balls with her pretty hands, and I
liked to do whatever she did); and, by-and-by, without
our noticing it, it grew dusk indoors, though it was still
light in the open air, and I was thinking of taking her
back into the nursery, when, all of a sudden, she cried
out,—

"Look, Hester! look! there is my poor little girl out
in the snow!"

I turned towards the long narrow windows, and there,
sure enough, I saw a little girl, less than my Miss
Rosamond—dressed all unfit to be out-of-doors such a
bitter night—crying, and beating against the window-
panes, as if she wanted to be let in. She seemed to
sob and wail, till Miss Rosamond could bear it no longer,
and was flying to the door to open it, when, all of a
sudden, and close upon us, the great organ pealed out
so loud and thundering, it fairly made me tremble; and
all the more, when I remembered me that, even in the
stillness of that dead-cold weather, I had heard no sound
of little battering hands upon the window-glass, although
the phantom child had seemed to put forth all its force;
and, although I had seen it wail and cry, no faintest
touch of sound had fallen upon my ears. Whether I
remembered all this at the very moment, I do not know;
the great organ sound had so stunned me into terror;
but this I know, I caught up Miss Rosamond before she
got the hall-door opened, and clutched her, and carried
her away, kicking and screaming, into the large, bright

kitchen, where Dorothy and Agnes were busy with their mince-pies.

" What is the matter with my sweet one ?" cried Dorothy, as I bore in Miss Rosamond, who was sobbing as if her heart would break.

" She won't let me open the door for my little girl to come in ; and she'll die if she is out on the Fells all night. Cruel, naughty Hester," she said, slapping me ; but she might have struck harder, for I had seen a look of ghastly terror on Dorothy's face, which made my very blood run cold.

" Shut the back-kitchen door fast, and bolt it well," said she to Agnes. She said no more ; she gave me raisins and almonds to quiet Miss Rosamond ; but she sobbed about the little girl in the snow, and would not touch any of the good things. I was thankful when she cried herself to sleep in bed. Then I stole down to the kitchen, and told Dorothy I had made up my mind. I would carry my darling back to my father's house in Applethwaite ; where, if we lived humbly, we lived at peace. I said I had been frightened enough with the old lord's organ-playing ; but now that I had seen for myself this little moaning child, all decked out as no child in the neighbourhood could be, beating and battering to get in, yet always without any sound or noise— with the dark wound on its right shoulder ; and that Miss Rosamond had known it again for the phantom that had nearly lured her to her death (which Dorothy knew was true) ; I would stand it no longer.

I saw Dorothy change colour once or twice. When I had done, she told me she did not think I could take Miss Rosamond with me, for that she was my lord's ward,

and I had no right over her; and she asked me would
I leave the child that I was so fond of just for sounds
and sights that could do me no harm; and that they
had all had to get used to in their turns?   I was all in
a hot, trembling passion; and I said it was very well for
her to talk, that knew what these sights and noises betokened, and that had, perhaps, had something to do with
the spectre child while it was alive.   And I taunted her
so, that she told me all she knew at last; and then I
wished I had never been told, for it only made me more
afraid than ever.

She said she had heard the tale from old neighbours
that were alive when she was first married; when folks
used to come to the hall sometimes, before it had got
such a bad name on the country side: it might not be
true, or it might, what she had been told.

The old lord was Miss Furnivall's father—Miss Grace,
as Dorothy called her, for Miss Maude was the elder,
and Miss Furnivall by rights.   The old lord was eaten
up with pride.   Such a proud man was never seen or
heard of; and his daughters were like him.   No one
was good enough to wed them, although they had choice
enough; for they were the great beauties of their day,
as I had seen by their portraits, where they hung in the
state drawing-room.   But, as the old saying is, " Pride
will have a fall;" and these two haughty beauties fell in
love with the same man, and he no better than a foreign
musician, whom their father had down from London to
play music with him at the Manor House.   For, above
all things, next to his pride, the old lord loved music.
He could play on nearly every instrument that ever was
heard of; and it was a strange thing it did not soften

him; but he was a fierce dour old man, and had broken his poor wife's heart with his cruelty, they said. He was mad after music, and would pay any money for it. So he got this foreigner to come; who made such beautiful music, that they said the very birds on the trees stopped their singing to listen. And, by degrees, this foreign gentleman got such a hold over the old lord, that nothing would serve him but that he must come every year; and it was he that had the great organ brought from Holland, and built up in the hall, where it stood now. He taught the old lord to play on it; but many and many a time, when Lord Furnivall was thinking of nothing but his fine organ, and his finer music, the dark foreigner was walking abroad in the woods with one of the young ladies; now Miss Maude, and then Miss Grace.

Miss Maude won the day and carried off the prize, such as it was; and he and she were married, all unknown to any one; and, before he made his next yearly visit, she had been confined of a little girl at a farm-house on the Moors, while her father and Miss Grace thought she was away at Doncaster Races. But though she was a wife and a mother, she was not a bit softened, but as haughty and as passionate as ever; and perhaps more so, for she was jealous of Miss Grace, to whom her foreign husband paid a deal of court—by way of blinding her—as he told his wife. But Miss Grace triumphed over Miss Maude, and Miss Maude grew fiercer and fiercer, both with her husband and with her sister; and the former—who could easily shake off what was disagreeable, and hide himself in foreign countries—went away a month before his usual time that summer, and half-threatened that he would never come back again. Meanwhile, the little girl was left at the farm-house, and her mother used to have her horse saddled and gallop wildly over the hills to see her once every week, at the very least; for where she loved she loved, and where she hated she hated. And the old lord went on playing—playing on his organ; and the servants thought the sweet music he made had soothed down his awful temper, of which (Dorothy said) some terrible tales could be told. He grew infirm too, and had to walk with a crutch; and his son—that was the present Lord Furnivall's father—was with the army in America, and the other son at sea; so Miss Maude had it pretty much her own way, and she and Miss Grace grew colder and bitterer to each other every day; till at last they hardly ever spoke, except when the old lord was by. The foreign musician came again the next summer, but it was for the last time; for they led him such a life with their jealousy and their passions, that he grew weary, and went away, and never was heard of again. And Miss Maude, who had always meant to have her marriage acknowledged when her father should be dead, was left now a deserted wife, whom nobody knew to have been married, with a child that she dared not own, although she loved it to distraction; living with a father whom she feared, and a sister whom she hated. When the next summer passed over, and the dark foreigner never came, both Miss Maude and Miss Grace grew gloomy and sad; they had a haggard look about them, though they looked handsome as ever. But, by-and-by, Miss Maude brightened; for her father grew more and more infirm, and more than ever carried away by his music; and she and Miss Grace lived almost entirely apart, having separate rooms, the one on the west side, Miss Maude on the east—those very rooms which were now shut up. So she thought she might have her little girl with her, and no one need ever know except those who dared not speak about it, and were bound to believe that it was, as she said, a cottager's child she had taken a fancy to. All this, Dorothy said, was pretty well known; but what came afterwards no one knew, except Miss Grace, and Mrs. Stark, who was even then her maid, and much more of a friend to her than ever her sister had been. But the servants supposed, from words that were dropped, that Miss Maude had triumphed over Miss Grace, and told her that all the time the dark foreigner had been mocking her with pretended love—he was her own husband. The colour left Miss Grace's cheek and lips that very day for ever, and she was heard to say many a time that sooner or later she would have her revenge; and Mrs. Stark was for ever spying about the east rooms.

One fearful night, just after the New Year had come in, when the snow was lying thick and deep, and the flakes were still falling—fast enough to blind any one who might be out and abroad—there was a great and violent noise heard, and the old lord's voice above all, cursing and swearing awfully, and the cries of a little child, and the proud defiance of a fierce woman, and the sound of a blow, and a dead stillness, and moans and wailings dying away on the hill-side! Then the old lord summoned all his servants, and told them, with terrible oaths, and words more terrible, that his daughter had disgraced herself, and that he had turned her out of

doors—her, and her child—and that if ever they gave
her help, or food, or shelter, he prayed that they might
never enter heaven.   And, all the while, Miss Grace
stood by him, white and still as any stone; and, when
he had ended, she heaved a great sigh, as much as to
say her work was done, and her end was accomplished.
But the old lord never touched his organ again, and died
within the year; and no wonder! for, on the morrow of
that wild and fearful night, the shepherds, coming down
the Fell side, found Miss Maude sitting, all crazy and
smiling, under the holly-trees, nursing a dead child, with
a terrible mark on its right shoulder.   "But that was not
what killed it," said Dorothy: " it was the frost and the
cold.   Every wild creature was in its hole, and every
beast in its fold, while the child and its mother were
turned out to wander on the Fells!   And now you know
all! and I wonder if you are less frightened now?"

I was more frightened than ever; but I said I was
not.   I wished Miss Rosamond and myself well out of
that dreadful house for ever; but I would not leave her,
and I dared not take her away.   But oh, how I watched
her, and guarded her!   We bolted the doors, and shut
the window-shutters fast, an hour or more before dark,
rather than leave them open five minutes too late.   But
my little lady still heard the weird child crying and
mourning; and not all we could do or say, could keep
her from wanting to go to her, and let her in from the
cruel wind and the snow.   All this time I kept away
from Miss Furnivall and Mrs. Stark, as much as ever I
could; for I feared them—I knew no good could be
about them, with their grey, hard faces, and their
dreamy eyes, looking back into the ghastly years that

were gone. But, even in my fear, I had a kind of pity for Miss Furnivall, at least. Those gone down to the pit can hardly have a more hopeless look than that which was ever on her face. At last I even got so sorry for her—who never said a word but what was quite forced from her—that I prayed for her; and I taught Miss Rosamond to pray for one who had done a deadly sin; but often when she came to those words, she would listen, and start up from her knees, and say, "I hear my little girl plaining and crying very sad—oh, let her in, or she will die!"

One night—just after New Year's Day had come at last, and the long winter had taken a turn, as I hoped— I heard the west drawing-room bell ring three times, which was the signal for me. I would not leave Miss Rosamond alone, for all she was asleep—for the old lord had been playing wilder than ever—and I feared lest my darling should waken to hear the spectre child; see her I knew she could not. I had fastened the windows too well for that. So I took her out of her bed, and wrapped her up in such outer clothes as were most handy, and carried her down to the drawing-room, where the old ladies sat at their tapestry work as usual. They looked up when I came in, and Mrs. Stark asked, quite astounded, "Why did I bring Miss Rosamond there, out of her warm bed?" I had begun to whisper, "Because I was afraid of her being tempted out while I was away, by the wild child in the snow," when she stopped me short (with a glance at Miss Furnivall), and said Miss Furnivall wanted me to undo some work she had done wrong, and which neither of them could see to unpick. So I laid my pretty dear on the sofa, and sat down on a stool by them, and hardened my heart against them, as I heard the wind rising and howling.

Miss Rosamond slept on sound, for all the wind blew so; and Miss Furnivall said never a word, nor looked round when the gusts shook the windows. All at once she started up to her full height, and put up one hand, as if to bid us listen.

"I hear voices!" said she. "I hear terrible screams —I hear my father's voice!"

Just at that moment my darling wakened with a sudden start: "My little girl is crying, oh, how she is crying!" and she tried to get up and go to her, but she got her feet entangled in the blanket, and I caught her up; for my flesh had begun to creep at these noises, which they heard while we could catch no sound. In a minute or two the noises came, and gathered fast, and filled our ears; we, too, heard voices and screams, and no longer heard the winter's wind that raged abroad. Mrs. Stark looked at me, and I at her, but we dared not speak. Suddenly Miss Furnivall went towards the door, out into the ante-room, through the west lobby, and opened the door into the great hall. Mrs. Stark followed, and I durst not be left, though my heart almost stopped beating for fear. I wrapped my darling tight in my arms, and went out with them. In the hall the screams were louder than ever; they seemed to come from the east wing—nearer and nearer—close on the other side of the locked-up doors—close behind them. Then I noticed that the great bronze chandelier seemed all alight, though the hall was dim, and that a fire was blazing in the vast hearth-place, though it gave no heat; and I shuddered up with terror, and folded my darling closer to me. But as I did so, the east door shook, and she, suddenly struggling to get free from me, cried, "Hester! I must go! My little girl is there! I hear her; she is coming! Hester, I must go!"

I held her tight with all my strength; with a set will, I held her. If I had died, my hands would have grasped her still, I was so resolved in my mind. Miss Furnivall stood listening, and paid no regard to my darling, who had got down to the ground, and whom I, upon my knees now, was holding with both my arms clasped round her neck; she still striving and crying to get free.

All at once, the east door gave way with a thundering crash, as if torn open in a violent passion, and there came into that broad and mysterious light, the figure of a tall old man, with grey hair and gleaming eyes. He drove before him, with many a relentless gesture of abhorrence, a stern and beautiful woman, with a little child clinging to her dress.

"Oh, Hester! Hester!" cried Miss Rosamond; "it's the lady! the lady below the holly-trees; and my little girl is with her. Hester! Hester! let me go to her; they are drawing me to them. I feel them—I feel them. I must go!"

Again she was almost convulsed by her efforts to get away; but I held her tighter and tighter, till I feared I should do her a hurt; but rather that than let her go towards those terrible phantoms. They passed along towards the great hall-door, where the winds howled and ravened for their prey; but before they reached that, the lady turned; and I could see that she defied the old man with a fierce and proud defiance; but then she quailed

—and then she threw up her arms wildly and piteously to save her child—her little child—from a blow from his uplifted crutch.

And Miss Rosamond was torn as by a power stronger than mine, and writhed in my arms, and sobbed (for by this time the poor darling was growing faint).

"They want me to go with them on to the Fells— they are drawing me to them. Oh, my little girl! I would come, but cruel, wicked Hester holds me very tight." But when she saw the uplifted crutch, she swooned away, and I thanked God for it. Just at this moment—when the tall old man, his hair streaming as in the blast of a furnace, was going to strike the little shrinking child—Miss Furnivall, the old woman by my side, cried out, "Oh, father! father! spare the little innocent child!" But just then I saw—we all saw— another phantom shape itself, and grow clear out of the blue and misty light that filled the hall; we had not seen her till now, for it was another lady who stood by the old man, with a look of relentless hate and trium- phant scorn. That figure was very beautiful to look upon, with a soft, white hat drawn down over the proud brows, and a red and curling lip. It was dressed in an open robe of blue satin. I had seen that figure before. It was the likeness of Miss Furnivall in her youth; and the terrible phantoms moved on, regardless of old Miss Furnivall's wild entreaty,—and the uplifted crutch fell on the right shoulder of the little child, and the younger sister looked on, stony, and deadly serene. But at that moment, the dim lights, and the fire that gave no heat, went out of themselves, and Miss Furnivall lay at our feet stricken down by the palsy—death-stricken.

Yes! she was carried to her bed that night never to rise again. She lay with her face to the wall, muttering low, but muttering always: " Alas! alas! what is done in youth can never be undone in age! What is done in youth can never be undone in age! "

TRAITS AND STORIES OF THE HUGUENOTS.

———◦◦———

I HAVE always been interested in the conversation of any one who could tell me anything about the Huguenots ; and, little by little, I have picked up many fragments of information respecting them. I will just recur to the well-known fact, that five years after Henry the Fourth's formal abjuration of the Protestant faith, in fifteen hundred and ninety-three, he secured to the French Protestants their religious liberty by the Edict of Nantes.   His unworthy son, however, Louis the Thirteenth, refused them the privileges which had been granted to them by this act ; and, when reminded of the claims they had, if the promises of Henry the Third and Henry the Fourth were to be regarded, he answered that " the first-named monarch feared them, and the latter loved them ; but he neither feared nor loved them."   The extermination of the Huguenots was a favourite project with Cardinal Richelieu, and it was at his instigation that the second siege of Rochelle was undertaken—known even to the most careless student of history for the horrors of famine which the besieged endured. Miserably disappointed as they were at the failure of the looked-for assistance from England, the mayor of the town, Guiton, rejected the conditions of peace which Cardinal Richelieu offered; namely, that they would raze their fortifications to the ground, and suffer the Catholics to enter. But there was a traitorous faction in the town; and, on Guiton's rejection of the terms, this faction collected in one night a crowd of women, and children, and aged persons, and drove them beyond the lines; they were useless, and yet they ate food. Driven out from the beloved city, tottering, faint, and weary, they were fired at by the enemy; and the survivors came pleading back to the walls of Rochelle, pleading for a quiet shelter to die in, even if their death were caused by hunger. When two-thirds of the inhabitants had perished; when the survivors were insufficient to bury their dead; when ghastly corpses out-numbered the living—miserable, glorious Rochelle, stronghold of the Huguenots, opened its gates to receive the Roman Catholic cardinal, who celebrated mass in the church of St. Marguerite, once the beloved sanctuary of Protestant worship. As we cling to the memory of the dead, so did the Huguenots remember Rochelle. Years—long years of suffering—gone by, a village sprang up, not twenty miles from New York, and the name of that village was New Rochelle; and the old men told with tears of the sufferings their parents had undergone when they were little children, far away across the sea, in the " pleasant " land of France.

Richelieu was otherwise occupied after this second siege of Rochelle, and had to put his schemes for the extermination of the Huguenots on one side. So they lived in a kind of trembling, uncertain peace during the remainder of the reign of Louis the Thirteenth. But they strove to avert persecution by untiring submission. It was not until sixteen hundred and eighty-three that the Huguenots of the south of France resolved to profess their religion, and refuse any longer to be registered among those of the Roman Catholic faith; to be martyrs rather than apostates or hypocrites. On an appointed Sabbath, the old deserted Huguenot churches were re-opened; nay, those in ruins, of which but a few stones remained to tell the tale of having once been holy ground, were peopled with attentive hearers, listening to the word of God as preached by reformed ministers. Languedoc, Cevennes, Dauphigny, seemed alive with Huguenots—even as the Highlands were, at the chieftain's call, alive with armed men, whose tartans had been hidden but a moment before in the harmonious and blending colours of the heather.

Dragonnades took place, and cruelties were perpetrated, which it is as well, for the honour of human nature, should be forgotten. Twenty-four thousand conversions were announced to Le Grand Louis, who fully believed in them. The more far-seeing Madame de Maintenon hinted at her doubts in the famous speech, " Even if the fathers are hypocrites, the children will be Catholics."

And then came the Revocation of the Edict of Nantes. A multitude of weak reasons were alleged, as is generally the case where there is not one that is really good, or presentable; such as that the Edict was never meant to be perpetual; that (by the blessing of Heaven and the dragonnades) the Huguenots had returned to the true faith, therefore the Edict was useless — a mere matter of form, &c., &c.

As a "mere matter of form," some penalties were decreed against the professors of the extinct heresy. Every Huguenot place of worship was to be destroyed; every minister who refused to conform was to be sent to the Hôpitaux des Forçats at Marseilles and at Valence. If he had been noted for his zeal he was to be considered "obstinate," and sent to slavery for life in such of the West-Indian islands as belonged to the French. The children of Huguenot parents were to be taken from them by force, and educated by the Roman Catholic monks or nuns.   These are but a few of the enactments contained in the Revocation of the Edict of Nantes.

And now come in some of the traditions which I have heard and collected.

A friend of mine, a descendant from some of the Huguenots who succeeded in emigrating to England, has told me the following particulars of her great-great-grandmother's escape. This lady's father was a Norman farmer, or rather small landed proprietor. His name was Lefebvre; he had two sons, grown men, stout and true; able to protect themselves, and choose their own line of conduct. But he had also one little daughter, Magdalen, the child of his old age, and the darling of his house; keeping it alive and glad with her innocent prattle. His small estate was far away from any large town, with its corn-fields and orchards surrounding the old ancestral house. There was plenty always in it; and though the wife was an invalid, there was always a sober cheerfulness present, to give a charm to the abundance.

The family Lefebvre lived almost entirely on the produce of the estate, and had little need for much communication with their nearest neighbours, with whom, however, as kindly, well-meaning people, they were on good terms, although they differed in their religion. In those days, coffee was scarcely known, even in large cities; honey supplied the place of sugar; and for the pottage the *bouilli*, the vegetables, the salad, the fruit, the garden, farm, and orchards of the Lefebvres was all-sufficient. The woollen cloth was spun by the men of the house on winter's evenings, standing by the great wheel, and carefully and slowly turning it to secure evenness of thread. The women took charge of the linen, gathering, and drying, and beating the bad-smelling hemp, the ugliest crop that grew about the farm; and reserving the delicate blue-flowered flax for the fine thread needed for the daughter's *trousseau;* for as soon as a woman child was born, the mother, lying too faint to work, smiled as she planned the web of dainty linen, which was to be woven at Rouen, out of the flaxen thread of gossamer fineness, to be spun by no hand, as you may guess, but that mother's own. And the farm-maidens took pride in the store of sheets and table napery which they were to have a share in preparing for the future wedding of the little baby, sleeping serene in her warm cot, by her mother's side. Such being the self-sufficient habits of the Norman farmers, it was no wonder that in the eventful year of sixteen hundred and eighty-five, Lefebvre remained ignorant for many days of that Revocation which was

stirring the whole souls of his co-religionists. But
there was to be a cattle fair at Avranches, and he
needed a barren cow to fatten up, and salt for the
winter's provision. Accordingly, the large-boned Norman horse was accoutred, summer as it was, with all
its paraphernalia of high-peaked wooden saddle, blue
sheep-skin, scarlet worsted fringe and tassels; and the
farmer Lefebvre, slightly stiff in his limbs after sixty
winters, got on from the horse-block by the stable wall,
his little daughter Magdalen nodding and kissing her
hand as he rode away. When he arrived at the fair,
in the great place before the cathedral in Avranches,
he was struck with the absence of many of those who
were united to him by the bond of their common persecuted religion; and on the faces of the Huguenot
farmers who were there, was an expression of gloom
and sadness. In answer to his inquiries, he learnt for
the first time of the Revocation of the Edict of Nantes.
He and his sons could sacrifice anything—would be
proud of martyrdom, if need were—but the clause which
cut him to the heart, was that which threatened that
his pretty, innocent, sweet Magdalen might be taken
from him and consigned to the teachings of a convent.
A convent, to the Huguenots' excited prejudices, implied
a place of dissolute morals, as well as of idolatrous
doctrine.

Poor Farmer Lefebvre thought no more of the cow he
went to purchase; the life and death—nay, the salvation or damnation—of his darling, seemed to him to
depend on the speed with which he could reach his
home, and take measures for her safety. What these
were to be he could not tell in this moment of bewildered

terror; for, even while he watched the stable-boy at the
inn arranging his horse's gear, without daring to help
him, for fear his early departure and undue haste might
excite suspicion in the malignant faces he saw gathering
about him—even while he trembled with impatience, his
daughter might be carried away out of his sight for ever
and ever. He mounted and spurred the old horse; but
the road was hilly, and the steed had not had his accustomed rest, and was poorly fed, according to the habit
of the country; and, at last, he almost stood still at the
foot of every piece of rising ground. Farmer Lefebvre
dismounted, and ran by the horse's side up every hill,
pulling him along, and encouraging his flagging speed
by every conceivable noise, meant to be cheerful, though
the tears were fast running down the old man's cheeks.
He was almost sick with the revulsion of his fears, when
he saw Magdalen sitting out in the sun, playing with
the "fromages" of the mallow-plant, which are such a
delight to Norman children. He got off his horse,
which found its accustomed way into the stable. He
kissed Magdalen over and over again, the tears coming
down his cheeks like rain. And then he went in to tell
his wife—his poor invalid wife. She received the news
more tranquilly than he had done. Long illness had
deadened the joys and fears of this world to her. She
could even think and suggest. "That night a fishing
smack was to sail from Granville to the Channel Islands.
Some of the people, who had called at the Lefebvre farm
on their way to Avranches, had told her of ventures they
were making, in sending over apples and pears to be sold in
Jersey, where the orchard crops had failed. The captain
was a friend of one of her absent sons: for his sake——"

"But we must part from *her*—from Magdalen, the apple of our eyes. And she—she has never left her home before, never been away from us—who will take care of her? Marie, I say, who is to take care of the precious child?" And the old man was choked with his sobs. Then his wife made answer, and said,—

"God will take care of our precious child, and keep her safe from harm, till we two—or you, at least, dear husband—can leave this accursed land. Or, if we cannot follow her, she will be safe for heaven; whereas, if she stays here to be taken to the terrible convent, hell will be her portion, and we shall never see her again—never!"

So they were stilled by their faith into sufficient composure to plan for the little girl. The old horse was again to be harnessed and put into the cart; and if any spying Romanist looked into the cart, what would they see but straw, and a new mattress rolled up, and peeping out of a sackcloth covering. The mother blessed her child, with a full conviction that she should never see her again. The father went with her to Granville. On the way the only relief he had was caring for her comfort in her strange imprisonment. He stroked her cheeks and smoothed her hair with his labour-hardened fingers, and coaxed her to eat the food her mother had prepared. In the evening her feet were cold; he took off his warm flannel jacket to wrap them in. Whether it was that chill coming on the heat of the excited day, or whether the fatigue and grief broke down the old man utterly, no one can say. The child Magdalen was safely extricated from her hiding-place at the Quai at Granville, and smuggled on board of the fishing-smack, with her great chest of clothes, and half-collected *trousseau;* the captain took her safe to Jersey, and willing friends received her eventually in London. But the father— moaning to himself, " If I am bereaved of my children, I am bereaved," saying that pitiful sentence over and over again, as if the repetition could charm away the deep sense of woe—went home, and took to his bed, and died; nor did the mother remain long after him.

One of these Lefebvre sons was the grandfather of the Duke of Dantzic, one of Napoleon's marshals. The little daughter's descendants, though not very numerous, are scattered over England; and one of them, as I have said, is the lady who told me this, and many other particulars relating to the exiled Huguenots.

At first, the rigorous decrees of the Revocation were principally enforced against the ministers of religion. They were all required to leave Paris at forty-eight hours' notice, under severe penalties for disobedience. Some of the most distinguished among them were igno- miniously forced to leave the country; but the expulsion of these ministers was followed by the emigration of the more faithful among their people. In Languedoc this was especially the case; whole congregations followed their pastors; and France was being rapidly drained of the more thoughtful and intelligent of the Huguenots (who, as a people, had distinguished themselves in manufacture and commerce), when the king's minister took the alarm, and prohibited emigration, under pain of imprisonment for life; imprisonment for life includ- ing abandonment to the tender mercies of the priests. Here again I may relate an anecdote told me by my friend :—A husband and wife attempted to escape separately from some town in Brittany; the wife succeeded, and reached England, where she anxiously awaited her husband. The husband was arrested in the attempt, and imprisoned. The priest alone was allowed to visit him; and, after vainly using argument to endeavour to persuade him to renounce his obnoxious religion, the priest, with cruel zeal, had recourse to physical torture. There was a room in the prison with an iron floor, and no seat, nor means of support or rest; into this room the poor Huguenot was introduced. The iron flooring was gradually heated (one remembers the gouty gentleman whose cure was effected by a similar process in *Sandford and Merton;* but there the heat was not carried up to torture, as it was in the Huguenot's case); still the brave man was faithful. The process was repeated; all in vain. The flesh on the soles of his feet was burnt off, and he was a cripple for life; but cripple or sound, dead or alive, a Huguenot he remained. And, by-and-by, they grew weary of their useless cruelty, and the poor man was allowed to hobble about on crutches. How it was that he obtained his liberty at last, my informant could not tell. He only knew that, after years of imprisonment and torture, a poor grey cripple was seen wandering about the streets of London, making vain inquiries for his wife in his broken English, as little understood by most as the Moorish maiden's cry for " Gilbert, Gilbert." Some one at last directed him to a coffee-house near Soho Square, kept by an emigrant, who thrived upon the art, even then national, of making good coffee. It was the resort of the Huguenots, many of whom by this time had turned their intelligence to good account in busy, commercial England.

To this coffee-house the poor cripple hied himself; but no one knew of his wife ; she might be alive, or she might be dead; it seemed as if her name had vanished from the earth.   In the corner sat a pedlar, listening to everything, but saying nothing.   He had come to London to lay in a stock of wares for his rounds.   Now the three harbours of the French emigrants were Norwich, where they established the manufacture of Norwich crape; Spitalfields, in London, where they embarked in the silk trade; and Canterbury, where a colony of them carried on one or two delicate employments, such as jewellery, wax-bleaching, &c.   The pedlar took Canterbury in his way, and sought among the French residents for a woman who might correspond to the missing wife. She was there, earning her livelihood as a milliner, and believing her husband to be either a galley-slave, or dead, long since, in some of the terrible prisons.   But, on hearing the pedlar's tale, she set off at once to London, and found her poor crippled husband, who lived many years afterwards in Canterbury, supported by his wife's exertions.

Another Huguenot couple determined to emigrate. They could disguise themselves; but their baby?   If they were seen passing through the gates of the town in which they lived, with a child, they would instantly be arrested, suspected Huguenots as they were.   Their expedient was to wrap the baby into a formless bundle, to one end of which was attached a string; and then, taking advantage of the deep gutter which runs in the centre of so many old streets in French towns, they placed the baby in this hollow, close to one of the gates, after dusk. The gend'arme came out to open the gate to them. They were suddenly summoned to see a sick relation, they said; they were known to have an infant child, which no Huguenot mother would willingly leave behind, to be brought up by Papists. So the sentinel concluded that they were not going to emigrate, at least this time; and locking the great town-gates behind them, he re-entered his little guard-room. "Now, quick! quick! the string under the gate! Catch it with your hook stick! There, in the shadow! There! Thank God! the baby is safe; it has not cried! Pray God the sleeping draught be not too strong!" It was not too strong. Father, mother, and babe escaped to England, and their descendants may be reading this very paper.

England, Holland, and the Protestant states of Germany, were the places of refuge for the Norman and Breton Protestants. From the south of France escape was more difficult. Algerine pirates infested the Mediterranean, and the small vessels in which many of the Huguenots embarked from the southern ports were an easy prey. There were Huguenot slaves in Algiers and Tripoli for years after the Revocation of the Edict of Nantes. Most Catholic Spain caught some of the fugitives, who were welcomed by the Spanish Inquisition with a different kind of greeting from that which the wise, far-seeing William the Third of England bestowed on such of them as sought English shelter after his accession. We will return to the condition of the English Huguenots presently. First, let us follow the fortunes of those French Protestants who sent a letter to the State of Massachusetts (among whose historical papers it is still extant), giving an account of the persecutions to which they were exposed, and the distress they were undergoing, stating the wish of many of them to emigrate to America, and asking how far they might have privileges allowed them for following out their pursuit of agriculture. What answer was returned may be guessed from the fact that a tract of land, comprising about eleven thousand acres at Oxford, near the present town of Worcester, Massachusetts, was granted to thirty Huguenots, who were invited to come over and settle there. The invitation came like a sudden summons to a land of hope across the Atlantic. There was no time for preparations; these might excite suspicion; they left the "pot boiling on the fire" (to use the expression of one of their descendants), and carried no clothes with them but what they wore. The New Englanders had too lately escaped from religious persecution themselves not to welcome, and shelter, and clothe these poor refugees when they once arrived at Boston. The little French colony at Oxford was called a plantation; and Gabriel Bernon, a descendant of a knightly name in Froissart, a Protestant merchant of Rochelle, was appointed undertaker for this settlement. They sent for a French Protestant minister, and assigned to him a salary of forty pounds a year. They bent themselves assiduously to the task of cultivating the half-cleared land, on the borders of which lay the dark forest, among which the Indians prowled and lurked, ready to spring upon the unguarded households. To protect themselves from this creeping, deadly enemy, the French built a fort, traces of which yet remain. But on the murder of

the Johnson family, the French dared no longer remain
on the bloody spot, although more than ten acres of
ground were in garden cultivation around the fort; and
long afterwards, those who told in hushed, awe-struck
voices of the Johnson murder, could point to the rose-
bushes, the apple and pear trees yet standing in the
Frenchmen's deserted gardens. Mrs. Johnson was a
sister of Andrew Sigourney, one of the first Huguenots
who came over. He saved his sister's life by dragging
her by main force through a back door, while the Indians
massacred her children, and shot down her husband at
his own threshold. To preserve her life was but a cruel
kindness.

Gabriel Bernon lived to a patriarchal age, in spite of
his early sufferings in France and the wild Indian cries
of revenge around his home in Massachusetts. He died
rich and prosperous. He had kissed Queen Anne's
hand, and become intimate with some of the English
nobility, such as Lord Archdale, the Quaker Governor
of Carolina, who had lands and governments in the
American States. The descendants of the Huguenot
refugees repaid in part their debt of gratitude to Massachusetts in various ways during the War of Independence; one, Gabriel Manigault, by advancing a
large loan to further the objects of it. Indeed, three
of the nine presidents of the old Congress which con-
ducted the United States through the revolutionary war,
were descendants of the French Protestant refugees.
General Francis Marion, who fought bravely under
Washington, was of Huguenot descent. In fact, both
in England and France, the Huguenot refugees showed
themselves temperate, industrious, thoughtful, and intel-

ligent people, full of good principle and strength of character. But all this is implied in the one circumstance that they suffered and emigrated to secure the rights of conscience.

In the State of New York they fondly called their plantation or settlement by the name of the precious city which had been their stronghold, and where they had suffered so much. New Rochelle was built on the shore of Long Island Sound, twenty-three miles from New York. On the Saturday afternoons, the inhabitants of New Rochelle harnessed their horses to their carts, to convey the women and little ones; and the men in the prime of life walked all the distance to New York, camping out in their carts in the environs of the city, through the night, till the bell summoned them on Sunday morning to service, in the old Church du Saint Esprit. In the same way they returned on Sunday evening. The old longing for home, recorded in Allan Cunningham's ballad—

It's hame, and it's hame, hame fain would I be;
O, hame, hame, hame, to my ain countree!—

clung to the breasts, and caused singular melancholy in some of them. There was one old man who went every day down to the seashore, to look and gaze his fill towards the beautiful cruel land where most of his life had been passed. With his face to the east—his eyes strained, as if by force of longing looks he could see the far distant France—he said his morning prayers, and sang one of Clément Marot's hymns. There had been an edition of the Psalms of David put into French rhyme, ("Pseaumes de David, mis en Rime françoise, par Clément Marot et Théodore de Bèze,") published in as small a form as possible, in order that the book might be concealed in their bosoms, if the Huguenots were surprised in their worship while they lived in France.

Nor were Oxford and New Rochelle the only settlements of the Huguenots in the United States. Farther south again they were welcomed, and found resting-places in Virginia and South Carolina.

I now return to the Huguenots in England. Even during James the Second's reign collections were made for the refugees; and, in the reign of his successor, fifteen thousand pounds were voted by Parliament "to be distributed among persons of quality, and all such as, by age or infirmity, were unable to support themselves." There are still, or were, not many years ago, a few survivors of the old Huguenot stock, who go, on quarter-day, to claim their small benefit from this fund at the Treasury; and doubtless, at the time it was granted, there were many friendless and helpless to whom the little pensions were inestimable boons. But the greater part were active, strong men, full of good sense and practical talent; and they preferred taking advantage of the national good-will in a more independent form. Their descendants bear honoured names among us. Sir Samuel Romilly, Mrs. Austin, and Miss Harriet Martineau, are three of those that come most prominently before me as I write; but each of these names is suggestive of others in the same families worthy of note. Sir Samuel Romilly's ancestors came from the south of France, where the paternal estate fell to a distant relation rather than to the son, because the former was a Catholic, while the latter had preferred a foreign country, with "freedom to worship God." In Sir Samuel Romilly's account of his father and grandfather, it is easy to detect the southern character predominating. Most affectionate, impulsive, generous, carried away by transports of anger and of grief, tender and true in all his relationships—the reader does not easily forget the father of Sir Samuel Romilly, with his fond adoption of Montaigne's idea, "playing on a flute by the side of his daughter's bed, in order to waken her in the morning." No wonder he himself was so beloved! But there was much more demonstration of affection in all these French households, if what I have gathered from their descendants be correct, than we English should ever dare to manifest.

French was the language still spoken among themselves sixty and seventy years after their ancestors had quitted France. In the Romilly family, the father established it as a rule, that French should be always spoken on a Sunday. Forty years later, the lady to whom I have so often alluded was living, an orphan child, with two maiden aunts, in the heart of London city. They always spoke French. English was the foreign language; and a certain pride was cultivated in the little damsel's mind by the fact of her being reminded every now and then that she was a little French girl, bound to be polite, gentle, and attentive in manners; to stand till her elders gave her leave to sit down; to curtsey on entering or leaving a room. She attended her relations to the early market near Spitalfields, where many herbs, not in general use in England, and some "weeds," were habitually brought by the market-women for the use of the French people. Burnet, chervil, dandelion, were

amongst the number, in order to form the salads which
were a principal dish at meals. There were still hereditary schools in the neighbourhood, kept by descendants of the first refugees who established them, and to
which the Huguenot families still sent their children. A
kind of correspondence was occasionally kept up with
the unseen and distant relations in France—third or
fourth cousins it might be. As was to be expected, such
correspondence languished and died by slow degrees.
But tales of their ancestors' sufferings and escapes
beguiled the long winter evenings. Though far away
from France, though cast off by her a hundred years
before, the gentle old ladies, who had lived all their
lives in London, considered France as their country,
and England as a strange land. Upstairs, too, was a
great chest—the very chest Magdalen Lefebvre had had
packed to accompany her in her flight, and escape in the
mattress. The stores her fond mother had provided for
her *trousseau* were not yet exhausted, though she slept in
her grave; and out of them her little orphan descendant was dressed; and when the quaintness of the pattern
made the child shrink from putting on so peculiar a
dress, she was asked, " Are you not a little French girl?
You ought to be proud of wearing a French print—there
are none like it in England." In all this, her relations
and their circle seem to have differed from the refugee
friends of old Mr. Romilly, who, we are told, " desired
nothing less than to preserve the memory of their origin;
and their chapels were therefore ill-attended. A large
uncouth room, the avenues to which were narrow courts
and dirty alleys, ... with irregular unpainted pews,
and dusty unplastered walls; a congregation consisting

11

principally of some strange-looking old women scattered
here and there," &c. Probably these old ladies looked
strange to the child, who recorded these early impressions in after-life, because they clung with fond pride to
the dress of their ancestors, and decked themselves out
in the rich grotesque raiment which had formed part of
their mother's *trousseau.* At any rate, there certainly
was a little colony in the heart of the city, at the end of
the last century, who took pride in their descent from the
suffering Huguenots, who mustered up relics of the old
homes and the old times in Normandy or Languedoc.
A sword wielded by some great grandfather in the wars
of the League ; a gold whistle, such as hung ever ready
at the master's girdle, before bells were known in houses,
or ready to summon out-of-door labourers ; some of the
very ornaments sold at the famous curiosity-shop at
Warwick for ladies to hang at their *châtelaines,* within
this last ten years, were brought over by the flying
Huguenots. And there were precious Bibles, secured
by silver clasps and corners ; strangely-wrought silver
spoons, the handle of which enclosed the bowl ; a travel-
ling-case, containing a gold knife, spoon, and fork, and a
crystal goblet, on which the coat-of-arms was engraved
in gold. All these, and many other relics, tell of the
affluence and refinement the refugees left behind for the
sake of their religion.

There is yet an hospital (or rather great almshouse)
for aged people of French descent somewhere near the
City Road, which is supported by the proceeds of land
bequeathed, I believe, by some of the first refugees, who
were prosperous in trade after settling in England. But
it has lost much of its distinctive national character.

Fifty or sixty years ago, a visitor might have heard the inmates of this hospital chattering away in antiquated French. Now they speak English, for the majority of their ancestors in four generations have been English, and probably some of them do not know a word of French. Each inmate has a comfortable bedroom, a small annuity for clothes, &c., and sits and has meals in a public dining-room. As a little amusing mark of deference to the land of their founders, I may mention that a Mrs. Stephens, who was admitted within the last thirty years, became Madame St. Etienne as soon as she entered the hospital.

I have now told all I know about the Huguenots. I pass the mark to some one else.

MORTON HALL.

——◦——

CHAPTER I.

Our old Hall is to be pulled down, and they are going to build streets on the site. I said to my sister, "Ethelinda! if they really pull down Morton Hall, it will be a worse piece of work than the Repeal of the Corn Laws." And, after some consideration, she replied, that if she must speak what was on her mind, she would own that she thought the Papists had something to do with it; that they had never forgiven the Morton who had been with Lord Monteagle when he discovered the Gunpowder Plot; for we knew that, somewhere in Rome, there was a book kept, and which had been kept for generations, giving an account of the secret private history of every English family of note, and registering the names of those to whom the Papists owed either grudges or gratitude.

We were silent for some time; but I am sure the same thought was in both our minds; our ancestor, a Sidebotham, had been a follower of the Morton of that day; it had always been said in the family that he had

been with his master when he went with the Lord
Monteagle, and found Guy Fawkes and his dark lantern
under the Parliament House ; and the question flashed
across our minds, were the Sidebothams marked with a
black mark in that terrible mysterious book which was
kept under lock and key by the Pope and the Cardinals
in Rome ? It was terrible, yet, somehow, rather pleasant to think of. So many of the misfortunes which had
happened to us through life, and which we had called
" mysterious dispensations," but which some of our
neighbours had attributed to our want of prudence and
foresight, were accounted for at once, if we were objects
of the deadly hatred of such a powerful order as the
Jesuits, of whom we had lived in dread ever since we
had read the *Female Jesuit*. Whether this last idea
suggested what my sister said next I can't tell ; we did
know the female Jesuit's second cousin, so might be
said to have literary connections, and from that the
startling thought might spring up in my sister's mind,
for, said she, " Biddy ! " (my name is Bridget, and no
one but my sister calls me Biddy,) " suppose you write
some account of Morton Hall ; we have known much in
our time of the Mortons, and it will be a shame if they
pass away completely from men's memories while we can
speak or write." I was pleased with the notion, I confess ; but I felt ashamed to agree to it all at once,
though even, as I objected for modesty's sake, it came
into my mind how much I had heard of the old place in
its former days, and how it was, perhaps, all I could
now do for the Mortons, under whom our ancestors had
lived as tenants for more than three hundred years. So
at last I agreed ; and, for fear of mistakes, I showed it

to Mr. Swinton, our young curate, who has put it quite in order for me.

Morton Hall is situated about five miles from the centre of Drumble. It stands on the outskirts of a village, which, when the Hall was built, was probably as large as Drumble in those days; and even I can remember when there was a long piece of rather lonely road, with high hedges on either side, between Morton village and Drumble. Now, it is all street, and Morton seems but a suburb of the great town near. Our farm stood where Liverpool Street runs now; and people used to come snipe-shooting just where the Baptist chapel is built. Our farm must have been older than the Hall, for we had a date of 1460 on one of the cross-beams. My father was rather proud of this advantage, for the Hall had no date older than 1554; and I remember his affronting Mrs. Dawson, the housekeeper, by dwelling too much on this circumstance one evening when she came to drink tea with my mother, when Ethelinda and I were mere children. But my mother, seeing that Mrs. Dawson would never allow that any house in the parish could be older than the Hall, and that she was getting very warm, and almost insinuating that the Sidebothams had forged the date to disparage the squire's family, and set themselves up as having the older blood, asked Mrs. Dawson to tell us the story of old Sir John Morton before we went to bed. I slily reminded my father that Jack, our man, was not always so careful as might be in housing the Alderney in good time in the autumn evenings. So he started up, and went off to see after Jack; and Mrs. Dawson and we drew nearer the fire to hear the story about Sir John.

Sir John Morton had lived some time about the Restoration. The Mortons had taken the right side; so when Oliver Cromwell came into power, he gave away their lands to one of his Puritan followers—a man who had been but a praying, canting, Scotch pedlar till the war broke out; and Sir John had to go and live with his royal master at Bruges. The upstart's name was Carr, who came to live at Morton Hall; and, I'm proud to say, we—I mean our ancestors—led him a pretty life. He had hard work to get any rent at all from the tenantry, who knew their duty better than to pay it to a Roundhead. If he took the law to them, the law officers fared so badly, that they were shy of coming out to Morton—all along that lonely road I told you of—again. Strange noises were heard about the Hall, which got the credit of being haunted; but, as those noises were never heard before or since that Richard Carr lived there, I leave you to guess if the evil spirits did not know well over whom they had power—over schismatic rebels, and no one else. They durst not trouble the Mortons, who were true and loyal, and were faithful followers of King Charles in word and deed. At last, Old Oliver died; and folks did say that, on that wild and stormy night, his voice was heard high up in the air, where you hear the flocks of wild geese skirl, crying out for his true follower Richard Carr to accompany him in the terrible chase the fiends were giving him before carrying him down to hell. Anyway, Richard Carr died within a week—summoned by the dead or not, he went his way down to his master, and his master's master.

Then his daughter Alice came into possession. Her

mother was somehow related to General Monk, who was
beginning to come into power about that time. So when
Charles the Second came back to his throne, and many
of the sneaking Puritans had to quit their ill-gotten
land, and turn to the right about, Alice Carr was still
left at Morton Hall to queen it there. She was taller
than most women, and a great beauty, I have heard.
But, for all her beauty, she was a stern, hard woman.
The tenants had known her to be hard in her father's
lifetime, but now that she was the owner, and had the
power, she was worse than ever. She hated the Stuarts
worse than ever her father had done; had calves' head
for dinner every thirtieth of January; and when the
first twenty-ninth of May came round, and every mother's
son in the village gilded his oak-leaves, and wore them
in his hat, she closed the windows of the great hall with
her own hands, and sate throughout the day in darkness
and mourning. People did not like to go against her
by force, because she was a young and beautiful woman.
It was said the King got her cousin, the Duke of Albemarle, to ask her to court, just as courteously as if she
had been the Queen of Sheba, and King Charles, Solo-
mon, praying her to visit him in Jerusalem. But she
would not go; not she! She lived a very lonely life,
for now the King had got his own again, no servant but
her nurse would stay with her in the hall; and none of
the tenants would pay her any money for all that her
father had purchased the lands from the Parliament, and
paid the price down in good red gold.

All this time, Sir John was somewhere in the Vir-
ginian plantations; and the ships sailed from thence
only twice a year: but his royal master had sent for

him home; and home he came, that second summer after
the restoration. No one knew if Mistress Alice had
heard of his landing in England or not; all the villagers
and tenantry knew, and were not surprised, and turned
out in their best dresses, and with great branches of
oak, to welcome him as he rode into the village one
July morning, with many gay-looking gentlemen by his
side, laughing, and talking, and making merry, and
speaking gaily and pleasantly to the village people.
They came in on the opposite side to the Drumble
Road; indeed Drumble was nothing of a place then, as
I have told you. Between the last cottage in the village
and the gates to the old hall, there was a shady part of
the road, where the branches nearly met overhead, and
made a green gloom. If you'll notice, when many
people are talking merrily out of doors in sunlight, they
will stop talking for an instant, when they come into the
cool green shade, and either be silent for some little
time, or else speak graver, and slower, and softer. And
so old people say those gay gentlemen did; for several
people followed to see Alice Carr's pride taken down.
They used to tell how the cavaliers had to bow their
plumed hats in passing under the unlopped and drooping
boughs. I fancy Sir John expected that the lady would
have rallied her friends, and got ready for a sort of
battle to defend the entrance to the house; but she had
no friends. She had no nearer relations than the Duke
of Albemarle, and he was mad with her for having
refused to come to court, and so save her estate,
according to his advice.

Well, Sir John rode on in silence; the tramp of the
many horses' feet, and the clumping sound of the clogs

of the village people were all that was heard. Heavy
as the great gate was, they swung it wide on its hinges,
and up they rode to the Hall steps, where the lady stood,
in her close, plain, Puritan dress, her cheeks one crimson
flush, her great eyes flashing fire, and no one behind
her, or with her, or near her, or to be seen, but the old
trembling nurse, catching at her gown in pleading terror.
Sir John was taken aback; he could not go out with
swords and warlike weapons against a woman; his very
preparations for forcing an entrance made him ridiculous
in his own eyes, and, he well knew, in the eyes of his
gay, scornful comrades too; so he turned him round
about, and bade them stay where they were, while he
rode close to the steps, and spoke to the young lady;
and there they saw him, hat in hand, speaking to her;
and she, lofty and unmoved, holding her own as if she
had been a sovereign queen with an army at her back.
What they said, no one heard; but he rode back, very
grave and much changed in his look, though his grey
eye showed more hawk-like than ever, as if seeing the
way to his end, though as yet afar off.   He was not one
to be jested with before his face ; so when he professed
to have changed his mind, and not to wish to disturb so
fair a lady in possession, he and his cavaliers rode back
to the village inn, and roystered there all day, and feasted
the tenantry, cutting down the branches that had incom-
moded them in their morning's ride, to make a bonfire
of on the village green, in which they burnt a figure,
which some called Old Noll, and others Richard Carr:
and it might do for either, folks said, for unless they
had given it the name of a man, most people would have
taken it for a forked log of wood.

But the lady's nurse told the villagers afterwards
that Mistress Alice went in from the sunny Hall steps
into the chill house shadow, and sate her down and
wept as her poor faithful servant had never seen her
do before, and could not have imagined her proud young
lady ever doing. All through that summer's day she
cried; and if for very weariness she ceased for a time,
and only sighed as if her heart was breaking, they
heard through the upper windows—which were open
because of the heat—the village bells ringing merrily
through the trees, and bursts of choruses to gay cava-
lier songs, all in favour of the Stuarts. All the young
lady said was once or twice, " Oh God! I am very
friendless! "—and the old nurse knew it was true, and
could not contradict her; and always thought, as she
said long after, that such weary weeping showed there
was some great sorrow at hand.

I suppose it was the dreariest sorrow that ever a
proud woman had; but it came in the shape of a gay
wedding. How, the village never knew. The gay
gentlemen rode away from Morton the next day as
lightly and carelessly as if they had attained their end,
and Sir John had taken possession; and, by-and-by,
the nurse came timorously out to market in the village,
and Mistress Alice was met in the wood walks just as
grand and as proud as ever in her ways, only a little
more pale, and a little more sad. The truth was, as
I have been told, that she and Sir John had each taken
a fancy to each other in that parley they held on the
Hall steps; she, in the deep, wild way in which she
took the impressions of her whole life, deep down, as
if they were burnt in. Sir John was a gallant-looking

man, and had a kind of foreign grace and courtliness about him. The way he fancied her was very different —a man's way, they tell me. She was a beautiful woman to be tamed, and made to come to his beck and call; and perhaps he read in her softening eyes that she might be won, and so all legal troubles about the possession of the estate come to an end in an easy, pleasant manner. He came to stay with friends in the neighbourhood; he was met in her favourite walks, with his plumed hat in his hand, pleading with her, and she looking softer and far more lovely than ever; and lastly, the tenants were told of the marriage then nigh at hand.

After they were wedded, he stayed for a time with her at the Hall, and then off back to court. They do say that her obstinate refusal to go with him to London was the cause of their first quarrel; but such fierce, strong wills would quarrel the first day of their wedded life. She said that the court was no place for an' honest woman; but surely Sir John knew best, and she might have trusted him to take care of her. However, he left her all alone; and at first she cried most bitterly, and then she sook to her old pride, and was more haughty and gloomy than ever. By-and-by she found out hidden conventicles; and, as Sir John never stinted her of money, she gathered the remnants of the old Puritan party about her, and tried to comfort herself with long prayers, snuffled through the nose, for the absence of her husband, but it was of no use. Treat her as he would, she loved him still with a terrible love. Once, they say, she put on her waiting-maid's dress, and stole up to London to find out what kept him there; and something she saw or heard that changed her altogether, for she came back as if her heart was broken. They say that the only person she loved with all the wild strength of her heart, had proved false to her; and if so, what wonder! At the best of times she was but a gloomy creature, and it was a great honour for her father's daughter to be wedded to a Morton. She should not have expected too much.

After her despondency came her religion. Every old Puritan preacher in the country was welcome at Morton Hall. Surely that was enough to disgust Sir John. The Mortons had never cared to have much religion, but what they had, had been good of its kind hitherto. So, when Sir John came down wanting a gay greeting and a tender show of love, his lady exhorted him, and prayed over him, and quoted the last Puritan text she had heard at him; and he swore at her, and at her preachers; and made a deadly oath that none of them should find harbour or welcome in any house of his. She looked scornfully back at him, and said she had yet to learn in what county of England the house he spoke of was to be found; but in the house her father purchased, and she inherited, all who preached the Gospel should be welcome, let kings make what laws, and kings' minions swear what oaths they would. He said nothing to this—the worst sign for her; but he set his teeth at her; and in an hour's time he rode away back to the French witch that had beguiled him.

Before he went away from Morton he set his spies. He longed to catch his wife in his fierce clutch, and punish her for defying him. She had made him hate her with her Puritanical ways. He counted the days till the messenger came, splashed up to the top of his deep leather boots, to say that my lady had invited the canting Puritan preachers of the neighbourhood to a prayer-meeting, and a dinner, and a night's rest at her house. Sir John smiled as he gave the messenger five gold pieces for his pains; and straight took post-horses, and rode long days till he got to Morton; and only just in time; for it was the very day of the prayer-meeting. Dinners were then at one o'clock in the country. The great people in London might keep late hours, and dine at three in the afternoon or so; but the Mortons they always clung to the good old ways, and as the church bells were ringing twelve when Sir John came riding into the village, he knew he might slacken bridle; and, casting one glance at the smoke which came hurrying up as if from a newly-mended fire, just behind the wood, where he knew the Hall kitchen chimney stood, Sir John stopped at the smithy, and pretended to question the smith about his horse's shoes; but he took little heed of the answers, being more occupied by an old serving-man from the Hall, who had been loitering about the smithy half the morning, as folk thought afterwards to keep some appointment with Sir John. When their talk was ended, Sir John lifted himself straight in his saddle; cleared his throat, and spoke out aloud :—

" I grieve to hear your lady is so ill." The smith wondered at this, for all the village knew of the coming feast at the Hall; the spring-chickens had been bought up, and the cade-lambs killed; for the preachers in those days, if they fasted they fasted, if they fought they fought, if they prayed they prayed, sometimes for three hours at a standing; and if they feasted they feasted, and knew what good eating was, believe me.

" My lady ill ? " said the smith, as if he doubted the old prim serving-man's word. And the latter would have chopped in with an angry asseveration (he had been at Worcester and fought on the right side), but Sir John cut him short.

" My lady is very ill, good Master Fox. It touches her here," continued he, pointing to his head. " I am come down to take her to London, where the King's own physician shall prescribe for her." And he rode slowly up to the hall.

The lady was as well as ever she had been in her life, and happier than she had often been; for in a few minutes some of those whom she esteemed so highly would be about her, some of those who had known and valued her father—her dead father, to whom her sorrowful heart turned in its woe, as the only true lover and friend she had ever had on earth. Many of the preachers would have ridden far,—was all in order in their rooms, and on the table in the great dining parlour? She had got into restless hurried ways of late. She went round below, and then she mounted the great oak staircase to see if the tower bed-chamber was all in order for old Master Hilton, the oldest among the preachers. Meanwhile, the maidens below were carrying in mighty cold rounds of spiced beef, quarters of lamb, chicken pies, and all such provisions, when, suddenly, they knew not how, they found themselves each seized by strong arms, their aprons thrown over their heads, after the manner of a gag, and themselves borne out of the house on to the poultry green behind, where, with threats of what worse might befall them, they were sent with many a shameful word (Sir John could not always command his men, many of whom had been soldiers in the French wars) back into the village. They scudded away like frightened hares. My lady was strewing the white-headed preacher's room with the last year's lavender, and stirring up the sweet-pot on the dressing-table, when she heard a step on the echoing stairs. It was no measured tread of any Puritan; it was the clang of a man of war coming nearer and nearer, with loud rapid strides. She knew the step; her heart stopped beating, not for fear, but because she loved Sir John even yet; and she took a step forward to meet him, and then stood still and trembled, for the flattering false thought came before her that he might have come yet in some quick impulse of reviving love, and that his hasty step might be prompted by the passionate tenderness of a husband. But when he reached the door, she looked as calm and indifferent as ever.

"My lady," said he, "you are gathering your friends to some feast. May I know who are thus invited to revel in my house? Some graceless fellows, I see, from the store of meat and drink below—wine-bibbers and drunkards, I fear."

But, by the working glance of his eye, she saw that he knew all; and she spoke with a cold distinctness.

"Master Ephraim Dixon, Master Zerubbabel Hopkins, Master Help-me-or-I-perish Perkins, and some other godly ministers, come to spend the afternoon in my house."

He went to her, and in his rage he struck her. She put up no arm to save herself, but reddened a little with the pain, and then drawing her neckerchief on one side, she looked at the crimson mark on her white neck.

"It serves me right," she said. "I wedded one of my father's enemies; one of those who would have hunted the old man to death. I gave my father's enemy house and lands, when he came as a beggar to my door; I followed my wicked, wayward heart in this, instead of minding my dying father's words. Strike again, and avenge him yet more!"

But he would not, because she bade him. He unloosed his sash, and bound her arms tight,—tight together, and she never struggled or spoke. Then pushing her so that she was obliged to sit down on the bed side,—

"Sit there," he said, "and hear how I will welcome the old hypocrites you have dared to ask to my house— my house and my ancestors' house, long before your father—a canting pedlar—hawked his goods about, and cheated honest men."

And, opening the chamber window right above these Hall steps where she had awaited him in her maiden beauty scarce three short years ago, he greeted the company of preachers as they rode up to the Hall with such terrible hideous language (my lady had provoked him past all bearing, you see), that the old men turned round aghast, and made the best of their way back to their own places.

Meanwhile, Sir John's serving-men below had obeyed their master's orders. They had gone through the house, closing every window, every shutter, and every door, but leaving all else just as it was—the cold meats on the table, the hot meats on the spit, the silver flagons

12

on the side-board, all just as if it were ready for a feast; and then Sir John's head-servant, he that I spoke of before, came up and told his master all was ready.

"Is the horse and the pillion all ready? Then you and I must be my lady's tire-women;" and as it seemed to her in mockery, but in reality with a deep purpose, they dressed the helpless woman in her riding things all awry, and strange and disorderly, Sir John carried her down stairs; and he and his man bound her on the pillion; and Sir John mounted before. The man shut and locked the great house-door, and the echoes of the clang went through the empty Hall with an ominous sound. "Throw the key," said Sir John, "deep into the mere yonder. My lady may go seek it if she lists, when next I set her arms at liberty. Till then I know whose house Morton Hall shall be called."

"Sir John! it shall be called the Devil's House, and you shall be his steward."

But the poor lady had better have held her tongue; for Sir John only laughed, and told her to rave on. As he passed through the village, with his serving-men riding behind, the tenantry came out and stood at their doors, and pitied him for having a mad wife, and praised him for his care of her, and of the chance he gave her of amendment by taking her up to be seen by the King's physician. But, somehow, the Hall got an ugly name; the roast and boiled meats, the ducks, the chickens had time to drop into dust, before any human being now dared to enter in; or, indeed, had any right to enter in, for Sir John never came back to Morton; and as for my lady, some said she was dead, and some said she was mad, and shut up in London, and some said Sir John had taken her to a convent abroad.

"And what did become of her?" asked we, creeping up to Mrs. Dawson.

"Nay, how should I know?"

"But what do you think?" we asked pertinaciously.

"I cannot tell. I have heard that after Sir John was killed at the battle of the Boyne she got loose, and came wandering back to Morton, to her old nurse's house; but, indeed, she was mad then, out and out, and I've no doubt Sir John had seen it coming on. She used to have visions and dream dreams: and some thought her a prophetess, and some thought her fairly crazy. What she said about the Mortons was awful. She doomed them to die out of the land, and their house to be razed to the ground, while pedlars and huxters, such as her own people, her father, had been, should dwell where the knightly Mortons had once lived. One winter's night she strayed away, and the next morning they found the poor crazy woman frozen to death in Drumble meeting-house yard; and the Mr. Morton who had succeeded to Sir John had her decently buried where she was found, by the side of her father's grave."

We were silent for a time. "And when was the old Hall opened, Mrs. Dawson, please?"

"Oh! when the Mr. Morton, our Squire Morton's grandfather, came into possession. He was a distant cousin of Sir John's, a much quieter kind of man. He had all the old rooms opened wide, and aired, and fumigated; and the strange fragments of musty food were collected and burnt in the yard; but somehow that old dining-parlour had always a charnel-house smell, and no

12—2

one ever liked making merry in it—thinking of the grey
old preachers, whose ghosts might be even then scenting
the meats afar off, and trooping unbidden to a feast,
that was not that of which they were baulked. I was
glad for one when the squire's father built another
dining-room; and no servant in the house will go an
errand into the old dining-parlour after dark, I can
assure ye."

"I wonder if the way the last Mr. Morton had to sell
his land to the people at Drumble had anything to do with
old Lady Morton's prophecy," said my mother, musingly.

"Not at all," said Mrs. Dawson, sharply. "My
lady was crazy, and her words not to be minded. I
should like to see the cotton-spinners of Drumble offer
to purchase land from the squire. Besides, there's a
strict entail now. They can't purchase the land if they
would. A set of trading pedlars, indeed!"

I remember Ethelinda and I looked at each other at
this word "pedlars;" which was the very word she had
put into Sir John's mouth when taunting his wife with
her father's low birth and calling. We thought, "We
shall see."

Alas! we have seen.

Soon after that evening our good old friend Mrs.
Dawson died. I remember it well, because Ethelinda
and I were put into mourning for the first time in our
lives. A dear little brother of ours had died only the
year before, and then my father and mother had decided
that we were too young; that there was no necessity for
their incurring the expense of black frocks. We mourned
for the little delicate darling in our hearts, I know; and
to this day I often wonder what it would have been to

have had a brother. But when Mrs. Dawson died it became a sort of duty we owed to the squire's family to go into black, and very proud and pleased Ethelinda and I were with our new frocks. I remember dreaming Mrs. Dawson was alive again, and crying, because I thought my new frock would be taken away from me. But all this has nothing to do with Morton Hall.

When I first became aware of the greatness of the squire's station in life, his family consisted of himself, his wife (a frail, delicate lady), his only son, "little master," as Mrs. Dawson was allowed to call him, "the young squire," as we in the village always termed him. His name was John Marmaduke. He was always called John; and after Mrs. Dawson's story of the old Sir John, I used to wish he might not bear that ill-omened name. He used to ride through the village in his bright scarlet coat, his long fair curling hair falling over his lace collar, and his broad black hat and feather shading his merry blue eyes. Ethelinda and I thought then, and I always shall think, there never was such a boy. He had a fine high spirit, too, of his own, and once horsewhipped a groom twice as big as himself who had thwarted him. To see him and Miss Phillis go tearing through the village on their pretty Arabian horses, laughing as they met the west wind, and their long golden curls flying behind them, you would have thought them brother and sister, rather than nephew and aunt; for Miss Phillis was the squire's sister, much younger than himself; indeed, at the time I speak of, I don't think she could have been above seventeen, and the young squire, her nephew, was nearly ten. I remember Mrs. Dawson sending for my mother and me up to the

Hall that we might see Miss Phillis dressed ready to go
with her brother to a ball given at some great lord's
house to Prince William of Gloucester, nephew to good
old George the Third.

When Mrs. Elizabeth, Mrs. Morton's maid, saw us
at tea in Mrs. Dawson's room, she asked Ethelinda and
me if we would not like to come into Miss Phillis's
dressing-room, and watch her dress ; and then she said,
if we would promise to keep from touching anything,
she would make interest for us to go.   We would have
promised to stand on our heads, and would have tried to
do so too, to earn such a privilege.   So in we went, and
stood together, hand-in-hand, up in a corner out of the
way, feeling very red, and shy, and hot, till Miss Phillis
put us at our ease by playing all manner of comical
tricks, just to make us laugh, which at last we did outright, in spite of all our endeavours to be grave, lest
Mrs. Elizabeth should complain of us to my mother.   I
recollect the scent of the *maréchale* powder with which
Miss Phillis's hair was just sprinkled ; and how she
shook her head, like a young colt, to work the hair
loose which Mrs. Elizabeth was straining up over a
cushion.   Then Mrs. Elizabeth would try a little of
Mrs. Morton's rouge ; and Miss Phillis would wash it
off with a wet towel, saying that she liked her own
paleness better than any performer's colour ; and when
Mrs. Elizabeth wanted just to touch her cheeks once
more, she hid herself behind the great arm-chair, peeping out, with her sweet, merry face, first at one side and
then at another, till we all heard the squire's voice at
the door, asking her, if she was dressed, to come and
show herself to madam, her sister-in-law ; for, as I

said, Mrs. Morton was a great invalid, and unable to
go out to any grand parties like this. We were all
silent in an instant; and even Mrs. Elizabeth thought
no more of the rouge, but how to get Miss Phillis's
beautiful blue dress on quick enough. She had cherry-
coloured knots in her hair, and her breast-knots were of
the same ribbon. Her gown was open in front, to a
quilted white silk skirt. We felt very shy of her as she
stood there fully dressed—she looked so much grander
than anything we had ever seen; and it was like a
relief when Mrs. Elizabeth told us to go down to
Mrs. Dawson's parlour, where my mother was sitting all
this time.

Just as we were telling how merry and comical Miss
Phillis had been, in came a footman. "Mrs. Dawson,"
said he, "the squire bids me ask you to go with Mrs.
Sidebotham into the west parlour, to have a look at
Miss Morton before she goes." We went, too, clinging
to my mother. Miss Phillis looked rather shy as we
came in, and stood just by the door. I think we all
must have shown her that we had never seen anything
so beautiful as she was in our lives before; for she went
very scarlet at our fixed gaze of admiration, and, to
relieve herself, she began to play all manner of antics—
whirling round, and making cheeses with her rich silk
petticoat; unfurling her fan (a present from madam, to
complete her dress), and peeping first on one side and
then on the other, just as she had done upstairs; and
then catching hold of her nephew, and insisting that he
should dance a minuet with her until the carriage came;
which proposal made him very angry, as it was an insult
to his manhood (at nine years old) to suppose he could

dance. " It was all very well for girls to make fools of themselves," he said, " but it did not do for men." And Ethelinda and I thought we had never heard so fine a speech before. But the carriage came before we had half feasted our eyes enough ; and the squire came from his wife's room to order the little master to bed, and hand his sister to the carriage.

I remember a good deal of talk about royal dukes and unequal marriages that night. I believe Miss Phillis did dance with Prince William ; and I have often heard that she bore away the bell at the ball, and that no one came near her for beauty and pretty, merry ways. In a day or two after I saw her scampering through the village, looking just as she did before she had danced with a royal duke. We all thought she would marry some one great, and used to look out for the lord who was to take her away. But poor madam died, and there was no one but Miss Phillis to comfort her brother, for the young squire was gone away to some great school down south ; and Miss Phillis grew grave, and reined in her pony to keep by the squire's side, when he rode out on his steady old mare in his lazy, careless way.

We did not hear so much of the doings at the Hall now Mrs. Dawson was dead ; so I cannot tell how it was ; but, by-and-by, there was a talk of bills that were once paid weekly, being now allowed to run to quarter-day ; and then, instead of being settled every quarter-day, they were put off to Christmas ; and many said they had hard enough work to get their money then. A buzz went through the village that the young squire played high at college, and that he made away with more money than his father could afford. But when he

came down to Morton, he was as handsome as ever; and
I, for one, never believed evil of him; though I'll allow
others might cheat him, and he never suspect it. His
aunt was as fond of him as ever; and he of her. Many
is the time I have seen them out walking together,
sometimes sad enough, sometimes merry as ever. By-
and-by, my father heard of sales of small pieces of land,
not included in the entail; and, at last, things got so
bad, that the very crops were sold yet green upon the
ground, for any price folks would give, so that there was
but ready money paid. The squire at length gave way
entirely, and never left the house; and the young master
in London; and poor Miss Phillis used to go about trying to see after the workmen and labourers, and save
what she could. By this time she would be above
thirty; Ethelinda and I were nineteen and twenty-one
when my mother died, and that was some years before
this. Well, at last the squire died; they do say of a
broken heart at his son's extravagance; and, though
the lawyers kept it very close, it began to be rumoured
that Miss Phillis's fortune had gone too. Any way, the
creditors came down on the estate like wolves. It was
entailed, and it could not be sold; but they put it into
the hands of a lawyer, who was to get what he could out
of it, and have no pity for the poor young squire, who
had not a roof for his head. Miss Phillis went to live
by herself in a little cottage in the village, at the end of
the property, which the lawyer allowed her to have
because he could not let it to any one, it was so tumble-
down and old. We never knew what she lived on, poor
lady; but she said she was well in health, which was all
we durst ask about. She came to see my father just

before he died, and he seemed made bold with the feeling that he was a dying man; so he asked, what I had longed to know for many a year, where was the young squire? he had never been seen in Morton since his father's funeral. Miss Phillis said he was gone abroad; but in what part he was then, she herself hardly knew; only she had a feeling that, sooner or later, he would come back to the old place; where she should strive to keep a home for him whenever he was tired of wandering about, and trying to make his fortune.

"Trying to make his fortune still?" asked my father, his questioning eyes saying more than his words. Miss Phillis shook her head, with a sad meaning in her face; and we understood it all. He was at some French gaming-table, if he was not at an English one.

Miss Phillis was right. It might be a year after my father's death when he came back, looking old and grey and worn. He came to our door just after we had barred it one winter's evening. Ethelinda and I still lived at the farm, trying to keep it up, and make it pay; but it was hard work. We heard a step coming up the straight pebble walk; and then it stopped right at our door, under the very porch, and we heard a man's breathing, quick and short.

"Shall I open the door?" said I.

"No, wait!" said Ethelinda; for we lived alone, and there was no cottage near us. We held our breaths. There came a knock.

"Who's there?" I cried.

"Where does Miss Morton live—Miss Phillis?"

We were not sure if we would answer him; for she, like us, lived alone.

" Who's there ? " again said I.

" Your master," he answered, proud and angry. " My name is John Morton. Where does Miss Phillis live ? "

We had the door unbarred in a trice, and begged him to come in ; to pardon our rudeness. We would have given him of our best, as was his due from us ; but he only listened to the directions we gave him to his aunt's, and took no notice of our apologies.

———◆———

CHAPTER II.

UP to this time we had felt it rather impertinent to tell each other of our individual silent wonder as to what Miss Phillis lived on ; but I know in our hearts we each thought about it, with a kind of respectful pity for her fallen low estate. Miss Phillis—that we remembered like an angel for beauty, and like a little princess for the imperious sway she exercised, and which was such sweet compulsion that we had all felt proud to be her slaves—Miss Phillis was now a worn, plain woman, in homely dress, tending towards old age ; and looking— (at that time I dared not have spoken so insolent a thought, not even to myself)—but she did look as if she had hardly the proper nourishing food she required. One day, I remember Mrs. Jones, the butcher's wife (she was a Drumble person) saying, in her saucy way, that she was not surprised to see Miss Morton so bloodless and pale, for she only treated herself to a Sunday's dinner of meat, and lived on slop and bread-and-butter all the rest of the week. Ethelinda put on her severe face—a look that I am afraid of to this day—and said, Mrs. Jones, do you suppose Miss Morton can eat your half-starved meat? You do not know how choice and dainty she is, as becomes one born and bred like her. What was it we had to bring for her only last Saturday from the grand new butcher's, in Drumble, Biddy?"—(We took our eggs to market in Drumble every Saturday, for the cotton-spinners would give us a higher price than the Morton people: the more fools they!)

I thought it rather cowardly of Ethelinda to put the story-telling on me; but she always thought a great deal of saving her soul; more than I did, I am afraid, for I made answer, as bold as a lion, "Two sweat-breads, at a shilling a-piece; and a forequarter of house-lamb, at eighteen-pence a pound." So off went Mrs. Jones, in a huff, saying, "their meat was good enough for Mrs. Donkin, the great mill-owner's widow, and might serve a beggarly Morton any day." When we were alone, I said to Ethelinda, " I'm afraid we shall have to pay for our lies at the great day of account;" and Ethelinda answered, very sharply—(she's a good sister in the main)—"Speak for yourself, Biddy. I never said a word. I only asked questions. How could I help it if you told lies? I'm sure I wondered at you, how glib you spoke out what was not true." But I knew she was glad I told the lies, in her heart.

After the poor squire came to live with his aunt, Miss Phillis, we ventured to speak a bit to ourselves. We were sure they were pinched. They looked like it.

He had a bad hacking cough at times; though he was so dignified and proud he would never cough when any one was near. I have seen him up before it was day, sweeping the dung off the roads, to try and get enough to manure the little plot of ground behind the cottage, which Miss Phillis had let alone, but which her nephew used to dig in and till; for, said he, one day, in his grand, slow way, "he was always fond of experiments in agriculture." Ethelinda and I do believe that the two or three score of cabbages he raised were all they had to live on that winter, besides the bit of meal and tea they got at the village shop.

One Friday night I said to Ethelinda, "It is a shame to take these eggs to Drumble to sell, and never to offer one to the squire, on whose lands we were born." She answered, "I have thought so many a time; but how. can we do it? I, for one, dare not offer them to the squire; and as for Miss Phillis, it would seem like impertinence." "I'll try at it," said I.

So that night I took some eggs—fresh yellow eggs from our own pheasant hen, the like of which there were not for twenty miles round—and I laid them softly after dusk on one of the little stone seats in the porch of Miss Phillis's cottage. But, alas! when we went to market at Drumble, early the next morning, there were my eggs all shattered and splashed, making an ugly yellow pool in the road just in front of the cottage. I had meant to have followed it up by a chicken or so; but I saw now that it would never do. Miss Phillis came now and then to call on us; she was a little more high and distant than she had been when a girl, and we felt we must keep our place. I suppose we had affronted the young squire, for he never came near our house.

Well, there came a hard winter, and provisions rose; and Ethelinda and I had much ado to make ends meet. If it had not been for my sister's good management, we should have been in debt, I know; but she proposed that we should go without dinner, and only have a breakfast and a tea, to which I agreed, you may be sure.

One baking day I had made some cakes for tea—potato-cakes we called them. They had a savoury, hot smell about them; and, to tempt Ethelinda, who was not quite well, I cooked a rasher of bacon. Just as we were sitting down, Miss Phillis knocked at our door. We let her in. God only knows how white and haggard she looked. The heat of our kitchen made her totter, and for a while she could not speak. But all the time she looked at the food on the table as if she feared to shut her eyes lest it should all vanish away. It was an eager stare like that of some animal, poor soul! "If I durst," said Ethelinda, wishing to ask her to share our meal, but being afraid to speak out. I did not speak, but handed her the good, hot, buttered cake; on which she seized, and putting it up to her lips as if to taste it, she fell back in her chair, crying.

We had never seen a Morton cry before; and it was something awful. We stood silent and aghast. She recovered herself, but did not taste the food; on the contrary, she covered it up with both her hands, as if afraid of losing it. "If you'll allow me," said she, in a stately kind of way, to make up for our having seen her crying, "I'll take it to my nephew." And she got up to go away; but she could hardly stand for very weakness, and had to sit down again; she smiled at us, and said she was a little dizzy, but it would soon go off; but as she smiled, the bloodless lips were drawn far back over her teeth, making her face seem somehow like a death's head. "Miss Morton," said I, "do honour us by taking tea with us this once. The squire, your father, once took a luncheon with my father, and we are proud of it to this day." I poured her out some tea, which she drank; the food she shrank away from as if the very sight of it turned her sick again. But when she rose to go, she looked at it with her sad, wolfish eyes, as if she could not leave it; and at last she broke into a low cry, and said, "Oh, Bridget, we are starving! we are starving for want of food! I can bear it; I don't mind; but he suffers—oh, how he suffers! Let me take him food for this one night."

We could hardly speak; our hearts were in our throats, and the tears ran down our cheeks like rain. We packed up a basket, and carried it to her very door, never venturing to speak a word, for we knew what it must have cost her to say that. When we left her at the cottage, we made her our usual deep courtesy, but she fell upon our necks, and kissed us. For several nights after she hovered round our house about dusk; but she would never come in again, and face us in candle or fire light, much less meet us by daylight. We took out food to her as regularly as might be, and gave it to her in silence, and with the deepest courtesies we could make, we felt so honoured. We had many plans now she had permitted us to know of her distress. We hoped she would allow us to go on serving her in some way as became us as Sidebothams. But one night she never came; we stayed out in the cold, bleak wind, looking into the dark for her thin, worn figure; all in vain. Late the next afternoon, the young squire lifted the latch, and stood right in the middle of our house-place. The roof was low overhead, and made lower by the deep beams supporting the floor above; he stooped as he looked at us, and tried to form words, but no sound came out of his lips. I never saw such gaunt woe; no, never! At last he took me by the shoulder, and led me out of the house.

"Come with me!" he said, when we were in the open air, as if that gave him strength to speak audibly. I needed no second word. We entered Miss Phillis's cottage; a liberty I had never taken before. What little furniture was there, it was clear to be seen were cast-off fragments of the old splendour of Morton Hall. No fire. Grey wood ashes lay on the hearth. An old settee, once white and gold, now doubly shabby in its fall from its former estate. On it lay Miss Phillis, very pale; very still; her eyes shut.

"Tell me!" he gasped. "Is she dead? I think she is asleep; but she looks so strange—as if she might be—" He could not say the awful word again. I stooped, and felt no warmth; only a cold chill atmosphere seemed to surround her.

"She is dead!" I replied at length. "Oh, Miss Phillis! Miss Phillis!" and, like a fool, I began to cry. But he sate down without a tear, and looked vacantly at the empty hearth. I dared not cry any more when I saw him so stony sad. I did not know what to do. I could not leave him; and yet I had no excuse for staying. I went up to Miss Phillis, and softly arranged the grey ragged locks about her face.

"Ay!" said he. "She must be laid out. Who so fit to do it as you and your sister, children of good old Robert Sidebotham?"

"Oh, my master," I said, "this is no fit place for you. Let me fetch my sister to sit up with me all night; and honour us by sleeping at our poor little cottage."

I did not expect he would have done it; but after a few minutes' silence he agreed to my proposal. I hastened home, and told Ethelinda, and both of us crying, we heaped up the fire, and spread the table with food, and made up a bed in one corner of the floor. While I stood ready to go, I saw Ethelinda open the great chest in which we kept our treasures; and out she took a fine Holland shift that had been one of my mother's wedding shifts; and, seeing what she was after, I went upstairs and brought down a piece of rare old lace, a good deal darned to be sure, but still old Brussels point, bequeathed to me long ago by my god-mother, Mrs. Dawson. We huddled these things under our cloaks, locked the door behind us, and set out to do all we could now for poor Miss Phillis. We found the squire sitting just as we left him; I hardly knew if he understood me when I told him how to unlock our door, and gave him the key, though I spoke as distinctly as ever I could for the choking in my throat. At last he rose and went; and Ethelinda and I composed her poor thin limbs to decent rest, and wrapped her in the fine Holland shift; and then I plaited up my lace into a close cap to tie up the wasted features.

13

When all was done we looked upon her from a little distance.

"A Morton to die of hunger!" said Ethelinda solemnly. "We should not have dared to think that such a thing was within the chances of life. Do you remember that evening, when you and I were little children, and she a merry young lady peeping at us from behind her fan?"

We did not cry any more; we felt very still and awe-struck. After a while I said, "I wonder if, after all, the young squire did go to our house. He had a strange look about him. If I dared I would go and see." I opened the door; the night was black as pitch; the air very still. "I'll go," said I; and off I went, not meeting a creature, for it was long past eleven. I reached our house; the window was long and low, and the shutters were old and shrunk. I could peep between them well, and see all that was going on. He was there, sitting over the fire, never shedding a tear; but seeming as if he saw his past life in the embers. The food we had prepared was untouched. Once or twice, during my long watch (I was more than an hour away), he turned towards the food, and made as though he would have eaten it, and then shuddered back; but at last he seized it, and tore it with his teeth, and laughed and rejoiced over it like some starved animal. I could not keep from crying then. He gorged himself with great morsels; and when he could eat no more, it seemed as if his strength for suffering had come back. He threw himself on the bed, and such a passion of despair I never heard of, much less ever saw. I could not bear to witness it. The dead Miss Phillis lay calm and still.

Her trials were over. I would go back and watch with Ethelinda.

When the pale grey morning dawn stole in, making us shiver and shake after our vigil, the squire returned. We were both mortal afraid of him, we knew not why. He looked quiet enough—the lines were worn deep before—no new traces were there. He stood and looked at his aunt for a minute or two. Then he went up into the loft above the room where we were; he brought a small paper parcel down; bade us keep on our watch yet a little time. First one and then the other of us went home to get some food. It was a bitter black frost; no one was out who could stop indoors; and those who were out cared not to stop to speak. Towards afternoon the air darkened, and a great snow-storm came on. We durst not be left only one alone; yet, at the cottage where Miss Phillis had lived, there was neither fire nor fuel. So we sate and shivered and shook till morning. The squire never came that night nor all next day.

" What must we do ? " asked Ethelinda, broken down entirely. " I shall die if I stop here another night. We must tell the neighbours and get help for the watch."

" So we must," said I, very low and grieved. I went out and told the news at the nearest house, taking care, you may be sure, never to speak of the hunger and cold Miss Phillis must have endured in silence. It was bad enough to have them come in, and make their remarks on the poor bits of furniture; for no one had known their bitter straits even as much as Ethelinda and me, and we had been shocked at the bareness of the place. I did hear that one or two of the more ill-conditioned had said, it was not for nothing we had kept the death to ourselves for two nights ; that, to judge from the lace on her cap, there must have been some pretty pickings. Ethelinda would have contradicted this, but I bade her let it alone ; it would save the memory of the proud Mortons from the shame that poverty is thought to be ; and as for us, why we could live it down. But, on the whole, people came forward kindly ; money was not wanting to bury her well, if not grandly, as became her birth ; and many a one was bidden to the funeral who might have looked after her a little more in her life-time. Among others was Squire Hargreaves from Both-wick Hall over the moors. He was some kind of far-away cousin to the Morton's ; so when he came he was asked to go chief mourner in Squire Morton's strange absence, which I should have wondered at the more if I had not thought him almost crazy when I watched his ways through the shutter that night. Squire Hargreaves started when they paidd him the compliment of asking him to take the head of the coffin.

" Where is her nephew ? " asked he.

" No one has seen him since eight o'clock last Thursday morning."

" But I saw him at noon on Thursday," said Squire Hargreaves, with a round oath. " He came over the moors to tell me of his aunt's death, and to ask me to give him a little money to bury her, on the pledge of his gold shirt-buttons. He said I was a cousin, and could pity a gentleman in such sore need ; that the buttons were his mother's first gift to him ; and that I was to keep them safe, for some day he would make his fortune, and come back to redeem them. He had not known his aunt was so ill, or he would have parted with these buttons sooner, though he held them as more precious than he could tell me. I gave him money; but I could not find in my heart to take the buttons. He bade me not tell of all this; but when a man is missing it is my duty to give all the clue I can."

And so their poverty was blazoned abroad! But folk forgot it all in the search for the squire on the moorside. Two days they searched in vain; the third, upwards of a hundred men turned out, hand-in-hand, step to step, to leave no foot of ground unsearched. They found him stark and stiff, with Squire Hargreaves' money, and his mother's gold buttons, safe in his waistcoat pocket.

And we laid him down by the side of his poor aunt Phillis.

After the squire, John Marmaduke Morton, had been found dead in that sad way, on the dreary moors, the creditors seemed to lose all hold on the property; which indeed, during the seven years they had had it, they had drained as dry as a sucked orange. But for a long time no one seemed to know who rightly was the owner of Morton Hall and lands. The old house fell out of repair; the chimneys were full of starlings' nests; the flags in the terrace in front were hidden by the long grass; the panes in the windows were broken, no one knew how or why, for the children of the village got up a tale that the house was haunted. Ethelinda and I went sometimes in the summer mornings, and gathered some of the roses that were being strangled by the bindweed that spread over all; and we used to try and weed the old flower-garden a little; but we were no longer

young, and the stooping made our backs ache. Still we
always felt happier if we cleared but ever such a little
space. Yet we did not go there willingly in the afternoons, and left the garden always long before the first
slight shade of dusk.

We did not choose to ask the common people—many
of them were weavers for the Drumble manufacturers,
and no longer decent hedgers and ditchers—we did not
choose to ask them, I say, who was squire now, or
where he lived. But one day, a great London lawyer
came to the Morton Arms, and made a pretty stir. He
came on behalf of a General Morton, who was squire
now, though he was far away in India. He had been
written to, and they had proved him heir, though he
was a very distant cousin, farther back than Sir John, I
think. And now he had sent word they were to take
money of his that was in England, and put the house in
thorough repair; for that three maiden sisters of his,
who lived in some town in the north, would come and
live at Morton Hall till his return. So the lawyer sent
for a Drumble builder, and gave him directions. We
thought it would have been prettier if he had hired John
Cobb, the Morton builder and joiner, he that had made
the squire's coffin, and the squire's father's before that.
Instead, came a troop of Drumble men, knocking and
tumbling about in the Hall, and making their jests up
and down all those stately rooms. Ethelinda and I never
went near the place till they were gone, bag and bag-
gage. And then what a change! The old casement
windows, with their heavy leaded panes half overgrown
with vines and roses, were taken away, and great staring
sash windows were in their stead. New grates inside;

all modern, new-fangled, and smoking, instead of the
brass dogs which held the mighty logs of wood in the
old squire's time. The little square Turkey carpet under
the dining-table, which had served Miss Phillis, was not
good enough for these new Mortons; the dining-room
was all carpeted over. We peeped into the old dining-
parlour—that parlour where the dinner for the Puritan
preachers had been laid out; the flag parlour, as it had
been called of late years. But it had a damp, earthy
smell, and was used as a lumber-room. We shut the door
quicker than we had opened it. We came away disappointed. The Hall was no longer like our own honoured
Morton Hall.

"After all, these three ladies are Mortons," said
Ethelinda to me. "We must not forget that: we must
go and pay our duty to them as soon as they have
appeared in church."

Accordingly we went. But we had heard and seen a
little of them before we paid our respects at the Hall.
Their maid had been down in the village; their maid,
as she was called now; but a maid-of-all-work she had
been until now, as she very soon let out when we questioned her. However, we were never proud; and she
was a good honest farmer's daughter out of Northumberland. What work she did make with the Queen's English! The folk in Lancashire are said to speak broad,
but I could always understand our own kindly tongue;
whereas, when Mrs. Turner told me her name, both
Ethelinda and I could have sworn she said Donagh, and
were afraid she was an Irishwoman. Her ladies were
what you may call past the bloom of youth; Miss
Sophronia—Miss Morton, properly—was just sixty;

Miss Annabella, three years younger; and Miss Dorothy (or Baby, as they called her when they were by themselves), was two years younger still. Mrs. Turner was very confidential to us, partly because, I doubt not, she had heard of our old connection with the family, and partly because she was an arrant talker, and was glad of anybody who would listen to her. So we heard the very first week how each of the ladies had wished for the east bed-room—that which faced the north-east—which no one slept in in the old squire's days; but there were two steps leading up into it, and, said Miss Sophronia, she would never let a younger sister have a room more elevated than she had herself. She was the eldest, and she had a right to the steps. So she bolted herself in for two days, while she unpacked her clothes, and then came out, looking like a hen that has laid an egg, and defies any one to take that honour from her.

But her sisters were very deferential to her in general; that must be said. They never had more than two black feathers in their bonnets; while she had always three. Mrs. Turner said that once, when they thought Miss Annabella had been going to have an offer of marriage made her, Miss Sophronia had not objected to her wearing three that winter; but when it all ended in smoke, Miss Annabella had to pluck it out as became a younger sister. Poor Miss Annabella! She had been a beauty (Mrs. Turner said), and great things had been expected of her. Her brother, the general, and her mother had both spoilt her, rather than cross her unnecessarily, and so spoil her good looks; which old Mrs. Morton had always expected would make the fortune of the family. Her sisters were angry with her for not having married

some great rich gentleman; though, as she used to say
to Mrs. Turner, how could she help it? She was willing
enough, but no rich gentleman came to ask her. We
agreed that it really was not her fault; but her sisters
thought it was; and now, that she had lost her beauty,
they were always casting it up what they would have
done if they had had her gifts. There were some Miss
Burrells they had heard of, each of whom had married a
lord; and these Miss Burrells had not been such great
beauties. So Miss Sophronia used to work the question
by the rule of three, and put it in this way—If Miss
Burrell, with a tolerable pair of eyes, a snub nose, and
a wide mouth, married a baron, what rank of peer ought
our pretty Annabella to have espoused? And the worst
was, Miss Annabella—who had never had any ambition—
wanted to have married a poor curate in her youth; but
was pulled up by her mother and sisters, reminding her
of the duty she owed to her family. Miss Dorothy had
done her best—Miss Morton always praised her for it.
With not half the good looks of Miss Annabella, she had
danced with an honourable at Harrogate three times
running; and, even now, she persevered in trying;
which was more than could be said of Miss Annabella,
who was very broken-spirited.

I do believe Mrs. Turner told us all this before we
had ever seen the ladies. We had let them know,
through Mrs. Turner, of our wish to pay them our
respects; so we ventured to go up to the front door,
and rap modestly. We had reasoned about it before,
and agreed that if we were going in our every-day
clothes, to offer a little present of eggs, or to call on
Mrs. Turner (as she had asked us to do), the back door

would have been the appropriate entrance for us. But going, however humbly, to pay our respects, and offer our reverential welcome to the Miss Mortons, we took rank as their visitors, and should go to the front door. We were shown up the wide stairs, along the gallery, up two steps, into Miss Sophronia's room. She put away some papers hastily as we came in. We heard afterwards that she was writing a book, to be called *The Female Chesterfield; or, Letters from a Lady of Quality to her Niece.* And the little niece sat there in a high chair, with a flat board tied to her back, and her feet in stocks on the rail of the chair; so that she had nothing to do but listen to her aunt's letters; which were read aloud to her as they were written, in order to mark their effect on her manners. I was not sure whether Miss Sophronia liked our interruption; but I know little Miss Cordelia Mannisty did.

"Is the young lady crooked?" asked Ethelinda, during a pause in our conversation. I had noticed that my sister's eyes would rest on the child; although, by an effort, she sometimes succeeded in looking at something else occasionally.

"No! indeed, 'ma'am," said Miss Morton. "But she was born in India, and her backbone has never properly hardened. Besides, I and my two sisters each take charge of her for a week; and their systems of education—I might say non-education—differ so totally and entirely from my ideas, that when Miss Mannisty comes to me, I consider myself fortunate if I can undo the—hem!—that has been done during a fortnight's absence. Cordelia, my dear, repeat to these good ladies the geography lesson you learnt this morning."

Poor little Miss Mannisty began to tell us a great deal about some river in Yorkshire of which we had never heard, though I dare say we ought to, and then a great deal more about the towns that it passed by, and what they were famous for; and all I can remember—indeed, could understand at the time—was that Pomfret was famous for Pomfret cakes, which I knew before. But Ethelinda gasped for breath before it was done, she was so nearly choked up with astonishment; and when it was ended, she said, "Pretty dear; it's wonderful!" Miss Morton looked a little displeased, and replied, "Not at all. Good little girls can learn anything they choose, even French verbs. Yes, Cordelia, they can. And to be good is better than to be pretty. We don't think about looks here. You may get down, child, and go into the garden; and take care you put your bonnet on, or you'll be all over freckles." We got up to take leave at the same time, and followed the little girl out of the room. Ethelinda fumbled in her pocket.

"Here's a sixpence, my dear, for you. Nay, I am sure you may take it from an old woman like me, to whom you've told over more geography than I ever thought there was out of the Bible." For Ethelinda always maintained that the long chapters in the Bible which were all names, were geography; and though I knew well enough they were not, yet I had forgotten what the right word was, so I let her alone; for one hard word did as well as another. Little miss looked as if she was not sure if she might take it; but I suppose we had two kindly old faces, for at last the smile came into her eyes—not to her mouth, she had lived too much with grave and quiet people for that—and, looking wistfully at us, she said,—

"Thank you. But won't you go and see aunt Annabella?" We said we should like to pay our respects to both her other aunts if we might take that liberty; and perhaps she would show us the way. But, at the door of a room, she stopped short, and said, sorrowfully, "I mayn't go in; it is not my week for being with aunt Annabella;" and then she went slowly and heavily towards the garden-door.

"That child is cowed by somebody," said I to Ethelinda.

"But she knows a deal of geography"——Ethelinda's speech was cut short by the opening of the door in answer to our knock. The once beautiful Miss Annabella Morton stood before us, and bade us enter. She was dressed in white, with a turned-up velvet hat, and two or three short drooping black feathers in it. I should not like to say she rouged, but she had a very pretty colour in her cheeks; that much can do neither good nor harm. At first she looked so unlike anybody I had ever seen, that I wondered what the child could have found to like in her; for like her she did, that was very clear. But, when Miss Annabella spoke, I came under the charm. Her voice was very sweet and plaintive, and suited well with the kind of things she said; all about charms of nature, and tears, and grief, and such sort of talk, which reminded me rather of poetry—very pretty to listen to, though I never could understand it as well as plain, comfortable prose. Still I hardly know why I liked Miss Annabella. I think I was sorry for her; though whether I should have been if she had

not put it in my head, I don't know. The room looked
very comfortable ; a spinnet in a corner to amuse herself
with, and a good sofa to lie down upon. By-and-by,
we got her to talk of her little niece, and she, too, had
her system of education. She said she hoped to develop
the sensibilities and to cultivate the tastes. While with
her, her darling niece read works of imagination, and
acquired all that Miss Annabella could impart of the fine
arts. We neither of us quite knew what she was hinting
at, at the time ; but afterwards, by dint of questioning
little miss, and using our own eyes and ears, we found
that she read aloud to her aunt while she lay on the
sofa. *Santo Sebastiano ; or, the Young Protector*, was
what they were deep in at this time ; and, as it was in
five volumes and the heroine spoke broken English—
which required to be read twice over to make it intel-
ligible—it lasted them a long time. She also learned
to play on the spinnet ; not much, for I never heard
above two tunes, one of which was God save the King,
and the other was not. But I fancy the poor child was
lectured by one aunt, and frightened by the other's sharp
ways and numerous fancies. She might well be fond of
her gentle, pensive (Miss Annabella told me she was
pensive, so I know I am right in calling her so) aunt,
with her soft voice, and her never-ending novels,
and the sweet scents that hovered about the sleepy
room.

No one tempted us towards Miss Dorothy's apartment
when we left Miss Annabella ; so we did not see the
youngest Miss Morton this first day. We had each of
us treasured up many little mysteries to be explained by
our dictionary, Mrs. Turner.

" Who is little Miss Mannisty ? " we asked in one breath, when we saw our friend from the Hall. And then we learnt that there had been a fourth—a younger Miss Morton, who was no beauty, and no wit, and no anything; so Miss Sophronia, her eldest sister, had allowed her to marry a Mr. Mannisty, and ever after spoke of her as " my poor sister Jane." She and her husband had gone out to India, and both had died there ; and the general had made it a sort of condition with his sisters that they should take charge of the child, or else none of them liked children except Miss Annabella.

" Miss Annabella likes children," said I. " Then that's the reason children like her."

" I can't say she likes children ; for we never have any in our house but Miss Cordelia ; but her she does like dearly."

" Poor little miss ! " said Ethelinda, " does she never get a game of play with other little girls ? " And I am sure from that time Ethelinda considered her in a diseased state from this very circumstance, and that her knowledge of geography was one of the symptoms of the disorder ; for she used often to say, " I wish she did not know so much geography ! I'm sure it is not quite right."

Whether or not her geography was right, I don't know ; but the child pined for companions. A very few days after we had called—and yet long enough to have passed her into Miss Annabella's week—I saw Miss Cordelia in a corner of the church green, playing, with awkward humility, along with some of the rough village girls, who were as expert at the game as she was unapt and slow. I hesitated a little, and at last I called to her.

"How do you, my dear?" I said. "How come you here, so far from home?"

She reddened, and then looked up at me with her large, serious eyes.

"Aunt Annabel sent me into the wood to meditate —and—and—it was very dull—and I heard these little girls playing and laughing—and I had my sixpence with me, and—it was not wrong, was it, ma'am?—I came to them, and told one of them I would give it to her if she would ask the others to let me play with them."

"But, my dear, they are—some of them—very rough little children, and not fit companions for a Morton."

"But I am a Mannisty, ma'am!" she pleaded, with so much entreaty in her ways, that if I had not known what naughty, bad girls some of them were, I could not have resisted her longing for companions of her own age. As it was, I was angry with them for having taken her sixpence; but, when she had told me which it was, and saw that I was going to reclaim it, she clung to me, and said,—

"Oh! don't, ma'am—you must not. I gave it to her quite of my own self."

So I turned away; for there was truth in what the child said. But to this day I have never told Ethelinda what became of her sixpence. I took Miss Cordelia home with me while I changed my dress to be fit to take her back to the Hall. And on the way, to make up for her disappointment, I began talking of my dear Miss Phillis, and her bright, pretty youth. I had never named her name since her death to any one but Ethe-

linda—and that only on Sundays and quiet times. And
I could not have spoken of her to a grown-up person;
but somehow to Miss Cordelia it came out quite natural.
Not of her latter days, of course; but of her pony, and
her little black King Charles's dogs, and all the living
creatures that were glad in her presence when first I
knew her. And nothing would satisfy the child but
I must go into the Hall garden and show her where
Miss Phillis's garden had been. We were deep in our
talk, and she was stooping down to clear the plot from
weeds, when I heard a sharp voice cry out, "Cordelia!
Cordelia! Dirtying your frock with kneeling on the
wet grass! It is not my week; but I shall tell your
aunt Annabella of you."

And the window was shut down with a jerk. It was
Miss Dorothy. And I felt almost as guilty as poor little
Miss Cordelia; for I had heard from Mrs. Turner that
we had given great offence to Miss Dorothy by not going
to call on her in her room that day on which we had
paid our respects to her sisters; and I had a sort of an
idea that seeing Miss Cordelia with me was almost as
much of a fault as the kneeling down on the wet grass.
So I thought I would take the bull by the horns.

"Will you take me to your aunt Dorothy, my dear?"
said I.

The little girl had no longing to go into her aunt
Dorothy's room, as she had so evidently had at Miss
Annabella's door. On the contrary, she pointed it out
to me at a safe distance, and then went away in the
measured step she was taught to use in that house;
where such things as running, going upstairs two steps
at a time, or jumping down three, were considered

undignified and vulgar. Miss Dorothy's room was the
least prepossessing of any. Somehow it had a north-
east look about it, though it did face direct south; and
as for Miss Dorothy herself, she was more like a "cousin
Betty" than anything else; if you know what a cousin
Betty is, and perhaps it is too old-fashioned a word to
be understood by any one who has learnt the foreign
languages: but when I was a girl, there used to be
poor crazy women rambling about the country, one or
two in a district. They never did any harm that I
know of; they might have been born idiots, poor
creatures! or crossed in love, who knows? But they
roamed the country, and were well known at the farm-
houses, where they often got food and shelter for as
long a time as their restless minds would allow them
to stay in any one place; and the farmer's wife would,
maybe, rummage up a ribbon, or a feather, or a smart
old breadth of silk, to please the harmless vanity of
these poor crazy women; and they would go about so
bedizened sometimes that, as we called them always
" cousin Betty," we made it into a kind of proverb for
any one dressed in a fly-away, showy style, and said
they were like a cousin Betty. So now you know what
I mean that Miss Dorothy was like. Her dress was
white, like Miss Annabella's; but, instead of the black
velvet hat her sister wore, she had on, even in the
house, a small black silk bonnet. This sounds as if
it should be less like a cousin Betty than a hat; but
wait till I tell you how it was lined—with strips of
red silk, broad near the face, narrow near the brim;
for all the world like the rays of the rising sun, as
they are painted on the public-house sign. And her

14

face was like the sun; as round as an apple; and with
rouge on, without any doubt.: indeed, she told me once,
a lady was not dressed unless she had put her rouge
on.   Mrs. Turner told us she studied reflections a great
deal; not that she was a thinking woman in general, I
should say; and that this rayed lining was the fruit of
her study.   She had her hair pulled together, so that
her forehead was quite covered with it; and I won't
deny that I rather wished myself at home, as I stood
facing her in the doorway.   She pretended she did not
know who I was, and made me tell all about myself;
and then it turned out she knew all about me, and she
hoped I had recovered from my fatigue the other day.

"What fatigue?" asked I, immovably.   Oh! she
had understood I was very much tired after visiting her
sisters; otherwise, of course, I should not have felt it
too much to come on to her room.   She kept hinting at
me in so many ways, that I could have asked her gladly
to slap my face and have done with it, only I wanted to
make Miss Cordelia's peace with her for kneeling down
and dirtying her frock.   I did say what I could to
make things straight; but I don't know if I did any
good.   Mrs. Turner told me how suspicious and jealous
she was of everybody, and of Miss Annabella in particular, who had been set over her in her youth because
of her beauty; but since it had faded, Miss Morton and
Miss Dorothy had never ceased pecking at her; and Miss
Dorothy worst of all.   If it had not been for little
Miss Cordelia's love, Miss Annabella might have wished
to die; she did often wish she had had the small-pox as
a baby.   Miss Morton was stately and cold to her, as
one who had not done her duty to her family, and was

put in the corner for her bad behaviour. Miss Dorothy was continually talking at her, and particularly dwelling on the fact of her being the older sister. Now she was but two years older; and was still so pretty and gentle-looking, that I should have forgotten it continually but for Miss Dorothy.

The rules that were made for Miss Cordelia! She was to eat her meals standing, that was one thing! Another was, that she was to drink two cups of cold water before she had any pudding; and it just made the child loathe cold water. Then there were ever so many words she might not use; each aunt had her own set of words which were ungenteel or improper for some reason or another. Miss Dorothy would never let her say "red;" it was always to be pink, or crimson, or scarlet. Miss Cordelia used at one time to come to us, and tell us she had a "pain at her chest" so often, that Ethelinda and I began to be uneasy, and questioned Mrs. Turner to know if her mother had died of consumption; and many a good pot of currant jelly have I given her, and only made her pain at the chest worse; for—would you believe it?—Miss Morton told her never to say she had got a stomach-ache, for that it was not proper to say so. I had heard it called by a worse name still in my youth, and so had Ethelinda; and we sat and wondered to ourselves how it was that some kinds of pain were genteel and others were not. I said that old families, like the Mortons, generally thought it showed good blood to have their complaints as high in the body as they could—brain-fevers and headaches had a better sound, and did perhaps belong more to the aristocracy. I thought I had got the right view in

14—2

saying this, when Ethelinda would put in that she had often heard of Lord Toffey having the gout and being lame, and that nonplussed me. If there is one thing I do dislike more than another, it is a person saying something on the other side when I am trying to make up my mind—how can I reason if I am to be disturbed by another person's arguments?

But though I tell all these peculiarities of the Miss Mortons, they were good women in the main: even Miss Dorothy had her times of kindness, and really did love her little niece, though she was always laying traps to catch her doing wrong. Miss Morton I got to respect, if I never liked her. They would ask us up to tea; and we would put on our best gowns; and taking the house-key in my pocket, we used to walk slowly through the village, wishing that people who had been living in our youth could have seen us now, going by invitation to drink tea with the family at the Hall—not in the housekeeper's room, but with the family, mind you. But since they began to weave in Morton, everybody seemed too busy to notice us; so we were fain to be content with reminding each other how we should never have believed it in our youth that we could have lived to this day. After tea, Miss Morton would set us to talk of the real old family, whom they had never known; and you may be sure we told of all their pomp and grandeur and stately ways: but Ethelinda and I never spoke of what was to ourselves like the memory of a sad, terrible dream. So they thought of the squire in his coach-and-four as high sheriff, and madam lying in her morning-room in her Genoa velvet wrapping-robe, all over peacock's eyes (it was a piece of velvet the squire brought back from Italy, when he had been the grand tour), and Miss Phillis going to a ball at a great lord's house and dancing with a royal duke. The three ladies were never tired of listening to the tale of the splendour that had been going on here, while they and their mother had been starving in genteel poverty up in Northumberland; and as for Miss Cordelia, she sate on a stool at her aunt Annabella's knee, her hand in her aunt's, and listened, open-mouthed and unnoticed, to all we could say.

One day, the child came crying to our house. It was the old story; aunt Dorothy had been so unkind to aunt Annabella! The little girl said she would run away to India, and tell her uncle the general, and seemed in such a paroxysm of anger, and grief, and despair, that a sudden thought came over me. I thought I would try and teach her something of the deep sorrow that lies awaiting all at some part of their lives, and of the way in which it ought to be borne, by telling her of Miss Phillis's love and endurance for her wasteful, handsome nephew. So from little, I got to more, and I told her all; the child's great eyes filling slowly with tears, which brimmed over and came rolling down her cheeks unnoticed as I spoke. I scarcely needed to make her promise not to speak about all this to any one. She said, " I could not—no ! not even to aunt Annabella." And to this day she never has named it again, not even to me; but she tried to make herself more patient, and more silently helpful in the strange household among whom she was cast.

By-and-by, Miss Morton grew pale, and grey, and worn, amid all her stiffness. Mrs. Turner whispered to

us that for all her stern, unmoved looks, she was ill
unto death; that she had been secretly to see the great
doctor at Drumble; and he had told her she must set
her house in order.   Not even her sisters knew this;
but it preyed upon Mrs. Turner's mind and she told us.
Long after this, she kept up her week of discipline with
Miss Cordelia; and walked in her straight, soldier-like
way about the village, scolding people for having too
large families, and burning too much coal, and eating too
much butter.   One morning she sent Mrs. Turner for
her sisters; and, while she was away, she rummaged
out an old locket made of the four Miss Mortons' hair
when they were all children; and, threading the eye of
the locket with a piece of brown ribbon, she tied it
round Cordelia's neck, and kissing her, told her she had
been a good girl, and had cured herself of stooping;
that she must fear God and honour the king; and that
now she might go and have a holiday.   Even while the
child looked at her in wonder at the unusual tenderness
with which this was said, a grim spasm passed over her
face, and Cordelia ran in affright to call Mrs. Turner.
But when she came, and the other two sisters came, she
was quite herself again.   She had her sisters in her
room alone when she wished them good-by; so no one
knows what she said, or how she told them (who were
thinking of her as in health) that the signs of near-
approaching death, which the doctor had foretold, were
upon her.   One thing they both agreed in saying—and
it was much that Miss Dorothy agreed in anything—
that she bequeathed her sitting-room, up the two steps,
to Miss Annabella as being next in age.   Then they
left her room crying, and went both together into Miss

Annabella's room, sitting hand in hand (for the first time since childhood I should think), listening for the sound of the little hand-bell which was to be placed close by her, in case, in her agony, she required Mrs. Turner's presence. But it never rang. Noon became twilight. Miss Cordelia stole in from the garden with its long, black, green shadows, and strange eerie sounds of the night wind through the trees, and crept to the kitchen fire. At last Mrs. Turner knocked at Miss Morton's door, and hearing no reply, went in and found her cold and dead in her chair.

I suppose that some time or other we had told them of the funeral the old squire had; Miss Phillis's father, I mean. He had had a procession of tenantry half-a-mile long to follow him to the grave. Miss Dorothy sent for me to tell her what tenantry of her brother's could follow Miss Morton's coffin; but what with people working in mills, and land having passed away from the family, we could but muster up twenty people, men and women and all; and one or two were dirty enough to be paid for their loss of time.

Poor Miss Annabella did not wish to go into the room up two steps; nor yet dared she stay behind; for Miss Dorothy, in a kind of spite for not having had it bequeathed to her, kept telling Miss Annabella it was her duty to occupy it; that it was Miss Sophronia's dying wish, and that she should not wonder if Miss Sophronia were to haunt Miss Annabella, if she did not leave her warm room, full of ease and sweet scent, for the grim north-east chamber. We told Mrs. Turner we were afraid Miss Dorothy would lord it sadly over Miss Annabella, and she only shook her head;

which, from so talkative a woman, meant a great
deal. But, just as Miss Cordelia had begun to droop,
the general came home, without any one knowing
he was coming. Sharp and sudden was the word with
him. He sent Miss Cordelia off to school; but not
before she had had time to tell us that she loved her
uncle dearly, in spite of his quick, hasty ways. He
carried his sisters off to Cheltenham; and it was astonishing how young they made themselves look before
they came back again. He was always here, there, and
everywhere: and very civil to us into the bargain;
leaving the key of the Hall with us whenever they went
from home. Miss Dorothy was afraid of him, which
was a blessing, for it kept her in order, and really I was
rather sorry when she died; and, as for Miss Annabella,
she fretted after her till she injured her health, and
Miss Cordelia had to leave school to come and keep her
company. Miss Cordelia was not pretty; she had too
sad and grave a look for that; but she had winning
ways, and was to have her uncle's fortune some day, so
I expected to hear of her being soon snapt up. But
the general said her husband was to take the name of
Morton; and what did my young lady do but begin to
care for one of the great mill-owners at Drumble, as if
there were not all the lords and commons to choose
from besides? Mrs. Turner was dead; and there was
no one to tell us about it; but I could see Miss Cordelia
growing thinner and paler every time they came back to
Morton Hall; and I longed to tell her to pluck up a
spirit, and be above a cotton-spinner. One day, not
half a year before the general's death, she came to see
us, and told us, blushing like a rose, that her uncle had

given his consent; and so, although "he" had refused to take the name of Morton, and had wanted to marry her without a penny, and without her uncle's leave, it had all come right at last, and they were to be married at once; and their house was to be a kind of home for her aunt Annabella, who was getting tired of being perpetually on the ramble with the general.

"Dear old friends!" said our young lady, "you must like him. I am sure you will; he is so handsome, and brave, and good. Do you know, he says a relation of his ancestors lived at Morton Hall in the time of the Commonwealth."

"His ancestors," said Ethelinda. "Has he got ancestors? That's one good point about him, at any rate. I didn't know cotton-spinners had ancestors."

"What is his name?" asked I.

"Mr. Marmaduke Carr," said she, sounding each r with the old Northumberland burr, which was softened into a pretty pride and effort to give distinctness to each letter of the beloved name.

"Carr," said I, "Carr and Morton! Be it so! It was prophesied of old!" But she was too much absorbed in the thought of her own secret happiness to notice my poor sayings.

He was and is a good gentleman; and a real gentleman, too. They never lived at Morton Hall. Just as I was writing this, Ethelinda came in with two pieces of news. Never again say I am superstitious! There is no one living in Morton that knows the tradition of Sir John Morton and Alice Carr; yet the very first part of the Hall the Drumble builder has pulled down is the old stone dining-parlour where the great dinner for the

preachers mouldered away—flesh from flesh, crumb
from crumb!   And the street they are going to build
right through the rooms through which Alice Carr was
dragged in her agony of despair at her husband's loathing hatred, is to be called Carr Street.

And Miss Cordelia has got a baby ; a little girl ; and
writes in pencil two lines at the end of her husband's
note, to say she means to call it Phillis.

Phillis Carr!   I am glad he did not take the name of
Morton.   I like to keep the name of Phillis Morton in
my memory very still and unspoken.

MY FRENCH MASTER.

CHAPTER I.

My father's house was in the country, seven miles away from the nearest town. He had been an officer in the navy; but as he had met with some accident that would disable him from ever serving again, he gave up his commission, and his half-pay. He had a small private fortune, and my mother had not been penniless; so he purchased a house, and ten or twelve acres of land, and set himself up as an amateur farmer on a very small scale. My mother rejoiced over the very small scale of his operations; and when my father regretted, as he did very often, that no more land was to be purchased in the neighbourhood, I could see her setting herself a sum in her head, "If on twelve acres he manages to lose a hundred pounds a year, what would be our loss on a hundred and fifty?" But when my father was pushed hard on the subject of the money he spent in his sailor-like farming, he had one constant retreat:

"Think of the health, and the pleasure we all of us take in the cultivation of the fields around us! It is something for us to do, and to look forward to every

day." And this was so true that, as long as my father
confined himself to these arguments, my mother left him
unmolested : but to strangers he was still apt to enlarge
on the returns his farm brought him in; and he had
often to pull up in his statements when he caught the
warning glance of my mother's eye, showing him that
she was not so much absorbed in her own conversation
as to be deaf to his voice. But as for the happiness
that arose out of our mode of life, that was not to be
calculated by tens or hundreds of pounds. There were
only two of us, my sister and myself; and my mother
undertook the greater part of our education. We helped
her in her household cares during part of the morning;
then came an old-fashioned routine of lessons, such as
she herself had learnt when a girl—Goldsmith's *History
of England*, Rollins's *Ancient History*, Lindley Murray's
Grammar, and plenty of sewing, and stitching.

My mother used sometimes to sigh, and wish that she
could buy us a piano, and teach us what little music she
knew; but many of my dear father's habits were expen-
sive; at least, for a person possessed of no larger an
income than he had. Besides the quiet and unsuspected
drain of his agricultural pursuits, he was of a social turn;
enjoying the dinners to which he was invited by his more
affluent neighbours; and especially delighted in returning them the compliment, and giving them choice little
entertainments, which would have been yet more fre-
quent in their recurrence than they were, if it had not
been for my mother's prudence. But we never were able
to purchase the piano; it required a greater outlay of
ready money than we ever possessed. I daresay we
should have grown up ignorant of any language but our

own if it had not been for my father's social habits, which led to our learning French in a very unexpected manner. He and my mother went to dine with General Ashburton, one of the forest rangers; and there they met with an emigrant gentleman, a Monsieur de Chalabre, who had escaped in a wonderful manner, and at terrible peril to his life; and was, consequently, in our small forest-circle, a great lion, and a worthy cause of a series of dinner parties. His first entertainer, General Ashburton, had known him in France, under very different circumstances; and he was not prepared for the quiet and dignified request made by his guest, one afternoon after M. de Chalabre had been about a fortnight in the forest, that the general would recommend him as a French teacher, if he could conscientiously do so.

To the general's remonstrances, M. de Chalabre smilingly replied, by an assurance that his assumption of his new occupation could only be for a short time; that the good cause would—*must* triumph. It was before the fatal 21st of January, 1793; and then, still smiling, he strengthened his position by quoting innumerable instances out of the classics, of heroes and patriots, generals and commanders, who had been reduced by Fortune's frolics to adopt some occupation far below their original one. He closed his speech with informing the general that, relying upon his kindness in acting as referee, he had taken lodgings for a few months at a small farm which was in the centre of our forest circle of acquaintances. The general was too thoroughly a gentleman to say anything more than that he should be most happy to do whatever he could to forward M. de

Chalabre's plans; and as my father was the first person whom he met with after this conversation, it was announced to us, on the very evening of the day on which it had taken place, that we were forthwith to learn French; and I verily believe that, if my father could have persuaded my mother to join him, we should have formed a French class of father, mother, and two head of daughters, so touched had my father been by the general's account of M. de Chalabre's present desires, as compared with the high estate from which he had fallen. Accordingly, we were installed in the dignity of his first French pupils. My father was anxious that we should have a lesson every other day, ostensibly that we might get on all the more speedily, but really that he might have a larger quarterly bill to pay; at any rate, until M. de Chalabre had more of his time occupied with instruction. But my mother gently interfered, and calmed her husband down into two lessons a week, which was, she said, as much as we could manage. Those happy lessons! I remember them now, at the distance of more than fifty years. Our house was situated on the edge of the forest; our fields were, in fact, cleared out of it. It was not good land for clover; but my father would always sow one particular field with clover seed, because my mother was so fond of the fragrant scent in her evening walks, and through this a footpath ran which led into the forest.

A quarter of a mile beyond—a walk on the soft, fine, springy turf, and under the long, low branches of the beech-trees—and we arrived at the old red-brick farm where M. de Chalabre was lodging. Not that we went there to take our lessons; that would have been an

offence to his spirit of politeness; but as my father and
mother were his nearest neighbours, there was a constant
interchange of small messages and notes, which we little
girls were only too happy to take to our dear M. de
Chalabre.   Moreover, if our lessons with my mother
were ended pretty early, she would say—" You have
been good girls; now you may run to the high point in
the clover-field, and see if M. de Chalabre is coming;
and if he is, you may walk with him; but take care and
give him the cleanest part of the path, for you know he
does not like to dirty his boots."

This was all very well in theory; but, like many
theories, the difficulty was to put it in practice. If we
slipped to the side of the path where the water lay
longest, he bowed and retreated behind us to a still
wetter place, leaving the clean part for us; yet when
we got home, his polished boots would be without a
speck, while our shoes were covered with mud.

Another little ceremony which we had to get accustomed to, was his habit of taking off his hat as we ap-
proached, and walking by us holding it in his hand. To be
sure, he wore a wig, delicately powdered, frizzed, and tied
in a queue behind; but we had always a feeling that he
would catch cold, and that he was doing us too great an
honour, and that he did not know how old or rather how
young we were, until one day we saw him (far away from
our house) hand a countrywoman over a stile with the
same kind of dainty, courteous politeness, lifting her
basket of eggs over first; and then, taking up the silk-
lined lapel of his coat, he spread it on the palm of his
hand for her to rest her fingers upon; instead of which,
she took his small white hand in her plump, vigorous

gripe, and leant her full weight upon him. He carried
her basket for her as far as their roads lay together;
and from that time we were less shy in receiving his
courtesies, perceiving that he considered them as deference due to our sex, however old or young, or rich or
poor. So, as I said, we came down from the clover-field
in rather a stately manner, and through the wicket-gate
that opened into our garden, which was as rich in its
scents of varied kinds as the clover-field had been in its
one pure fragrance. My mother would meet us here;
and somehow—our life was passed as much out of doors
as in-doors, both winter and summer—we seemed to
have our French lessons more frequently in the garden
than in the house; for there was a sort of arbour on the
lawn near the drawing-room window, to which we always
found it easy to carry a table and chairs, and all the rest
of the lesson paraphernalia, if my mother did not prohibit
a lesson al fresco.

M. de Calabre wore, as a sort of morning costume,
a coat, waistcoat, and breeches, all made of a kind of
coarse grey cloth, which he had bought in the neighbourhood. His three-cornered hat was brushed to a
nicety, his wig sat as no one else's did. (My father's
was always awry.) And the only thing wanting to his
costume when he came was a flower. Sometimes I
fancied he purposely omitted gathering one of the roses
that clustered up the farm-house in which he lodged, in
order to afford my mother the pleasure of culling her
choicest carnations and roses to make him up his nose-
gay, or " posy," as he liked to call it. He had picked up
that pretty country word, and adopted it as an especial
favourite, dwelling on the first syllable with all the

"We came down from the clover-field in rather a stately manner"

p. 224.

languid softness of an Italian accent. Many a time have Mary and I tried to say it like him, we did so admire his way of speaking.

Once seated round the table, whether in the house or out of it, we were bound to attend to our lessons; and somehow he made us perceive that it was a part of the same chivalrous code that made him so helpful to the helpless, to enforce the slightest claim of duty to the full. No half-prepared lessons for him! The patience, and the resource with which he illustrated and enforced every precept; the untiring gentleness with which he made our stubborn English tongues pronounce, and mispronounce, and re-pronounce certain words; above all, the sweetness of temper which never varied, were such as I have never seen equalled. If we wondered at these qualities when we were children, how much greater has been our surprise at their existence since we have been grown up, and have learnt that, until his emigration, he was a man of rapid and impulsive action, with the imperfect education implied in the circumstance, that at fifteen he was a sous-lieutenant in the Queen's regiment, and must, consequently, have had to apply himself hard and conscientiously to master the language which he had in after-life to teach.

Twice we had holidays to suit his sad convenience. Holidays with us were not at Christmas, and Midsummer, Easter, and Michaelmas. If my mother was unusually busy, we had what we called a holiday, though, in reality, it involved harder work than our regular lessons; but we fetched, and carried, and ran errands, and became rosy, and dusty, and sang merry songs in the gaiety of our hearts. If the day was

15

remarkably fine, my dear father—whose spirits were
rather apt to vary with the weather—would come bursting in with his bright, kind, bronzed face, and carry
the day by storm with my mother. "It was a shame to
coop such young things up in a house," he would say,
"when every other young animal was frolicking in the
air and sunshine. Grammar!—what was that but the
art of arranging words?—and he never knew a woman
but could do that fast enough. Geography!—he would
undertake to teach us more geography in one winter
evening, telling us of the countries where he had been,
with just a map before him, than we could learn in ten
years with that stupid book, all full of hard words. As
for the French—why, that must be learnt; for he should
not like M. de Chalabre to think we slighted the lessons
he took so much pains to give us; but surely we could
get up the earlier to learn our French." We promised
by acclamation; and my mother—sometimes smilingly,
sometimes reluctantly—was always compelled to yield.
And these were the usual occasions for our holidays.
But twice we had a fortnight's entire cessation of French
lessons: once in January, and once in October. Nor
did we even see our dear French master during those
periods. We went several times to the top of the clover-
field, to search the dark green outskirts of the forest
with our busy eyes; and if we could have seen his figure
in that shade, I am sure we should have scampered to
him, forgetful of the prohibition which made the forest
forbidden ground. But we did not see him.

It was the fashion in those days to keep children much
less informed than they are now on the subjects which
interest their parents. A sort of hieroglyphic or cypher

talk was used in order to conceal the meaning of much
that was said if children were present. My mother was
a proficient in this way of talking, and took, we fancied, a
certain pleasure in perplexing my father by inventing
a new cypher, as it were, every day. For instance, for
some time, I was called Martia, because I was very tall
of my age; and, just as my father began to understand
the name—and, it must be owned, a good while after I
had learnt to prick up my ears whenever Martia was
named — my mother suddenly changed me into the
" buttress," from the habit I had acquired of leaning my
languid length against a wall. I saw my father's per-
plexity about this " buttress " for some days, and could
have helped him out of it, but I durst not. And so, when
the unfortunate Louis the Sixteenth was executed, the
news was too terrible to be put into plain English, and
too terrible also to be made known to us children, nor
could we at once find the clue to the cypher in which it
was spoken about. We heard about " the Iris being
blown down; " and saw my father's honest loyal excitement about it, and the quiet reserve which always
betokened some secret grief on my mother's part.

We had no French lessons; and somehow the poor,
battered, storm-torn Iris was to blame for this. It was
many weeks after this before we knew the full reason of
M. de Chalabre's deep depression when he again came
amongst us; why he shook his head when my mother
timidly offered him some snowdrops on that first morning on which we began lessons again; why he wore the
deep mourning of that day, when all of the dress that
could be black was black, and the white muslin frills
and ruffles were unstarched and limp, as if to bespeak the

15—2

very abandonment of grief. We knew well enough the
meaning of the next hieroglyphic announcement—" The
wicked, cruel boys had broken off the White Lily's
head ! " That beautiful queen, whose portrait once had
been shown to us, with her blue eyes, and her fair reso-
lute look, her profusion of lightly-powdered hair, her
white neck adorned with strings of pearls. We could
have cried, if we had dared, when we heard the trans-
parent mysterious words. We did cry at night, sitting
up in bed, with our arms round each other's necks, and
vowing, in our weak, passionate, childish way, that if
we lived long enough, that lady's death avenged should
be. No one who cannot remember that time can tell
the shudder of horror that thrilled through the country
at hearing of this last execution. At the moment, there
was no time for any consideration of the silent horrors
endured for centuries by the people, who at length rose
in their madness against their rulers. This last blow
changed our dear M. de Chalabre. I never saw him
again in quite the same gaiety of heart as before this time.
There seemed to be tears very close behind his smiles
for ever after. My father went to see him when he had
been about a week absent from us—no reason given, for
did not we, did not every one, know the horror the sun
had looked upon ! As soon as my father had gone, my
mother gave it in charge to us to make the dressing-
room belonging to our guest-chamber as much like a
sitting-room as possible. My father hoped to bring back
M. de Chalabre for a visit to us; but he would probably
like to be a good deal alone; and we might move any
article of furniture we liked, if we only thought it would
make him comfortable.

I believe General Ashburton had been on a somewhat similar errand to my father's before ; but he had failed. My father gained his point, as I afterwards learnt, in a very unconscious and characteristic manner. He had urged his invitation on M. de Chalabre, and received such a decided negative that he was hopeless, and quitted the subject. Then M. de Chalabre began to relieve his heart by telling him all the details ; my father held his breath to listen—at last, his honest heart could contain itself no longer, and the tears ran down his face. His unaffected sympathy touched M. de Chalabre inexpressibly ; and in an hour after we saw our dear French master coming down the clover-field slope, leaning on my father's arm, which he had involuntarily offered as a support to one in trouble—although he was slightly lame, and ten or fifteen years older than M. de Chalabre.

For a year after that time, M. de Chalabre never wore any flowers ; and after that, to the day of his death, no gay or coloured rose or carnation could tempt him. We secretly observed his taste, and always took care to bring him white flowers for his posy. I noticed, too, that on his left arm, under his coat sleeve (sleeves were made very open then), he always wore a small band of black crape. He lived to be eighty-one, but he had the black crape band on when he died.

M. de Chalabre was a favourite in all the forest circle. He was a great acquisition to the sociable dinner parties that were perpetually going on ; and though some of the families piqued themselves on being aristocratic, and turned up their noses at any one who had been engaged in trade, however largely, M. de Chalabre, in right of his good blood, his loyalty, his daring *preux chevalier* actions, was ever an honoured guest. He took his poverty, and the simple habits it enforced, so naturally and gaily, as a mere trifling accident of his life, about which neither concealment nor shame could be necessary, that the very servants—often so much more pseudo-aristocratic than their masters—loved and respected the French gentleman, who, perhaps, came to teach in the mornings, and in the evenings made his appearance dressed with dainty neatness as a dinner guest. He came lightly prancing through the forest mire; and, in our little hall, at any rate, he would pull out a neat minute case containing a blacking-brush and blacking, and repolish his boots, speaking gaily, in his broken English, to the footman all the time. That blacking-case was his own making; he had a genius for using his fingers. After our lessons were over, he relaxed into the familiar house friend, the merry playfellow. We lived far from any carpenter or joiner; if a lock was out of order, M. de Chalabre made it right for us. If any box was wanted, his ingenious fingers had made it before our lesson day. He turned silk-winders for my mother, made a set of chessmen for my father, carved an elegant watch-case out of a rough beef-bone, dressed up little cork dolls for us—in short, as he said, his heart would have been broken but for his joiner's tools. Nor were his ingenious gifts employed for us alone. The farmer's wife where he lodged had numerous contrivances in her house which he had made. One particularly which I remember was a paste-board, made after a French pattern, which would not slip about on a dresser, as he had observed her English paste-board do. Susan, the farmer's ruddy daughter, had her work-box, too, to show us; and her cousin-lover had a wonderful stick, with an extraordinary demon head carved upon it;—all by M. de Chalabre. Farmer, farmer's wife, Susan, Robert, and all were full of his praises.

We grew from children into girls—from girls into women; and still M. de Chalabre taught on in the forest; still he was beloved and honoured; still no dinner-party within five miles was thought complete without him, and ten miles' distance strove to offer him a bed sooner than miss his company. The pretty, merry Susan of sixteen had been jilted by the faithless Robert, and was now a comely, demure damsel of thirty-one or two; still waiting upon M. de Chalabre, and still constant in respectfully singing his praises. My own poor mother was dead; my sister was engaged to be married to a young lieutenant, who was with his ship in the Mediterranean. My father was as youthful as ever in heart, and, indeed, in many of his ways; only his hair was quite white, and the old lameness was more frequently troublesome than it had been. An uncle of his had left him a considerable fortune, so he farmed away to his heart's content, and lost an annual sum of money with the best grace and the lightest heart in the world. There were not even the gentle reproaches of my mother's eyes to be dreaded now.

Things were in this state when the peace of 1814 was declared. We had heard so many and such contradictory rumours that we were inclined to doubt even the *Gazette* at last, and were discussing probabilities with some vehemence, when M. de Chalabre entered the room unannounced and breathless:

"My friends, give me joy!" he said. "The Bourbons"—he could not go on; his features, nay, his very fingers, worked with agitation, but he could not speak. My father hastened to relieve him.

"We have heard the good news (you see, girls, it is quite true this time). I do congratulate you, my dear friend. I *am* glad." And he seized M. de Chalabre's hand in his own hearty gripe, and brought the nervous agitation of the latter to a close by unconsciously administering a pretty severe dose of wholesome pain.

"I go to London. I go straight this afternoon to see my sovereign. My sovereign holds a court to-morrow at Grillon's Hotel; I go to pay him my *devoirs*. I put on my uniform of Gardes du Corps, which have lain by these many years; a little old, a little worm-eaten, but never mind; they have been seen by Marie Antoinette, which gives them a grace for ever." He walked about the room in a nervous, hurried way. There was something on his mind, and we signed to my father to be silent for a moment or two, and let it come out. "No!" said M. de Chalabre, after a moment's pause. "I cannot say adieu; for I shall return to say, dear friends, my adieux. I did come a poor emigrant; noble Englishmen took me for their friend, and welcomed me to their houses. Chalabre is one large mansion, and my English friends will not forsake me; they will come and see me in my own country; and, for their sakes, not an English beggar shall pass the doors of Chalabre without being warmed and clothed and fed. I will not say adieu. I go now but for two days."

CHAPTER II.

My father insisted upon driving M. de Chalabre in his gig to the nearest town through which the London mail passed; and, during the short time that elapsed before my father was ready, he told us something more about Chalabre. He had never spoken of his ancestral home to any of us before; we knew little of his station in his own country. General Ashburton had met with him in Paris, in a set where a man was judged of by his wit and talent for society, and general brilliance of character, rather than by his wealth and hereditary position. Now we learned for the first time that he was heir to considerable estates in Normandy; to an old Château Chalabre; all of which he had forfeited by his emigration, it was true, but that was under another régime.

"Ah! if my dear friend, your poor mother, were alive now, I could send her such slips of rare and splendid roses from Chalabre. Often when I did see her nursing up some poor little specimen, I longed in secret for my rose garden at Chalabre. And the orangerie! Ah! Miss Fanny, the bride must come to Chalabre who wishes for a beautiful wreath." This was an allusion to my sister's engagement; a fact well known to him, as the faithful family friend.

My father came back in high spirits; and began to plan that very evening how to arrange his crops for the ensuing year, so as best to spare time for a visit to

Château Chalabre ; and as for us, I think we believed
that there was no need to delay our French journey
beyond the autumn of the present year.

M. de Chalabre came back in a couple of days; a
little damped, we girls fancied, though we hardly liked
to speak about it to my father. However, M. de
Chalabre explained it to us by saying that he had found
London more crowded and busy than he had expected;
that it was smoky and dismal after leaving the country,
where the trees were already coming into leaf; and,
when we pressed him a little more respecting the reception at Grillon's, he laughed at himself for having forgotten the tendency of the Count de Provence in former
days to become stout, and so being dismayed at the
mass of corpulence which Louis the Eighteenth presented, as he toiled up the long drawing-room of the
hotel.

"But what did he say to you?" Fanny asked. "How
did he receive you when you were presented?"

A flash of pain passed over his face; but it was gone
directly.

"Oh! his majesty did not recognize my name. It
was hardly to be expected he would; though it is a name
of note in Normandy; and I have——well! that is
worth nothing. The Duc de Duras reminded him of
a circumstance or two, which I had almost hoped his
majesty would not have forgotten; but I myself forgot
the pressure of long years of exile; it was no wonder he
did not remember me. He said he hoped to see me at
the Tuileries. His hopes are my laws. I go to prepare
for my departure. If his majesty does not need my
sword, I turn it into a ploughshare at Chalabre. Ah!

my friend, I will not forget there all the agricultural science I have learned from you.

A gift of a hundred pounds would not have pleased my father so much as this last speech. He began forthwith to inquire about the nature of the soil, &c., in a way which made our poor M. de Chalabre shrug his shoulders in despairing ignorance.

"Never mind!" said my father. "Rome was not built in a day. It was a long time before I learnt all that I know now. I was afraid I could not leave home this autumn, but I perceive you'll need some one to advise you about laying out the ground for next year's crops."

So M. de Chalabre left our neighbourhood, with the full understanding that we were to pay him a visit in his Norman château in the following September; nor was he content until he had persuaded every one who had shown him kindness to promise him a visit at some appointed time. As for his old landlord at the farm, the comely dame, and buxom Susan—they, we found, were to be franked there and back, under the pretence that the French dairymaids had no notion of cleanliness, any more than that the French farming men were judges of stock; so it was absolutely necessary to bring over some one from England to put the affairs of the Château Chalabre in order; and Farmer Dobson and his wife considered the favour quite reciprocal.

For some time we did not hear from our friend. The war had made the post between France and England very uncertain; so we were obliged to wait, and we tried to be patient; but, somehow, our autumn visit to France was silently given up; and my father gave us long expo-

sitions of the disordered state of affairs in a country
which had suffered so much as France, and lectured us
severely on the folly of having expected to hear so
soon.   We knew, all the while, that the exposition was
repeated to soothe his own impatience, and that the
admonition to patience was what he felt that he himself
was needing.

At last the letter came.   There was a brave attempt
at cheerfulness in it, which nearly made me cry, more
than any complaints would have done.   M. de Chalabre
had hoped to retain his commission as sous-lieutenant in
the Gardes du Corps—a commission signed by Louis the
Sixteenth himself, in 1791.   But the regiment was to
be remodelled, or re-formed, I forget which; and M. de
Chalabre assured us that his was not the only case
where applicants had been refused.   He had then tried
for a commission in the Cent Suisses, the Gardes du
Porte, the Mousquetaires—but all were full.   "Was it
not a glorious thing for France to have so many brave
sons ready to fight on the side of honour and loyalty?"
To which question Fanny replied "that it was a shame;"
and my father, after a grunt or two, comforted himself
by saying, "that M. de Chalabre would have the more
time to attend to his neglected estate."

That winter was full of incidents in our home.   As it
often happens when a family has seemed stationary, and
secure from change for years, and then at last one important event happens, another is sure to follow.   Fanny's
lover returned, and they were married, and left us alone
—my father and I.   Her husband's ship was stationed
in the Mediterranean, and she was to go and live at
Malta, with some of his relations there.   I know not if

it was the agitation of parting with her, but my father was stricken down from health into confirmed invalidism, by a paralytic stroke, soon after her departure, and my interests were confined to the fluctuating reports of a sick room. I did not care for the foreign intelligence which was shaking Europe with an universal tremour. My hopes, my fears were centred in one frail human body—my dearly beloved, my most loving father. I kept a letter in my pocket for days from M. de Chalabre, unable to find the time to decipher his French hieroglyphics; at last I read it aloud to my poor father, rather as a test of his power of enduring interest, than because I was impatient to know what it contained. The news in it was depressing enough, as everything else seemed to be that gloomy winter. A rich manufacturer of Rouen had bought the Château Chalabre; forfeited to the nation by its former possessor's emigration. His son, M. du Fay, was well-affected towards Louis the Eighteenth—at least as long as his government was secure and promised to be stable, so as not to affect the dyeing and selling of Turkey-red wools; and so the natural legal consequence was, that M. du Fay, Fils, was not to be disturbed in his purchased and paid-for property. My father cared to hear of this disappointment to our poor friend—cared just for one day, and forgot all about it the next. Then came the return from Elba—the hurrying events of that spring—the battle of Waterloo; and to my poor father, in his second childhood, the choice of a daily pudding was far more important than all.

One Sunday, in that August of 1815, I went to church. It was many weeks since I had been able

to leave my father for so long a time before. Since I
had been last there to worship, it seemed as if my youth
had passed away—gone without a warning—leaving no
trace behind. After service, I went through the long
grass to the unfrequented part of the churchyard where
my dear mother lay buried. A garland of brilliant
yellow immortelles lay on her grave; and the unwonted
offering took me by surprise. I knew of the foreign
custom, although I had never seen the kind of wreath
before. I took it up, and read one word in the black
floral letters; it was simply " Adieu." I knew, from
the first moment I saw it, that M. de Chalabre must
have returned to England. Such a token of regard
was like him, and could spring from no one else. But I
wondered a little that we had never heard or seen anything of him; nothing, in fact, since Lady Ashburton
had told me that her husband had met with him in
Belgium, hurrying to offer himself as a volunteer to one
of the eleven generals appointed by the Duc de Feltre
to receive such applications. General Ashburton himself had since this died at Brussels, in consequence of
wounds received at Waterloo. As the recollection of all
these circumstances gathered in my mind, I found I was
drawing near the field-path which led out of the direct
road home, to farmer Dobson's; and thither I suddenly
determined to go, and hear if they had learnt anything
respecting their former lodger. As I went up the garden-
walk leading to the house, I caught M. de Chalabre's
eye; he was gazing abstractedly out of the window of
what used to be his sitting-room. In an instant he had
joined me in the garden. If my youth had flown, his
youth, and middle-age as well, had vanished altogether.

He looked older by at least twenty years than when he had left us twelve months ago. How much of this was owing to the change in the arrangement of his dress, I cannot tell. He had formerly been remarkably dainty in all these things; now he was careless, even to the verge of slovenliness. He asked after my sister, after my father, in a manner which evinced the deepest, most respectful interest; but, somehow, it appeared to me as if he hurried question after question, rather to stop any inquiries which I, in my turn, might wish to make.

"I return here to my duties; to my only duties. The good God has not seen me fit to undertake any higher. Henceforth I am the faithful French teacher; the diligent, punctual French teacher: nothing more. But I do hope to teach the French language as becomes a gentleman and a Christian; to do my best. Henceforth the grammar and the syntax are my estate, my coat of arms." He said this with a proud humility which prevented any reply. I could only change the subject, and urge him to come and see my poor sick father. He replied,—

"To visit the sick, that is my duty as well as my pleasure. For the mere society—I renounce all that. That is now beyond my position, to which I accommodate myself with all my strength."

Accordingly, when he came to spend an hour with my father, he brought a small bundle of printed papers, announcing the terms on which M. Chalabre (the " de " was dropped now and for evermore) was desirous of teaching French, and a little paragraph at the bottom of the page solicited the patronage of schools. Now this was a great coming-down. In former days, non-

teaching at schools had been the line which marked
that M. de Chalabre had taken up teaching rather as an
amateur profession, than with any intention of devoting
his life to it. He respectfully asked me to distribute
these papers where I thought fit. I say " respectfully "
advisedly; there was none of the old deferential gal-
lantry, as offered by a gentleman to a lady, his equal in
birth and fortune—instead, there was the matter-of-fact
request and statement which a workman offers to his
employer. Only in my father's room, he was the former
M. de Chalabre; he seemed to understand how vain would
be all attempts to recount or explain the circumstances
which had led him so decidedly to take a lower level
in society. To my father, to the day of his death,
M. de Chalabre maintained the old easy footing; assumed
a gaiety which he never even pretended to feel anywhere
else; listened to my father's childish interests with a
true and kindly sympathy for which I ever felt grateful,
although he purposely put a deferential reserve between
him and me, as a barrier to any expression of such feeling on my part.

His former lessons had been held in such high esteem
by those who were privileged to receive them, that he
was soon sought after on all sides. The schools of the
two principal county towns put forward their claims, and
considered it a favour to receive his instructions. Morning, noon, and night he was engaged; even if he had
not proudly withdrawn himself from all merely society
engagements, he would have had no leisure for them.
His only visits were paid to my father, who looked for
them with a kind of childish longing. One day, to my
surprise, he asked to be allowed to speak to me for an

instant alone. He stood silent for a moment, turning his hat in his hand.

"You have a right to know—you, my first pupil; next Tuesday, I marry myself to Miss Susan Dobson—good, respectable woman, to whose happiness I mean to devote my life, or as much of it as is not occupied with the duties of instruction." He looked up at me, expecting congratulations, perhaps; but I was too much stunned with my surprise: the buxom, red-armed, apple-cheeked Susan, who, when she blushed, blushed the colour of beet-root; who did not know a word of French; who regarded the nation (always excepting the gentleman before me) as frog-eating Mounseers, the national enemies of England! I afterwards thought that perhaps this very ignorance constituted one of her charms. No word, nor allusion, nor expressive silence, nor regretful sympathetic sighs, could remind M. de Chalabre of the bitter past, which he was evidently striving to forget. And, most assuredly, never man had a more devoted and admiring wife than poor Susan made M. de Chalabre. She was a little awed by him, to be sure; never quite at her ease before him; but I imagine husbands do not dislike such a tribute to their Jupiter-ship. Madame Chalabre received my call, after their marriage, with a degree of sober, rustic, happy dignity, which I could not have foreseen in Susan Dobson. They had taken a small cottage on the borders of the forest; it had a garden round it; and the cow, pigs, and poultry, which were to be her charge, found their keep in the forest. She had a rough country servant to assist her in looking after them; and in what scanty leisure he had, her husband attended to the garden and the bees. Madame

16

Chalabre took me over the neatly furnished cottage with evident pride. "Moussire," as she called him, had done this; Moussire had fitted up that. Moussire was evidently a man of resource. In a little closet of a dressing-room belonging to Moussire, there hung a pencil drawing, elaborately finished to the condition of a bad pocket-book engraving. It caught my eye, and I lingered to look at it. It represented a high, narrow house, of considerable size, with four pepper-box turrets at each corner; and a stiff avenue formed the foreground.

"Château Chalabre?" said I, inquisitively.

"I never asked," my companion replied. "Moussire does not always like to be asked questions. It is the picture of some place he is very fond of, for he won't let me dust it for fear I should smear it."

M. de Chalabre's marriage did not diminish the number of his visits to my father. Until that beloved parent's death, he was faithful in doing all he could to lighten the gloom of the sick-room. But a chasm, which he had opened, separated any present intercourse with him from the free, unreserved friendship that had existed formerly. And yet for his sake I used to go and see his wife. I could not forget early days, nor the walks to the top of the clover-field, nor the daily posies, nor my mother's dear regard for the emigrant gentleman; nor a thousand little kindnesses which he had shown to my absent sister and myself. He did not forget either in the closed and sealed chambers of his heart. So, for his sake, I tried to become a friend to his wife; and she learned to look upon me as such. It was my employment in the sick chamber to make clothes for the little expected Chalabre baby; and its mother would fain (as she told me) have asked me to carry the little infant to the font, but that her husband somewhat austerely reminded her that they ought to seek a *marraine* among those of their own station in society. But I regarded the pretty little Susan as my god-child never-theless in my heart; and secretly pledged myself always to take an interest in her. Not two months after my father's death, a sister was born; and the human heart in M. de Chalabre subdued his pride; the child was to bear the pretty name of his French mother, although France could find no place for him, and had cast him out. That youngest little girl was called Aimée.

When my father died, Fanny and her husband urged me to leave Brookfield, and come and live with them at Valetta. The estate was left to us; but an eligible tenant offered himself; and my health, which had suf-fered materially during my long nursing, did render it desirable for me to seek some change to a warmer climate. So I went abroad, ostensibly for a year's residence only; but, somehow, that year has grown into a lifetime. Malta and Genoa have been my dwell-ing-places ever since. Occasionally, it is true, I have paid visits to England, but I have never looked upon it as my home since I left it thirty years ago. During these visits I have seen the Chalabres. He had become more absorbed in his occupation than ever; had pub-lished a French grammar on some new principle, of which he presented me with a copy, taking some pains to explain how it was to be used. Madame looked plump and prosperous; the farm, which was under her management, had thriven; and as for the two daughters,

16—2

behind their English shyness, they had a good deal of French piquancy and *esprit*. I induced them to take some walks with me, with a view of asking them some questions which should make our friendship an individual reality, not merely an hereditary feeling; but the little monkeys put me through my catechism, and asked me innumerable questions about France, which they evidently regarded as their country. "How do you know all about French habits and customs?" asked I. "Does Monsieur de—does your father talk to you much about France?"

"Sometimes, when we are alone with him—never when any one is by," answered Susan, the elder, a grave, noble-looking girl, of twenty or thereabouts. "I think he does not speak about France before my mother, for fear of hurting her."

"And I think," said little Aimée, "that he does not speak at all, when he can help it; it is only when his heart gets too full with recollections, that he is obliged to talk to us, because many of the thoughts could not be said in English."

"Then, I suppose, you are two famous French scholars?"

"Oh, yes! Papa always speaks to us in French; it is our own language."

But with all their devotion to their father and to his country, they were most affectionate, dutiful daughters to their mother. They were her companions, her comforts in the pleasant household labours; most practical, useful young women. But in a privacy not the less sacred, because it was understood rather than prescribed, they kept all the enthusiasm, all the romance of their nature, for their father. They were the confidantes of that poor exile's yearnings for France; the eager listeners for what he chose to tell them of his early days. His words wrought up Susan to make the resolution that, if ever she felt herself free from home duties and responsibilities, she would become a Sister of Charity, like Anne-Marguérite de Chalabre, her father's great-aunt, and model of woman's sanctity. As for Aimée, come what might, she never would leave her father; and that was all she was clear about in picturing her future.

Three years ago I was in Paris. An English friend of mine who lives there—English by birth, but married to a German professor, and very French in manners and ways—asked me to come to her house one evening. I was far from well, and disinclined to stir out.

"Oh, but come!" said she. "I have a good reason; really a tempting reason. Perhaps this very evening a piece of poetical justice will be done in my *salon*. A living romance! Now, can you resist?"

"What is it?" said I; for she was rather in the habit of exaggerating trifles into romances.

"A young lady is coming; not in the first youth, but still young, very pretty; daughter of a French *émigré*, whom my husband knew in Belgium, and who has lived in England ever since."

"I beg your pardon, but what is her name?" interrupted I, roused to interest.

"De Chalabre. Do you know her?"

"Yes; I am much interested in her. I will gladly come to meet her. How long has she been in Paris? Is it Susan or Aimée?"

"Now I am not to be baulked of the pleasure of telling you my romance; my hoped-for bit of poetical justice. You must be patient, and you will have answers to all your questions."

I sank back in my easy chair. Some of my friends are rather long-winded, and it is as well to be settled in a comfortable position before they begin to talk.

"I told you a minute ago, that my husband had become acquainted with M. de Chalabre in Belgium, in 1815. They have kept up a correspondence ever since; not a very brisk one, it is true, for M. de Chalabre was a French master in England, and my husband a professor in Paris; but still they managed to let each other know how they were going on, and what they were doing, once, if not twice every year. For myself, I never saw M. de Chalabre."

"I know him well," said I. "I have known him all my life."

"A year ago his wife died (she was an Englishwoman); she had had a long and suffering illness; and his eldest daughter had devoted herself to her with the patient sweetness of an angel, as he told us, and I can well believe. But after her mother's death, the world, it seems, became distasteful to her: she had been inured to the half-lights, the hushed voices, the constant thought for others required in a sick-room, and the noise and rough bustle of healthy people jarred upon her. So she pleaded with her father to allow her to become a Sister of Charity. She told him that he would have given a welcome to any suitor who came to offer to marry her, and bear her away from her home, and her father and sister; and now, when she was called by

religion, would he grudge to part with her? He gave
his consent, if not his full approbation; and he wrote to
my husband to beg me to receive her here, while we
sought out a convent into which she could be received.
She has been with me two months, and endeared herself to me unspeakably; she goes home next week
unless——"

"But, I beg your pardon; did you not say she wished
to become a Sister of Charity?"

"It is true; but she was too old to be admitted into
their order. She is eight-and-twenty. It has been a
grievous disappointment to her; she has borne it very
patiently and meekly, but I can see how deeply she has
felt it. And now for my romance. My husband had a
pupil some ten years ago, a M. du Fay, a clever,
scientific young man, one of the first merchants of
Rouen. His grandfather purchased M. de Chalabre's
ancestral estate. The present M. du Fay came on
business to Paris two or three days ago, and invited my
husband to a little dinner; and somehow this story of
Suzette Chalabre came out, in consequence of inquiries
my husband was making for an escort to take her to
England. M. du Fay seemed interested with the story;
and asked my husband if he might pay his respects
to me, some evening when Suzette should be in,—
and so is coming to-night, he, and a friend of his,
who was at the dinner party the other day; will you
come?"

I went, more in the hope of seeing Susan Chalabre,
and hearing some news about my early home, than with
any expectation of "poetical justice." And in that I
was right; and yet I was wrong. Susan Chalabre was

a grave, gentle woman, of an enthusiastic and devoted appearance, not unlike that portrait of his daughter which arrests every eye in Ary Scheffer's sacred pictures. She was silent and sad; her cherished plan of life was uprooted. She talked to me a little in a soft and friendly manner, answering any questions I asked; but, as for gentlemen, her indifference and reserve made it impossible for them to enter into any conversation with her; and the meeting was indisputably " flat."

" Oh! my romance! my poetical justice! Before the evening was half over, I would have given up all my castles in the air for one well-sustained conversation of ten minutes long. Now don't laugh at me, for I can't bear it to-night." Such was my friend's parting speech. I did not see her again for two days. The third she came in glowing with excitement.

" You may congratulate me after all; if it was not poetical justice, it is prosaic justice; and, except for the empty romance, that is a better thing! "

" What do you mean? " said I. " Surely M. du Fay has not proposed for Susan? "

" No! but that charming M. de Frez, his friend, has; that is to say, not proposed but spoken; no, not spoken, but it seems he asked M. du Fay—whose confidant he was—if he was intending to proceed in his idea of marrying Suzette; and on hearing that he was not, M. de Frez said that he should come to us, and ask us to put him in the way of prosecuting the acquaintance, for that he had been charmed with her; looks, voice, silence, he admires them all; and we have arranged that he is to be the escort to England; he has business there, he says; and as for Suzette (she knows nothing of all this, of course, for who dared tell her?), all her anxiety is to return home, and the first person travelling to England will satisfy her, if it does us. And, after all, M. de Frez lives within five leagues of the Château Chalabre, so she can go and see the old place whenever she will."

When I went to bid Susan good-by, she looked as unconscious and dignified as ever. No idea of a lover had ever crossed her mind. She considered M. de Frez as a kind of necessary incumbrance for the journey. I had not much hopes for him; and yet he was an agreeable man enough, and my friends told me that his character stood firm and high.

In three months, I was settled for the winter in Rome. In four, I heard that the marriage of Susan Chalabre had taken place. What were the intermediate steps between the cold, civil indifference with which I had last seen her regarding her travelling companion, and the full love with which such a woman as Suzette Chalabre must love a man before she could call him husband, I never learnt. I wrote to my old French master to congratulate him, as I believed I honestly might, on his daughter's marriage. It was some months before I received his answer. It was—

"Dear friend, dear old pupil, dear child of the beloved dead, I am an old man of eighty, and I tremble towards the grave. I cannot write many words; but my own hand shall bid you come to the home of Aimée and her husband. They tell me to ask you to come and see the old father's birth-place, while he is yet alive to show it to you. I have the very apartment in Château Chalabre that was mine when I was a boy, and my mother came in to bless me every night. Susan lives near us. The good God bless my sons-in-law, Bertrand de Frez and Alphonse du Fay, as He has blest me all my life long. I think of your father and mother, my dear; and you must think no harm when I tell you I have had masses said for the repose of their souls. If I make a mistake, God will forgive."

My heart could have interpreted this letter, even without the pretty letter of Aimée and her husband which accompanied it; and which told how, when M. du Fay came over to his friend's wedding, he had seen the younger sister, and in her seen his fate. The soft caressing, timid Aimée was more to his taste than the grave and stately Susan. Yet little Aimée managed to rule imperiously at Château Chalabre; or, rather, her husband was delighted to indulge her every wish; while Susan, in her grand way, made rather a pomp of her conjugal obedience. But they were both good wives, good daughters.

This last summer, you might have seen an old, old man, dressed in grey, with white flowers in his button-hole (gathered by a grand-child as fair as they), leading an elderly lady about the grounds of Château Chalabre, with tottering, unsteady eagerness of gait.

"Here!" said he to me, "just here my mother bade me adieu when first I went to join my regiment. I was impatient to go. I mounted—I rode to yonder great chestnut, and then, looking back, I saw my mother's sorrowful countenance. I sprang off, threw the reins to the groom, and ran back for one more embrace. 'My brave boy!'

she said; 'my own! Be faithful to God and your king!' I never saw her more; but I shall see her soon; and I think I may tell her I have been faithful both to my God and my king."

Before now, he has told his mother all.

THE SQUIRE'S STORY.

———◦◇◦———

IN the year 1769, the little town of Barford was thrown into a state of great excitement by the intelligence that a gentleman (and " quite the gentleman," said the land-land of the George Inn) had been looking at Mr. Cla-vering's old house.   This house was neither in the town nor in the country.   It stood on the outskirts of Barford, on the road-side leading to Derby.   The last occupant had been a Mr. Clavering—a Northumberland gentleman of good family—who had come to live in Barford while he was but a younger son; but when some elder branches of the family died, he had returned to take possession of the family estate.   The house of which I speak was called the White House, from its being covered with a greyish kind of stucco.   It had a good garden to the back, and Mr. Clavering had built capital stables, with what were then considered the latest improvements.   The point of good stabling was expected to let the house, as it was in a hunting county; other-wise it had few recommendations.   There were many bedrooms; some entered through others, even to the number of five, leading one beyond the other; several sitting-rooms of the small and poky kind, wainscotted round with wood, and then painted a heavy slate colour; one good dining-room, and a drawing-room over it, both looking into the garden, with pleasant bow-windows.

Such was the accommodation offered by the White House. It did not seem to be very tempting to strangers, though the good people of Barford rather piqued themselves on it as the largest house in the town, and as a house in which "townspeople" and "county people" had often met at Mr. Clavering's friendly dinners. To appreciate this circumstance of pleasant recollection, you should have lived some years in a little country town, surrounded by gentlemen's seats. You would then understand how a bow or a courtesy from a member of a county family elevates the individuals who receive it almost as much, in their own eyes, as the pair of blue garters fringed with silver, did Mr. Bickerstaff's ward. They trip lightly on air for a whole day afterwards. Now Mr. Clavering was gone, where could town and county mingle?

I mention these things that you may have an idea of the desirability of the letting of the White House in the Barfordites' imagination; and to make the mixture thick and slab, you must add for yourselves the bustle, the mystery, and the importance which every little event either causes or assumes in a small town; and then, perhaps, it will be no wonder to you that twenty ragged little urchins accompanied the "gentleman" aforesaid to the door of the White House; and that, although he was above an hour inspecting it, under the auspices of Mr. Jones, the agent's clerk, thirty more had joined themselves on to the wondering crowd before his exit,

and awaited such crumbs of intelligence as they could
gather before they were threatened or whipped out of
hearing distance. Presently, out came the "gentleman"
and the lawyer's clerk. The latter was speaking as he
followed the former over the threshold. The gentleman
was tall, well-dressed, handsome; but there was a
sinister cold look in his quick-glancing, light blue eye,
which a keen observer might not have liked. There
were no keen observers among the boys, and ill-conditioned gaping girls. But they stood too near; incon-
veniently close; and the gentleman, lifting up his right
hand, in which he carried a short riding-whip, dealt one
or two sharp blows to the nearest, with a look of savage
enjoyment on his face as they moved away whimpering
and crying. An instant after, his expression of countenance had changed.

"Here!" said he, drawing out a handful of money,
partly silver, partly copper, and throwing it into the
midst of them. "Scramble for it! fight it out, my
lads! come this afternoon, at three, to the George, and
I'll throw you out some more." So the boys hurrahed
for him as he walked off with the agent's clerk. He
chuckled to himself, as over a pleasant thought. "I'll
have some fun with those lads," he said; "I'll teach
'em to come prowling and prying about me. I'll tell
you what I'll do. I'll make the money so hot in the
fire-shovel that it shall burn their fingers. You come
and see the faces and the howling. I shall be very glad
if you will dine with me at two; and by that time I may
have made up my mind respecting the house."

Mr. Jones, the agent's clerk, agreed to come to the
George at two, but, somehow, he had a distaste for his

entertainer. Mr. Jones would not like to have said,
even to himself, that a man with a purse full of money,
who kept many horses, and spoke familiarly of noble-
men — above all, who thought of taking the White
House—could be anything but a gentleman; but still
the uneasy wonder as to who this Mr. Robinson Higgins
could be, filled the clerk's mind long after Mr. Higgins,
Mr. Higgins's servants, and Mr. Higgins's stud had
taken possession of the White House.

The White House was re-stuccoed (this time of a
pale yellow colour), and put into thorough repair by the
accommodating and delighted landlord, while his tenant
seemed inclined to spend any amount of money on
internal decorations, which were showy and effective in
their character, enough to make the White House a
nine days' wonder to the good people of Barford. The
slate-coloured paints became pink, and were picked out
with gold; the old-fashioned banisters were replaced
by newly gilt ones; but, above all, the stables were a
a sight to be seen. Since the days of the Roman
Emperor, never was there such provision made for the
care, the comfort, and the health of horses. But every
one said it was no wonder, when they were led through
Barford, covered up to their eyes, but curving their
arched and delicate necks, and prancing with short, high
steps, in repressed eagerness. Only one groom came
with them; yet they required the care of three men.
Mr. Higgins, however, preferred engaging two lads out
of Barford; and Barford highly approved of his prefer-
ence. Not only was it kind and thoughtful to give
employment to the lounging lads themselves, but they
were receiving such a training in Mr. Higgins's stables

as might fit them for Doncaster or Newmarket. The district of Derbyshire in which Barford was situated was too close to Leicestershire not to support a hunt and a pack of hounds. The master of the hounds was a certain Sir Harry Manley, who was *aut* a huntsman *aut nullus*. He measured a man by the " length of his fork," not by the expression of his countenance, or the shape of his head. But, as Sir Harry was wont to observe, there was such a thing as too long a fork, so his approbation was withheld until he had seen a man on horseback; and if his seat there was square and easy, his hand light, and his courage good, Sir Harry hailed him as a brother.

Mr. Higgins attended the first meet of the season, not as a subscriber but as an amateur. The Barford huntsmen piqued themselves on their bold riding; and their knowledge of the country came by nature; yet this new strange man, whom nobody knew, was in at the death, sitting on his horse, both well breathed and calm, without a hair turned on the sleek skin of the latter, supremely addressing the old huntsman as he hacked off the tail of the fox; and he, the old man, who was testy even under Sir Harry's slightest rebuke, and flew out on any other member of the hunt that dared to utter a word against his sixty years' experience as stable-boy, groom, poacher, and what not—he, old Isaac Wormeley, was meekly listening to the wisdom of this stranger, only now and then giving one of his quick, up-turning, cunning glances, not unlike the sharp, o'er-canny looks of the poor deceased Reynard, round whom the hounds were howling, unadmonished by the short whip which was now tucked into Wormeley's well-worn pocket.

When Sir Harry rode into the copse—full of dead brushwood and wet tangled grass—and was followed by the members of the hunt, as one by one they cantered past, Mr. Higgins took off his cap and bowed—half deferentially, half insolently—with a lurking smile in the corner of his eye at the discomfited looks of one or two of the laggards. "A famous run, sir," said Sir Harry. "The first time you have hunted in our country, but I hope we shall see you often."

"I hope to become a member of the hunt, sir," said Mr. Higgins.

"Most happy—proud, I am sure, to receive so daring a rider among us. You took the Cropper-gate, I fancy, while some of our friends here"—scowling at one or two cowards by way of finishing his speech. "Allow me to introduce myself—master of the hounds." He fumbled in his waistcoat pocket for the card on which his name was formally inscribed. "Some of our friends here are kind enough to come home with me to dinner; might I ask for the honour?"

"My name is Higgins," replied the stranger, bowing low. "I am only lately come to occupy the White House at Barford, and I have not as yet presented my letters of introduction."

"Hang it!" replied Sir Harry; "a man with a seat like yours, and that good brush in your hand, might ride up to any door in the county (I'm a Leicestershire man!), and be a welcome guest. Mr. Higgins, I shall be proud to become better acquainted with you over my dinner-table."

Mr. Higgins knew pretty well how to improve the acquaintance thus begun. He could sing a good song,

17

tell a good story, and was well up in practical jokes; with plenty of that keen, worldly sense, which seems like an instinct in some men, and which in this case taught him on whom he might play off such jokes, with impunity from their resentment, and with a security of applause from the more boisterous, vehement, or prosperous.   At the end of twelve months Mr. Robinson Higgins was, out-and-out, the most popular member of the Barford hunt; had beaten all the others by a couple of lengths, as his first patron, Sir Harry, observed one evening, when they were just leaving the dinner-table of an old hunting squire in the neighbourhood.

"Because, you know," said Squire Hearn, holding Sir Harry by the button—"I mean, you see, this young spark is looking sweet upon Catherine; and she's a good girl, and will have ten thousand pounds down, the day she's married, by her mother's will; and, excuse me, Sir Harry, but I should not like my girl to throw herself away."

Though Sir Harry had a long ride before him, and but the early and short light of a new moon to take it in, his kind heart was so much touched by Squire Hearn's trembling, tearful anxiety, that he stopped and turned back into the dining-room to say, with more asseverations than I care to give,—

" My good squire, I may say, I know that man pretty well by this time; and a better fellow never existed. If I had twenty daughters he should have the pick of them."

Squire Hearn never thought of asking the grounds for his old friend's opinion of Mr. Higgins; it had been given with too much earnestness for any doubts to cross the old man's mind as to the possibility of its not being well founded. Mr. Hearn was not a doubter, or a thinker, or suspicious by nature; it was simply his love for Catherine, his only child, that prompted his anxiety in this case; and, after what Sir Harry had said, the old man could totter with an easy mind, though not with very steady legs, into the drawing-room, where his bonny, blushing daughter Catherine and Mr. Higgins stood close together on the hearth-rug; he whispering, she listening with downcast eyes. She looked so happy, so like her dead mother had looked when the squire was a young man, that all his thought was how to please her most. His son and heir was about to be married, and bring his wife to live with the squire; Barford and the White House were not distant an hour's ride; and, even as these thoughts passed through his mind, he asked Mr. Higgins if he could not stay all night—the young moon was already set—the roads would be dark— and Catherine looked up with a pretty anxiety, which, however, had not much doubt in it, for the answer.

With every encouragement of this kind from the old squire, it took everybody rather by surprise when, one morning, it was discovered that Miss Catherine Hearn was missing; and when, according to the usual fashion in such cases, a note was found, saying that she had eloped with "the man of her heart," and gone to Gretna Green, no one could imagine why she could not quietly have stopped at home, and been married in the parish church. She had always been a romantic, sentimental girl; very pretty and very affectionate, and very much spoiled, and very much wanting in common sense. Her indulgent father was deeply hurt at

17—2

this want of confidence in his never-varying affection ; but when his son came, hot with indignation from the baronet's (his future father-in-law's house, where every form of law and of ceremony was to accompany his own impending marriage), Squire Hearn pleaded the cause of the young couple with imploring cogency, and protested that it was a piece of spirit in his daughter, which he admired and was proud of. However, it ended with Mr. Nathaniel Hearn's declaring that he and his wife would have nothing to do with his sister and her husband. "Wait till you've seen him, Nat!" said the old squire, trembling with his distressful anticipations of family discord. "He's an excuse for any girl. Only ask Sir Harry's opinion of him." "Confound Sir Harry! So that a man sits his horse well, Sir Harry cares nothing about anything else. Who is this man— this fellow ? Where does he come from ? What are his means ? Who are his family ? "

"He comes from the south—Surrey or Somersetshire, I forget which ; and he pays his way well and liberally. There's not a tradesmen in Barford but says he cares no more for money than for water ; he spends like a prince, Nat. I don't know who his family are ; but he seals with a coat of arms, which may tell you if you want to know ; and he goes regularly to collect his rents from his estates in the south. Oh, Nat! if you would but be friendly, I should be as well pleased with Kitty's marriage as any father in the county."

Mr. Nathaniel Hearn gloomed, and muttered an oath or two to himself. The poor old father was reaping the consequences of his weak indulgence to his two children. Mr. and Mrs. Nathaniel Hearn kept apart from Catherine and her husband; and Squire Hearn durst never ask them to Levison Hall, though it was his own house. Indeed, he stole away as if he were a culprit whenever he went to visit the White House; and if he passed a night there, he was fain to equivocate when he returned home the next day; an equivocation which was well interpreted by the surly, proud Nathaniel. But the younger Mr. and Mrs. Hearn were the only people who did not visit at the White House. Mr. and Mrs. Higgins were decidedly more popular than their brother and sister-in-law. She made a very pretty, sweet-tempered hostess, and her education had not been such as to make her intolerant of any want of refinement in the associates who gathered round her husband. She had gentle smiles for townspeople as well as county people; and unconsciously played an admirable second in her husband's project of making himself universally popular.

But there is some one to make ill-natured remarks, and draw ill-natured conclusions from very simple premises, in every place; and in Barford this bird of ill-omen was a Miss Pratt. She did not hunt—so Mr. Higgins's admirable riding did not call out her admiration. She did not drink—so the well-selected wines, so lavishly dispensed among his guests, could never mollify Miss Pratt. She could not bear comic songs, or buffo stories —so, in that way, her approbation was impregnable. And these three secrets of popularity constituted Mr. Higgins's great charm. Miss Pratt sat and watched. Her face looked immovably grave at the end of any of Mr. Higgins's best stories; but there was a keen, needle-like glance of her unwinking little eyes, which

Mr. Higgins felt rather than saw, and which made him shiver, even on a hot day, when it fell upon him. Miss Pratt was a Dissenter, and, to propitiate this female Mordecai, Mr. Higgins asked the Dissenting minister whose services she attended, to dinner; kept himself and his company in good order; gave a handsome donation to the poor of the chapel. All in vain— Miss Pratt stirred not a muscle more of her face towards graciousness; and Mr. Higgins was conscious that, in spite of all his open efforts to captivate Mr. Davis, there was a secret influence on the other side, throwing in doubts and suspicions, and evil interpretations of all he said or did. Miss Pratt, the little, plain old maid, living on eighty pounds a year, was the thorn in the popular Mr. Higgins's side, although she had never spoken one uncivil word to him; indeed, on the contrary, had treated him with a stiff and elaborate civility.

The thorn—the grief to Mrs. Higgins was this. They had no children! Oh! how she would stand and envy the careless, busy motion of half-a-dozen children; and then, when observed, move on with a deep, deep sigh of yearning regret. But it was as well.

It was noticed that Mr. Higgins was remarkably careful of his health. He ate, drank, took exercise, rested, by some secret rules of his own; occasionally bursting into an excess, it is true, but only on rare occasions—such as when he returned from visiting his estates in the south, and collecting his rents. That unusual exertion and fatigue—for there were no stage-coaches within forty miles of Barford, and he, like most country gentlemen of that day, would have preferred riding if there had been — seemed to require some strange excess to compensate for it ; and rumours went through the town, that he shut himself up, and drank enormously for some days after his return. But no one was admitted to these orgies.

One day—they remembered it well afterwards—the hounds met not far from the town ; and the fox was found in a part of the wild heath, which was beginning to be enclosed by a few of the more wealthy townspeople, who were desirous of building themselves houses rather more in the country than those they had hitherto lived in. Among these, the principal was a Mr. Dudgeon, the attorney of Barford, and the agent for all the county families about. The firm of Dudgeon had managed the leases, the marriage settlements, and the wills, of the neighbourhood for generations. Mr. Dudgeon's father had the responsibility of collecting the land-owners' rents just as the present Mr. Dudgeon had at the time of which I speak ; and as his son and his son's son have done since. Their business was an hereditary estate to them ; and with something of the old feudal feeling, was mixed a kind of proud humility at their position towards the squires whose family secrets they had mastered, and the mysteries of whose fortunes and estates were better known to the Messrs. Dudgeon than to themselves.

Mr. John Dudgeon had built himself a house on Wildbury Heath—a mere cottage, as he called it ; but though only two storeys high, it spread out far and wide, and work-people from Derby had been sent for on purpose to make the inside as complete as possible. The gardens, too, were exquisite in arrangement, if not very extensive ; and not a flower was grown in them, but of the rarest species. It must have been somewhat of a mortification to the owner of this dainty place when, on the day of which I speak, the fox after a long race, during which he had described a circle of many miles, took refuge in the garden; but Mr. Dudgeon put a good face on the matter when a gentleman hunter, with the careless insolence of the squires of those days and that place, rode across the velvet lawn, and tapping at the window of the dining-room with his whip-handle, asked permission—no! that is not it—rather, informed Mr. Dudgeon of their intention—to enter his garden in a body, and have the fox unearthed. Mr. Dudgeon compelled himself to smile assent, with the grace of a masculine Griselda; and then he hastily gave orders to have all that the house afforded of provision set out for luncheon, guessing rightly enough that a six hours' run would give even homely fare an acceptable welcome. He bore without wincing the entrance of the dirty boots into his exquisitely clean rooms; he only felt grateful for the care with which Mr. Higgins strode about laboriously and noiselessly moving on the tip of his toes, as he reconnoitred the rooms with a curious eye.

"I'm going to build a house myself, Dudgeon; and, upon my word, I don't think I could take a better model than yours."

"Oh! my poor cottage would be too small to afford any hints for such a house as you would wish to build, Mr. Higgins," replied Mr. Dudgeon, gently rubbing his hands nevertheless at the compliment.

"Not at all! not at all! Let me see. You have dining-room, drawing-room,—" he hesitated, and Mr. Dudgeon filled up the blank as he expected.

"Four sitting-rooms and the bed-rooms. But allow me to show you over the house. I confess I took some pains in arranging it, and, though far smaller than what you would require, it may, nevertheless, afford you some hints."

So they left the eating gentlemen with their mouths and their plates quite full, and the scent of the fox overpowering that of the hasty rashers of ham; and they carefully inspected all the ground-floor rooms. Then Mr. Dudgeon said,—

"If you are not tired, Mr. Higgins—it is rather my hobby, so you must pull me up if you are—we will go upstairs, and I will show you my sanctum."

Mr. Dudgeon's sanctum was the centre room, over the porch, which formed a balcony, and which was carefully filled with choice flowers in pots. Inside, there were all kinds of elegant contrivances for hiding the real strength of all the boxes and chests required by the particular nature of Mr. Dudgeon's business; for although his office was in Barford, he kept (as he informed Mr. Higgins) what was the most valuable here, as being safer than an office which was locked up and left every night. But, as Mr. Higgins reminded him with a sly poke in the side, when next they met, his own house was not over secure. A fortnight after the gentlemen of the Barford hunt lunched there, Mr. Dudgeon's strong box,—in his sanctum upstairs, with the mysterious spring-bolt to the window invented by himself, and the secret of which was only known to the inventor and a few of his most intimate friends, to whom he had proudly shown it;—this strong-box, containing the collected Christmas rents of half-a-dozen landlords, (there was then no bank nearer than Derby,) was rifled; and the secretly rich Mr. Dudgeon had to stop his agent in his purchases of paintings by Flemish artists, because the money was required to make good the missing rents.

The Dogberries and Verges of those days were quite incapable of obtaining any clue to the robber or robbers; and though one or two vagrants were taken up and brought before Mr. Dunover and Mr. Higgins, the magistrates who usually attended in the court-room at Barford, there was no evidence brought against them, and after a couple of nights' durance in the lock-ups they were set at liberty. But it became a standing joke with Mr. Higgins to ask Mr. Dudgeon, from time to time, whether he could recommend him a place of safety for his valuables; or, if he had made any more inventions lately for securing houses from robbers.

About two years after this time—about seven years after Mr. Higgins had been married—one Tuesday evening, Mr. Davis was sitting reading the news in the coffee-room of the George Inn. He belonged to a club of gentlemen who met there occasionally to play at whist, to read what few newspapers and magazines were published in those days, to chat about the market at Derby, and prices all over the country. This Tuesday night it was a black frost, and few people were in the room. Mr. Davis was anxious to finish an article in the *Gentleman's Magazine*; indeed, he was making extracts from it, intending to answer it, and yet unable with his small income to purchase a copy. So he stayed late; it was past nine, and at ten o'clock the room was closed. But while he wrote, Mr. Higgins came in. He was pale and haggard with cold. Mr. Davis, who had

had for some time sole possession of the fire, moved
politely on one side, and handed to the new comer
the sole London newspaper which the room afforded.
Mr. Higgins accepted it, and made some remark on the
intense coldness of the weather; but Mr. Davis was too
full of his article, and intended reply, to fall into conversation readily.   Mr. Higgins hitched his chair nearer to
the fire, and put his feet on the fender, giving an audible
shudder.   He put the newspaper on one end of the table
near him, and sat gazing into the red embers of the fire,
crouching down over them as if his very marrow were
chilled.   At length he said,—

"There is no account of the murder at Bath in that
paper?"   Mr. Davis, who had finished taking his notes,
and was preparing to go, stopped short, and asked,—

"Has there been a murder at Bath?   No! I have
not seen anything of it—who was murdered?"

"Oh! it was a shocking, terrible murder!" said
Mr. Higgins, not raising his look from the fire, but
gazing on with his eyes dilated till the whites were
seen all round them.   "A terrible, terrible murder!
I wonder what will become of the murderer?   I can
fancy the red glowing centre of that fire—look and see
how infinitely distant it seems, and how the distance
magnifies it into something awful and unquenchable."

"My dear sir, you are feverish; how you shake and
shiver!" said Mr. Davis, thinking, privately, that his
companion had symptoms of fever, and that he was wandering in his mind.

"Oh, no!" said Mr. Higgins.   "I am not feverish.
It is the night which is so cold."   And for a time he
talked with Mr. Davis about the article in the *Gentle-*

man's Magazine, for he was rather a reader himself, and could take more interest in Mr. Davis's pursuits than most of the people at Barford. At length it drew near to ten, and Mr. Davis rose up to go home to his lodgings.

" No, Davis, don't go. I want you here. We will have a bottle of port together, and that will put Saunders into good humour. I want to tell you about this murder," he continued, dropping his voice, and speaking hoarse and low. " She was an old woman, and he killed her, sitting reading her Bible by her own fireside!" He looked at Mr. Davis with a strange, searching gaze, as if trying to find some sympathy in the horror which the idea presented to him.

" Whom do you mean, my dear sir? What is this murder you are so full of? No one has been murdered here."

" No, you fool! I tell you it was in Bath!" said Mr. Higgins, with sudden passion; and then calming himself to most velvet-smoothness of manner, he laid his hand on Mr. Davis's knee, there, as they sat by the fire, and gently detaining him, began the narration of the crime he was so full of; but his voice and manner were constrained to a stony quietude: he never looked in Mr. Davis's face; once or twice, as Mr. Davis remembered afterwards, his grip tightened like a compressing vice.

" She lived in a small house in a quiet, old-fashioned street, she and her maid. People said she was a good old woman; but, for all that, she hoarded and hoarded, and never gave to the poor. Mr. Davis, it is wicked not to give to the poor—wicked—wicked, is it not? I

always give to the poor, for once I read in the Bible that
'Charity covereth a multitude of sins.' The wicked
old woman never gave, but hoarded her money, and
saved and saved. Some one heard of it; I say she
threw a temptation in his way, and God will punish her
for it. And this man—or it might be a woman, who
knows?—and this person—heard also that she went to
church in the mornings and her maid in the afternoons;
and so, while the maid was at church, and the street
and the house quite still, and the darkness of a winter
afternoon coming on, she was nodding over her Bible—
and that, mark you! is a sin, and one that God will
avenge sooner or later,—and a step came, in the dusk,
up the stair, and that person I told you of stood in the
room. At first, he—no! At first, it is supposed—for,
you understand, all this is mere guess-work—it is supposed that he asked her civilly enough to give him her
money, or to tell him where it was; but the old miser
defied him, and would not ask for mercy and give up her
keys, even when he threatened her, but looked him in
the face as if he had been a baby.—Oh, God! Mr. Davis,
I once dreamt, when I was a little, innocent boy, that I
should commit a crime like this, and I wakened up
crying; and my mother comforted me—that is the reason
I tremble so now—that and the cold, for it is very, very
cold!"

"But did he murder the old lady?" asked Mr. Davis,
"I beg your pardon, sir, but I am interested by your
story."

"Yes; he cut her throat; and there she lies yet, in
her quiet little parlour, with her face upturned and all
ghastly white, in the middle of a pool of blood. Mr.

Davis, this wine is no better than water; I must have some brandy!"

Mr. Davis was horror-struck by the story, which seemed to have fascinated him as much as it had done his companion.

"Have they got any clue to the murderer?" said he. Mr. Higgins drank down half a tumbler of raw brandy before he answered.

"No! no clue whatever. They will never be able to discover him; and I should not wonder, Mr. Davis—I should not wonder if he repented after all, and did bitter penance for his crime; and if so—will there be mercy for him at the last day?"

"God knows!" said Mr. Davis, with solemnity. "It is an awful story," continued he, rousing himself; "I hardly like to leave this warm, light room and go out into the darkness after hearing it. But it must be done"—buttoning on his great coat—"I can only say, I hope and trust they will find out the murderer and hang him. If you'll take my advice, Mr. Higgins, you'll have your bed warmed, and drink a treacle posset just the last thing; and, if you'll allow me, I'll send you my answer to Philologus before it goes up to old Urban."

The next morning, Mr. Davis went to call on Miss Pratt, who was not very well, and, by way of being agreeable and entertaining, he related to her all he had heard the night before about the murder at Bath; and really he made a very pretty connected story out of it, and interested Miss Pratt very much in the fate of the old lady—partly because of a similarity in their situations; for she also privately hoarded money, and had but one servant, and stopped at home alone on Sunday afternoons to allow her servant to go to church.

"And when did all this happen?" she asked.

"I don't know if Mr. Higgins named the day; and yet I think it must have been on this very last Sunday."

"And to-day is Wednesday. Ill news travels fast."

"Yes, Mr. Higgins thought it might have been in the London newspaper."

"That it could never be. Where did Mr. Higgins learn all about it?"

"I don't know; I did not ask. I think he only came home yesterday: he had been south to collect his rents, somebody said."

Miss Pratt grunted. She used to vent her dislike and suspicions of Mr. Higgins in a grunt whenever his name was mentioned.

"Well, I shan't see you for some days. Godfrey Merton asked me to go and stay with him and his sister; and I think it will do me good. Besides," added she, "these winter evenings—and these murderers at large in the country—I don't quite like living with only Peggy to call to in case of need.

Miss Pratt went to stay with her cousin, Mr. Merton. He was an active magistrate, and enjoyed his reputation as such. One day he came in, having just received his letters.

"Bad account of the morals of your little town here, Jessy!" said he, touching one of his letters. "You've either a murderer among you, or some friend of a murderer. Here's a poor old lady at Bath had her throat cut last Sunday week; and I've a letter from the Home

Office, asking to lend them 'my very efficient aid,' as they are pleased to call it, towards finding out the culprit.   It seems he must have been thirsty, and of a comfortable jolly turn; for before going to his horrid work he tapped a barrel of ginger wine the old lady had set by to work; and he wrapped the spigot round with a piece of a letter taken out of his pocket, as may be supposed: and this piece of a letter was found afterwards; there are only these letters on the outside, 'ns, *Esq., -arford, -egworth*,' which some one has ingeniously made out to mean Barford, near Kegworth.   On the other side, there is some allusion to a race-horse, I conjecture, though the name is singular enough— 'Church-and-King-and-down-with-the-Rump.'"

Miss Pratt caught at this name immediately.   It had hurt her feelings as a Dissenter only a few months ago, and she remembered it well.

"Mr. Nat Hearn has, or had (as I am speaking in the witness-box, as it were, I must take care of my tenses), a horse with that ridiculous name."

"Mr. Nat Hearn," repeated Mr. Merton, making a note of the intelligence; then he recurred to his letter from the Home Office again.

"These is also a piece of a small key, broken in the futile attempt to open a desk—well, well.   Nothing more of consequence.   The letter is what we must rely upon."

"Mr. Davis said that Mr. Higgins told him—" Miss Pratt began.

"Higgins!" exclaimed Mr. Merton, 'ns.   Is it Higgins, the blustering fellow that ran away with Nat Hearn's sister?"

"Yes!" said Miss Pratt. "But though he has never been a favourite of mine—"

"ns," repeated Mr. Merton. "It is too horrible to think of; a member of the hunt—kind old Squire Hearn's son-in-law! Who else have you in Barford with names that end in *ns?*"

"There's Jackon, and Higginson, and Blenkinsop, and Davis and Jones. Cousin! one thing strikes me—how did Mr. Higgins know all about it to tell Mr. Davis on Tuesday what had happened on Sunday afternoon?"

There is no need to add much more. Those curious in lives of the highwayman may find the name of Higgins as conspicuous among those annals as that of Claude Duval. Kate Hearn's husband collected his rents on the highway, like many another "gentleman" of the day; but, having been unlucky in one or two of his adventures, and hearing exaggerated accounts of the hoarded wealth of the old lady at Bath, he was led on from robbery to murder, and was hung for his crime at Derby, in 1775.

He had not been an unkind husband; and his poor wife took lodgings in Derby to be near him in his last moments—his awful last moments. Her old father went with her everywhere, but into her husband's cell; and wrung her heart by constantly accusing himself of having promoted her marriage with a man of whom he knew so little. He abdicated his squireship in favour of his son Nathaniel. Nat was prosperous, and the helpless silly father could be of no use to him; but to his widowed daughter, the foolish, fond old man was all in all—her knight, her protector, her companion, her most faithful loving companion. Only, he ever declined assuming the

18

office of her counsellor; shaking his head sadly, and saying,

"Ah! Kate, Kate! if I had had more wisdom to have advised thee better, thou need'st not have been an exile here in Brussels, shrinking from the sight of every English person as if they knew thy story."

I saw the White House not a month ago; it was to let, perhaps for the twentieth time since Mr. Higgins occupied it; but still the tradition goes in Barford that, once upon a time, a highwayman lived there, and amassed untold treasures; and that the ill-gotten wealth yet remains walled up in some unknown concealed chamber; but in what part of the house no one knows.

Will any of you become tenants, and try to find out this mysterious closet? I can furnish the exact address to any applicant who wishes for it.

19 JA 66

London: SMITH, ELDER and Co., 15½, Old Bailey, E.C.

CHEAP EDITIONS

OF

STANDARD WORKS.

Well Printed, on Good Paper, and Strongly Bound in Cloth.

The following Volumes sell at 2s. 6d. each.

JANE EYRE. By CHARLOTTE BRONTË.

SHIRLEY. By CHARLOTTE BRONTË.

VILLETTE. By CHARLOTTE BRONTË.

WUTHERING HEIGHTS AND AGNES GREY
By EMILY and ANNE BRONTË. With Preface and Memoir of the Sisters.
By CHARLOTTE BRONTË.

THE TENANT OF WILDFELL HALL. By ANNE BRONTË.

THE PROFESSOR. By CHARLOTTE BRONTË. To which are
added the Poems of CURRER, ELLIS, and ACTON BELL.

THE LIFE OF CHARLOTTE BRONTË. By Mrs. GASKELL.
    ₊ The above can also be had in cloth, gilt edges, 3s. 6d. each, or
    handsomely bound in half-morocco, 6s. each.

AGNES OF SORRENTO. By Mrs. H. B. STOWE, Author of
"Uncle Tom's Cabin," &c.

AUTOBIOGRAPHY OF LUTFULLAH, A Mohamedan Gentle-
man; And his Transactions with his Fellow-Creatures. Edited by EDWARD
B. EASTWICK, F.R.S., F.S.A.

AGAINST WIND AND TIDE. By HOLME LEE.

SYLVAN HOLT'S DAUGHTER. By HOLME LEE.

KATHIE BRANDE: The Fireside History of a Quiet Life.
By HOLME LEE.

THE TOWN: Its Memorable Characters and Events.
By LEIGH HUNT. Forty-five Wood Engravings.

AUTOBIOGRAPHY OF LEIGH HUNT. Edited by his
Eldest Son.

[*Continued next page.*

TALES OF THE COLONIES ; or, Adventures of an Emigrant.
By C. ROWCROFT.

LAVINIA. By the Author of "Doctor Antonio," and "Lorenzo
Benoni."

TRANSFORMATION ; or, the Romance of Monte Beni.
By NATHANIEL HAWTHORNE, Author of "The Scarlet Letter," "Our Old
Home," &c.

DEERBROOK ; a Tale of English Country Life.
By Mrs. HARRIET MARTINEAU.

HOUSEHOLD EDUCATION. By Mrs. HARRIET MARTINEAU.

BRITISH RULE IN INDIA. A Historical Sketch.
By Mrs. HARRIET MARTINEAU.

ROMANTIC TALES. By the Author of "John Halifax."

DOMESTIC STORIES. By the Author of "John Halifax."

AFTER DARK. By WILKIE COLLINS.

BELOW THE SURFACE. By Sir A. H. ELTON, Bart.

THE POLITICAL ECONOMY OF ART. By JOHN RUSKIN.

LECTURES ON THE ENGLISH HUMOURISTS.
By W. M. THACKERAY.

The following Volumes sell at 2s. each.

THE SCHOOL FOR FATHERS ; An Old English Story.
By TALBOT GWYNNE.

PAUL FERROLL ; A Tale. By the Author of "IX Poems by V."

A LOST LOVE. By ASHFORD OWEN.

LONDON : SMITH, ELDER AND CO., 65, CORNHILL.

CPSIA information can be obtained at www.ICGtesting.com
Printed in the USA
LVOW052054271011

252164LV00002BA/221/P